Advanced Security Solutions for Multimedia

Advanced Security Solutions for Multimedia

Edited by

Irshad Ahmad Ansari and Varun Bajaj

Electronics and Communication Engineering, PDPM Indian Institute of Information Technology, Design & Manufacturing (IIITDM) Jabalpur, India

IOP Publishing, Bristol, UK

ISBN   978-0-7503-3735-9 (ebook)
ISBN   978-0-7503-3733-5 (print)
ISBN   978-0-7503-3736-6 (myPrint)
ISBN   978-0-7503-3734-2 (mobi)

DOI   10.1088/978-0-7503-3735-9

Version: 20210901

IOP ebooks

British Library Cataloguing-in-Publication Data: A catalogue record for this book is available from the British Library.

Published by IOP Publishing, wholly owned by The Institute of Physics, London

IOP Publishing, Temple Circus, Temple Way, Bristol, BS1 6HG, UK

US Office: IOP Publishing, Inc., 190 North Independence Mall West, Suite 601, Philadelphia, PA 19106, USA

Dedicated to my family members.

— Irshad Ahmad Ansari

Dedicated to my father Late Mahendra Bajaj and Family members.

— Varun Bajaj

Contents

8 New lightweight image encryption algorithm for the Internet of Things and wireless multimedia sensor networks

8-1

Amina Msolli, Abdelhamid Helali, Hassen Maaref and Ridha Mghaieth

9 Applying the capabilities of machine learning for multimedia security: an analysis

9-1

Suja Cherukullapurath Mana and T Sasipraba

12 Ear recognition for multimedia security 12-1

Sagar G Sangodkar, Niranjan Suthar, Akash Palde,
Parmeshwar Birajadar and Vikram M Gadre

13 Secure multimedia management: currents trends and future avenues 13-1

Vishal Rajput and Sunil Kumar Jauhar

Preface

The use of multimedia data has seen tremendous growth in the recent past due to the excessive use of smartphones, easy availability of internet services and fast communication technologies. The shared data is mostly sensitive, personal or contains confidential information, which is only intended for the end user. A large amount of these digital data can easily be accessed by attackers. This digital data can easily be modified using efficient image and video processing tools. After modification, it can be used in an unlawful manner that can cause personal as well as financial loss to the owner of the original content.

There are various techniques such as digital watermarking, cryptography, stenography, data encryption, etc, which turn out to be very useful for multimedia data security. In addition, the sharing platform and connected nodes themselves might be faulty in nature and can cause security breaches. Many times, paid multimedia content gets stolen by attackers and owners find no way to protect the content/track the attackers.

Recent developments in machine learning techniques seems very promising for various fields. The use of machine learning along with advanced signal processing techniques can be an effective step in the field of data security since they can help in getting blueprints of data/attacks by detecting patterns. Most of the real-world multimedia applications generate important information in the form of image and video, where efficient outcomes and security against illegal use are expected. This demands the need of advanced security solutions for multimedia.

This book tries to make reader familiar with these multimedia security issues, its potential solutions and future research directions.

The chapter-wise description of the book is as follows:

- Chapter 1 proposes a blind image watermarking scheme for color images. One of the unique offerings of the scheme is its efficient dual restoration feature. A dual restoration feature allows color and gray image restoration in case of tampering. It utilizes block-wise embedding strategy and provides promising results.
- Chapter 2 deals with a robust and secure image watermarking algorithm based on sharp frequency localized contourlet transform (SFLCT). The algorithm is independent of the size of the embedded watermark; this is the significant contribution of their work. The proposed method is imperceptible and analysis shows its robustness towards different attacks.
- Chapter 3 provides a comprehensive summary of two well-known data security techniques, which are content watermarking and data hiding or steganography. A thorough review of both the methods is provided that covers multiple facets like history, applications, advancement, etc.
- Chapter 4 provides an insight of reversible watermarking (RW) in encrypted domain. It explores two different categories for RW in encrypted domain, namely data embedding before encryption and data embedding after

encryption. A detailed description of state-of-the-art RW methods in an encrypted domain is provided.

- Chapter 5 deals with application of deep learning in image steganography and steganalysis. Steganography is the art of hiding information in media without altering its form. Steganalysis is the technique of identifying stego files as distinct clean files. The chapter highlights the effect of deep learning in steganography and steganalysis.

- Chapter 6 provides a comprehensive analysis of reversible image watermarking techniques. Also, the importance and applications of reversible image watermarking are explored in this chapter. The review of research challenges and gaps in the field of reversible data hiding are the main offering of the chapter.

- Chapter 7 deals with the security concerns of multimedia wireless networks. Wireless networks have made possible uninterrupted connectivity with mobility. With the advancement of mobile devices wireless networks are ubiquitous, and data security is a major concern. Therefore, in this chapter, a thorough analysis of data security in multimedia wireless networks is presented.

- Chapter 8 proposes an advanced encryption standard (AES) algorithm for Internet of Things (IoT) application. With the aim of providing security solutions that are fast, and less costly in terms of resource consumption, a lightweight encryption algorithm for IoT applications is proposed in this chapter. The authors have updated the AES algorithm to make it suitable for IoT applications.

- Chapter 9 analyzes the application of machine learning (ML) algorithms for data security. A detailed description of various ML based techniques for multimedia security is provided. The advantages of ML based techniques over traditional techniques are also discussed.

- Chapter 10 proposes a service model for patient monitoring on the hospital–home axis in the context of elderly care as well as related security issues and ethical responses. With the help of the proposed model, family members could be better informed of a patient's health status through a home video connection during the patient's hospital stay, especially during time periods when normal visiting protocols and co-operation are restricted.

- Chapter 11 discusses the application of deep learning for abnormality detection in videos. Two different stages are analyzed, in the first stage understanding and labeling video clips based on their semantic content is studied. In the second stage, videos are identified based on normal and abnormal behavior. The authors also provide a review on popular competition and benchmarks, which helps to evaluate the growth of this vibrant security domain.

- Chapter 12 provides an insight into biometric feature based security of multimedia content. In this chapter, an ear recognition system is proposed. A deep learning approach is analyzed for ear detection based on you only look once (YOLO) object detection architecture. Two different approaches are proposed for feature extraction: the first approach is the use of a multi-resolution scattering wavelet network and the second approach is based on convolutional neural network (CNN). The authors have discussed potential applications of their system.

- Chapter 13 focuses on the current and future trends for Security of OTT (Over-the-top) media platforms. OTT platforms have gained immense popularity in the last few years. Therefore, this chapter attempts to provide current trends in OTT media market. Different parameters like rate of content creation and user management are thoroughly studied. A brief discussion of recent research in the OTT domain is also provided.

Acknowledgements

Dr Ansari expresses his gratitude and sincere thanks to his family members and teachers for their constant support and motivation.

Dr Bajaj expresses his heartfelt appreciation to his mother Prabha, wife Anuja, daughter Avadhi, for their wonderful support and encouragement throughout the completion of this important book *Advanced Security Solutions for Multimedia*. His deepest gratitude goes to his mother-in-law and father-in-law for their constant motivation. This book is an outcome of sincere efforts that could be given to the book only due to great support of the family.

We thank Professor Sanjeev Jain, Director of PDPM IIITDM Jabalpur for his support and encouragement. We would like to thank all our friends, well-wishers and all those who keep us motivated in doing more and more; better and better. We sincerely thank all contributors for writing relevant theoretical background and applications of this book on advanced security solutions for multimedia.

We express our humble thanks to Dr Navas John and all editorial staff of IOP for great support, necessary help, appreciation and quick responses. We also wish to thank IOP for giving us this opportunity to contribute on such a relevant topic with a reputed publisher. Finally we want to thank everyone, in one way or another, who helped us editing this book.

Dr Bajaj specially thanks his family who encouraged us throughout the time of editing the book. This book is heartily dedicated to his father who took the lead to heaven before the completion of this book.

Last but not least, we would also like to thank God for showering us his blessings and strength to do this type of novel and quality work.

— Irshad Ahmad Ansari
— Varun Bajaj

Editor biographies

Irshad Ahmad Ansari

Irshad Ahmad Ansari, Electronics and Communication Engineering, PDPM Indian Institute of Information Technology Design and Manufacturing, Jabalpur, India. Irshad Ahmad Ansari has been working as a faculty in the discipline of Electronics and Communication Engineering, at PDPM Indian Institute of Information Technology, Design and Manufacturing (IIITDM) Jabalpur, India since 2017. He received BTech degree in Electronics and Communication Engineering from Gautam Buddha Technical University, Lucknow, India in 2010, MTech degree in Control and Instrumentation from Dr B R Ambedkar National Institute of Technology Jalandhar, Punjab, India in 2012. He completed his PhD from IIT Roorkee with MHRD teaching assistantship, and subsequently joined Gwangju Institute of Science and Technology, South Korea as a Postdoctoral fellow. His major research interests include image processing, signal processing, soft computing, brain–computer interface and machine learning. He is a Senior IEEE member. He is presently guiding three PhD scholars. He has authored more than 32 research papers in various reputed international journals/conferences of publishers like IEEE, Elsevier, Springer etc. He is also serving as an active and potential technical reviewer for various journals of repute.

Varun Bajaj

Varun Bajaj, Electronics and Communication Engineering, PDPM Indian Institute of Information Technology Design and Manufacturing, Jabalpur, India. Varun Bajaj (PhD, MIEEE 16 SMIEEE20) has been working as a faculty in the discipline of Electronics and Communication Engineering, at Indian Institute of Information Technology, Design and Manufacturing (IIITDM) Jabalpur, India since 2014. He worked as a visiting faculty in IIITDM Jabalpur from September 2013 to March 2014. He worked as Assistant Professor at Department of Electronics and Instrumentation, Shri Vaishnav Institute of Technology and Science, Indore, India during 2009–2010. He received BE degree in Electronics and Communication Engineering from Rajiv Gandhi Technological University, Bhopal, India in 2006, MTech degree with Honors in Microelectronics and VLSI design from Shri Govindram Seksaria Institute of Technology and Science, Indore, India in 2009. He received his PhD degree in the Discipline of Electrical Engineering, at Indian Institute of Technology Indore, India in 2014.

He is an Associate Editor of *IEEE Sensor Journal* and Subject Editor-in-Chief of *IET Electronics Letters*. He served as a Subject Editor of *IET Electronics Letters* from Nov 2018 to June 2020. He is Senior Member IEEE June 2020, MIEEE 16–20, and also contributing as active technical reviewer of leading International journals of IEEE, IET, and Elsevier, etc. He has authored more than 110 research papers in various reputed international journals/conferences like *IEEE Transactions*, Elsevier, Springer, IOP etc. He has edited IOP Books, and CRC Press (Taylor & Francis Group). The citation impact of his publications is around 2365 citations, h index of 24, and i10 index of 55 (Google Scholar Sep 2020). He has guided six (three completed and three in progress) PhD Scholars, and six MTech scholars. He is a recipient of various reputed national and international awards. His research interests include biomedical signal processing, image processing, time-frequency analysis, and computer-aided medical diagnosis.

Contributor biographies

Mahdie Abazar

Mahdie Abazar, Department of Computer Engineering and Information Technology, Shiraz University, Shiraz, Iran. Mahdie Abazar received the BS degree in Computer Engineering and Information Technology from the Persian Gulf University, Bushehr, Iran, in 2016 and the MS degree in Computer Engineering, Secure Computing from Shiraz University, Shiraz, Iran, in 2020. Her research interests include steganalysis, steganography, information security, machine learning, image processing, and deep learning.

Parmeshwar Birajadar

Parmeshwar Birajadar, Indian Institute of Technology Bombay, Mumbai, Maharashtra, India. Dr Parmeshwar Birajadar completed the PhD in the field of Biometrics from IIT Bombay in the year 2018. He completed his Master's degree in the field of Electronics and Telecommunication from Mumbai University in the year 2018 and his Bachelor's degree in the field of Electronics from BAMU University, Aurangabad. He has a total teaching experience of 18 years. He is currently working as an assistant professor at VES Institute of Technology in the Department of Electronics Engineering. He has also worked as a technical advisor for the AMBIS project of Cyber Maharashtra.

Seyed Mostafa FakhrAhmad

Seyed Mostafa FakhrAhmad, Department of Computer Engineering and Information Technology, Shiraz University, Shiraz, Iran. Seyed Mostafa FakhrAhmad received his BSc in Computer Engineering from Kharazmi University of Tehran (Iran) in 2003. His MSc and PhD degrees were received in Computer Engineering both from Department of Computer Science and Engineering, Shiraz University (Iran), in 2006 and 2011, respectively. He is currently as an associate professor in Department of Computer Science and Engineering, at Shiraz University. His research interests include natural language processing, data mining, social network analysis and fuzzy systems.

Vikram M Gadre

Vikram M Gadre, Indian Institute of Technology Bombay, Mumbai, Maharashtra, India. Dr Vikram M Gadre is currently a Professor in the Department of Electrical Engineering. He has served as the faculty of the same department since July 27, 1994. He received his BTech and PhD degrees from the Electrical Engineering Department, Indian Institute of Technology, Delhi in the years 1989 and 1994, respectively. His areas of research interest are, broadly: signal and image processing with emphasis on multiresolution principles, multi-rate techniques, wavelets, and time-frequency methods. Further details of his curriculum vitae can be obtained from the site: https://www.ee.iitb.ac.in/web/people/faculty/home/vmgadre'

Ali Ghorbani

Ali Ghorbani, Department of Computer Engineering and Information Technology, Shiraz University, Shiraz, Iran. Ali Ghorbani received his BSc in Computer Engineering from Shahid Chamran University of Ahwaz, Ahwaz, Iran, in 2017. His MSc was received in information technology, secure computing from Shiraz University, Shiraz, Iran, in 2020. His research interests include network security, wireless security, steganography, machine learning and cryptoanalysis.

Jay Gohil

Jay Gohil, Department of Chemical Engineering, Pandit Deendayal Petroleum University, Raisan, Gandhinagar, Gujarat, India. Mr Jay Gohil is a BTech student pursuing Information and Communication Technology from Pandit Deendayal Petroleum University. He possesses specialization in machine learning (ML) from University of Washington, Python from University of Michigan, IT Automation from Google, deep learning from deeplearning.ai., financial technology from University of Michigan and international business essentials from University of London. He has earned a dozen badges from IBM in the fields of data science and cybersecurity, and is a certified Six Sigma Executive (green belt). His areas of interest and expertise include data science (ML and artificial intelligence (AI)) in the field of business and finance. He has communicated various research papers and conference papers in reputed journals and conferences, respectively.

Abdelhamid Helali

Abdelhamid Helali, Micro-Opto-electronics and Nanostructures Laboratory LMON LR99ES29, Monastir, Tunisia. Abdelhamid Helali, received his doctoral degree in electronic physics from the Science Faculty of Monastir Tunisia (2008). He is currently an associate Professor at the Institute of Informatics and Mathematics of Monastir, Tunisia. His research interests include multimedia integration in real-time computer networks, traffic management and quality of service for wireless sensor network (WSN). His recent work has been in security of image transmission in Internet of Things.

Sunil Kumar Jauhar

Sunil Kumar Jauhar, Operations Management and Decision Sciences, Indian Institute of Management Kashipur, Kundeshwari, Kashipur, Udham Singh Nagar, India. Dr Sunil Kumar Jauhar holds an MTech in Industrial Engineering from Visvesvaraya National Institute of Technology Nagpur and PhD in Operations and Supply Chain Management from the Indian Institute of Technology Roorkee. He was a Postdoctoral Fellow at Ted Rogers School of Management, Ryerson University, Canada. Prior to joining IIM Kashipur, he was a faculty at the Indian Institute of Management Jammu. His research interests include supply chain sustainability, circular economy, multi-criteria decision making, performance measurement, and soft computing techniques. He has published in reputable journals including *Journal of Computational Science*, and *International Journal of System Assurance Engineering and Management*.

Ameya Kshirsagar

Ameya Kshirsagar, Department of Information Technology, Symbiosis Institute of Technology, Pune, Maharashtra, India. Mr Ameya Kshirsagar, is a BTech in Information Technology from Symbiosis Institute of Technology. He has published several articles in reputed international journals in the area of computer science, data science, machine learning, finance sector etc. Moreover, he has also served as a reviewer for a reputable international journal, Elsevier.

S Kuppa

S Kuppa, Department of PG Studies and Research in Computer Science, Kuvempu University, Shankarghatta, India. S Kuppa, received a Master's degree in Computer Science from Kuvempu University, India. Currently, he is pursuing a doctoral degree in Computer Science from 2017 and his areas of research include image processing, computer vision and deep learning.

Hassen Maaref

Hassen Maaref, Micro-Opto-electronics and Nanostructures Laboratory LMON LR99ES29, Monastir, Tunisia. Hassen Maaref, received his MPhys in Solid State Physics in 1974 and PhD in Electronic of Semiconductor Materials in 1978 from the University of Paul Sabatier and the National Institute of Applied Sciences at Toulouse in France. He has been a Professor in Semiconductor Physics and Quantum Mechanics in the Department of Physics-Electronic at the Faculty of Sciences of Monastir, University of Monastir since 1979. At the same university, he leads an active research group in the area of epitaxial growth of III–V semiconductor materials and heterostructures (QW, Qdots, HEMT), modelling and characterizations of semiconductor devices for high speed and photonic applications.

V M Manikandan

V M Manikandan, SRM University-AP, Mangalagiri, Guntur, Andhra Pradesh, India. Dr V M Manikandan received his PhD in Computer Science and Engineering from the Indian Institute of Information Technology Design and Manufacturing Kancheepuram, Chennai, Tamilnadu, India after his MTech in Software Engineering from Cochin University of Science and Technology, Kerala, India. Currently, he is working as an Assistant Professor in Computer Science and Engineering at SRM University-AP, Andhra Pradesh, India. His research interests mainly include the design and development of reversible data hiding schemes, digital image watermarking, and content-based image retrieval. He has more than 30 peer-reviewed publications. He is a lifetime member of the Institution of Engineers (India).

Suja Cherukullapurath Mana

Suja Cherukullapurath Mana, Sathyabama Institute of Science and Technology, Jeppiaar Nagar, Chennai, Tamilnadu, India. Ms Suja Cherukullapurath Mana is currently doing research in the area of data science. She is interested in the areas of machine learning, deep learning and related applications. She has published many research papers in renowned journals and conferences.

Peyman Masjedi

Peyman Masjedi, Department of Computer Engineering and Information Technology, Shiraz University, Shiraz, Iran. Peyman Masjedi received His BS and MS degrees in Computer Engineering and Information Technology, Secure Computing from Shiraz University, Shiraz, Iran, in 2016 and 2020, respectively. He is currently pursuing a PhD degree in Artificial Intelligence at Shiraz University, Shiraz, Iran. His research interests include steganography, information security, machine learning and optimization.

Ridha Mghaieth

Ridha Mghaieth, Micro-Opto-electronics and Nanostructures Laboratory LMON LR99ES29, Monastir, Tunisia. Ridha Mghaieth, received his MSc (1985) and PhD (1989) from INSA at the University of Lyon I, France. Between 1989 and 2006 he was Assistant, Master Assistant and Lecturer in physics at the Faculty of sciences of Monastir in Tunisia. He received his State Doctorate Es Sciences from the University of Tunis and has been a professor at the University of Monastir, Tunisia since 2006. His research interests include material sciences and optoelectronics: porous silicon, photovoltaic, nano structuring and epitaxial growth of III–V semiconductors on silicon wafers. He conducts design and assembly of an evaporation rack using the closed spaced vapor transport technique, and the design and assembly of a photocurrent spectroscopy technique. He is the author/co-author of a book chapter, and 49 international publications in refereed journals. Since 2013, he has been the Head of Micro-Optoelectronic and Nanostructures Laboratory and is the Head of two joint Research Services Unit platforms: molecular beam epitaxy and femtosecond characterization chain.

Amina Msolli

Amina Msolli, Micro-Opto-electronics and Nanostructures Laboratory LMON LR99ES29, Monastir, Tunisia. Amina Msolli, received her Master in Microelectronics and Instrumentation from the Institute of Informatics and Mathematics of Monastir, University of Moanstir, Tunisia (2011). Currently, she is a PhD student in Microelectronics at the Monastir University. Her research interests include wireless sensor network, multimedia and information security.

Esmaeil Najafi

Esmaeil Najafi, Department of Mathematics, Faculty of Science, Urmia University, Urmia, Iran. Dr Esmaeil Najafi received his PhD degree in Applied Mathematics—Numerical Analysis from Iran University of Science and Technology, Tehran, Iran in 2012, MSc degree in Applied Mathematics from Iran University of Science and Technology, Tehran, Iran in 2008 and BSc degree in Applied Mathematics from Payam-e-Noor University, Tabriz, Iran in 2006. He is currently an assistant professor in Faculty of Science, Department of Mathematics at Urmia University, Urmia, Iran. His research interests are in the area of image processing and image watermarking as well as numerical analysis and computations of weakly singular integral equations.

Akash S Palde

Akash Palde, Indian Institute of Technology Bombay, Powai, Mumbai, Maharashtra, India. Mr Akash S Palde is currently pursuing his MTech degree (specialization: Communication and Signal Processing) from the Electrical Engineering Department, Indian Institute of Technology Bombay, Mumbai, India, from the year 2019. He completed his BTech degree in Electronics and Telecommunication Engineering from Vishwakarma Institute of Technology Pune, Maharashtra, India, in the year 2017. His main research interests include machine learning, deep learning, and image processing. His other interests are cycling, playing cricket and badminton, and watching animated movies.

Jay Patel

Jay Patel, Department of Chemical Engineering, Pandit Deendayal Petroleum University, Raisan, Gandhinagar, Gujarat, India. Mr Jay Patel is pursuing Bachelor's degree (BTech) in the field of Information and Communication Technology from Pandit Deendayal Petroleum University. He has strong research interest in IT domains including machine learning, artificial intelligence, deep learning and big data. He has communicated research papers in esteemed journals in the area of big data in environmental sustainability and has completed specialization in Python from University of Michigan.

D S Raghukumar

D S Raghukumar, Department of PG Studies and Research in Computer Science, Kuvempu University, Shankarghatta, India. D S Raghukumar, received a Master's degree in Computer Science from Kuvempu University, India. He has been pursuing a doctoral degree in Computer Science from 2017 and his area of research includes image processing and computer vision.

Vishal Rajput

Vishal Rajput, Katholieke Universiteit Leuven, Leuven, Belgiu. Mr Vishal Rajput holds a Bachelor's degree in Electronics and Communication Engineering for Indian Institute of Information Technology, Design and Manufacturing, Jabalpur. Currently he is pursuing his master's from KU Leuven in artificial intelligence. Presently, he also works at the Medical Image Research Centre, UZ Leuven, Belgium. He is a researcher in the field of computer vision and image processing. He has published several book chapters and papers in international journals. His research work includes, watermarking, data analysis, explainable artificial intelligence (AI).

Antti Rissanen

Antti Rissanen, Department of Military Technology, National Defence University, Helsinki, Finland. Dr Antti Rissanen, PhD received his BSc, MA and PhD degrees in Physics from Helsinki University, Finland in 1981, 1984 and 2011, respectively. He obtained licentiate in technology degree (biomedical engineering) in 1992 in University of Technology in Tampere. In 1997 he joined the National Defence University (Finland) as a Senior Lecturer for General Technology. Where he currently works as a researcher. He is also the leader of the Educational Research Group at the Military Technology Department. His research interests include science education, e-learning, and simulations or artificial intelligence in an educational context. Previous research interests are biomedical engineering, signal analysis, technology transfer and thin film technology. Dr Rissanen has authored/co-authored 37 publications in peer-reviewed journals. Dr Rissanen has written three book chapters and he presented about 50 papers in international conferences.

Marjo Rissanen

Marjo Rissanen, Prime Multimedia Ltd, Helsinki, Finlan. Mrs Marjo Rissanen is a senior consultant, focusing on the health informatics design area. She received her master degree from Helsinki University, Faculty of Medicine, Finland. She has worked in Helsinki University, in Ministry of Social Affairs and Health, and in consultancy companies in research and design activities. She has worked also in international projects, e.g., in Sri Lanka in a cost-control information system project for an orthopaedic hospital. She has lectured for the academia, health organizations, and industry also in international contexts. Her research interests cover topics connected to translational health technology and design, consumer-targeted health informatics, related quality and design challenges. She has written 16 peer-reviewed articles about timely topics.

T Saipraba

T Saipraba, Sathyabama Institute of Science and Technology, Jeppiaar Nagar, Rajiv Gandhi Salai, Chennai, Tamilnadu, India. Dr T Saipraba is working as the vice chancellor of Sathyabama Institute of Science and Technology. Her research interests are in the areas of decision support systems, distributed data mining, machine learning, and related applications. She has authored many publications in high impact, peer reviewed journals and conferences.

Sagar G Sangodkar

Sagar G Sangodkar, Indian Institute of Technology Bombay, Powai, Mumbai, Maharashtra, India. Mr Sagar G Sangodkar received his MTech (by Research) degree from the Electrical Engineering Department, Indian Institute of Technology Bombay, Mumbai, India, in the year 2020. He completed his BTech degree in Electronics and Communication Engineering from National Institute of Technology Goa, Goa, India, in the year 2015. In Jan 2021, he joined Hitachi Central Research Laboratory, Kokubunji, Japan as a Researcher. Before that, in 2020, he worked as an artificial intelligence research apprentice in a German-based AI company, Tvarit GmbH. His main research interests include image processing, computer vision, machine learning, and deep learning. His other interests/hobbies include reading fiction books, playing sports such as badminton, lawn tennis, and musical instruments such as guitar and piano.

Manan Shah

Manan Shah, Department of Chemical Engineering, Pandit Deendayal Petroleum University, Raisan, Gandhinagar, Gujarat, India. Dr Manan Shah is a BE in Chemical Engineering from LD College of Engineering and MTech in Petroleum Engineering from School of Petroleum Technology, PDPU. He has completed his PhD in the area of exploration and exploitation of Geothermal Energy in the state of Gujarat. He is currently working as an Assistant Professor in Department of Chemical Engineering, School of Technology (SOT), PDPU and Research Scientist in Centre of Excellence for Geothermal energy (CEGE). His research interests include renewable energy sector, pattern recognition, image processing, data analysis, and artificial intelligence. He has published several articles in reputed international journals in the area of many sectors. He serves as an active reviewer for several reputable international journals from Springer and Elsevier. Dr Shah is a young and dynamic academician and researcher in the various engineering fields. Dr Shah has guided more than 150+ students for profile building activities.

Tarun Kumar Sharma

Tarun Kumar Sharma, Department of Computer Science and Engineering, Shobhit University Gangoh, Saharanpur, India. Tarun Kumar Sharma has his PhD in the field of Computational Intelligence from Indian Institute of Technology (IIT), Roorkee, India. His current research interest encompasses evolutionary algorithms, software engineering, inventory systems and image processing. He has published more than 60 papers in refereed international journals and conferences of repute. He received the MCA degree from SGRRITS, Dehradun, affiliated to H.N.B. Garhwal University, Srinagar, UK, India; MTech (IT) from KSOU Karnataka and MBA (Mktg.) from VMOU Kota, Rajasthan. He has more than fourteen years of experience. Presently he is affiliated with Amity University Rajasthan as an Associate Professor in the Department of Computer Science Engineering. He is Program Chair of Soft Computing: Theories and Applications (SoCTA2016).

Rishi Sinhal

Rishi Sinhal, Electronics and Communication Engineering, PDPM Indian Institute of Information Technology Design and Manufacturing, Jabalpur, India. Rishi Sinhal received the BE degree in electronics and communication engineering from the Jabalpur Engineering College, Jabalpur, India, and the ME degree in digital techniques and instrumentation from SGSITS, Indore, India. He is currently pursuing a PhD degree in electronics and communication engineering with the PDPM Indian Institute of Information Technology, Design and Manufacturing Jabalpur, India. His research interests include image watermarking, image processing, signal and image processing applications, multimedia security and machine learning techniques.

M Suresha

M Suresha, Department of PG Studies and Research in Computer Science, Kuvempu University, Shankarghatta, India. Dr M Suresha is an Assistant Professor at the Department of Computer Science, Kuvempu University, India. He received the Master's and Doctoral degree from Kuvempu University, he has 14 years of teaching and research experience and two years of IT industry experience. He published more than 80 articles in peer-reviewed international journals and his area of research includes image processing, computer vision, and deep learning.

Niranjan Suthar

Niranjan Suthar, Indian Institute of Technology Bombay, Powai, Mumbai, Maharashtra, India. Mr Niranjan Suthar received his BTech + MTech dual degree with a specialization in Communication and Signal Processing from Electrical Engineering Department, Indian Institute of Technology Bombay, Mumbai, India, in the year 2020. In Dec. 2020, he joined AVA Retail, Surat, India, as a Computer Vision Engineer. His main research interests include artificial intelligence, image processing, computer vision, machine learning, and deep learning. His other interests include playing computer games, badminton, and dance.

Mohammad Taheri

Mohammad Taheri, Department of Computer Engineering and Information Technology, Shiraz University, Shiraz, Iran. Mohammad Taheri was born in 1983. He achieved BS, MS and PhD degrees as an outstanding student in Computer Science Department of Shiraz University (Iran) between 2001 and 2013. He started his job, as the faculty member (2014), with researches in machine learning, fuzzy systems, large margin classifiers, optimization, modeling and information hiding.

Hanzhou Wu

 **Hanzhou Wu**, Shanghai University, Baoshan District, Shanghai, China. Dr Hanzhou Wu, PhD, received his BE and PhD degrees in information security from Southwest Jiaotong University, Chengdu, China, in June 2011 and June 2017, respectively. He was a visiting scholar in New Jersey Institute of Technology from October 2014 to October 2016. From July 2017 to March 2019, he was a research staff in Institute of Automation, Chinese Academy of Sciences, Beijing, China. Currently, he is an assistant professor in School of Communication and Information Engineering, Shanghai University, Shanghai, China. His research interests include steganography/steganalysis, watermarking, graph optimization and AI security. Dr Wu has authored/co-authored more than 40 papers in peer-reviewed journals and conferences such as IEEE TDSC, IEEE TCSVT, ACM IH&MMSec, and IEEE WIFS. Dr Wu has written two book chapters, and served as a reviewer for more than 30 peer journals and conferences such as IEEE TIFS, IEEE TCSVT, IEEE TSMCS, IEEE IoT Journal, and IEEE ICASSP. Dr Wu has received more than 600 citations from Google Scholar.

Chapter 1

Blind image watermarking with efficient dual restoration feature

Rishi Sinhal, Tarun Kumar Sharma, Irshad Ahmad Ansari and Varun Bajaj

The use of digital images is increasing day by day due to easy availability of handy and user friendly digital devices. Thus, the security, authentication, and restoration issues of digital images have been increased. This work presents a blind color image watermarking scheme with dual restoration (color and gray) features. The host image is first divided into blocks and then block-wise watermark embedding is done using the least significant bit replacement approach. A key based random binary sequence is used to authenticate the blocks against different tampering attacks. The block-wise recovery information is also inserted randomly (key based) into different blocks. Block neighborhood and block averaging approaches are employed during tamper localization and restoration procedure, respectively. The dual restoration feature enhances the practicability for the applications like the identification of face, text/number, or article. Experimental outcomes show that the scheme can efficiently detect, localize and restore (both color and gray) the tampered watermarked images even for severe tampering.

1.1 Introduction

Nowadays, the use of the internet is an incorporated piece of individuals' lives. Individuals utilize computerized ways for different purposes, for example, charge installments, cash transfer, sharing information (pictures, recordings, and so forth), and so on [1–3]. By and large, online accessible information is effectively open to clients even without legitimate approval [4]. Along these lines, the chance of information falsification/adjustment cannot be overlooked. The validity of computerized information has been an inevitable security issue [5]. Digital data (e.g. images) are commonly utilized in online communications. This information can be modified effectively to misguide consumers [6]. Therefore, tamper detection/localization and the recovery of the tampered with (modified) part of the image are greatly required [7]. Many techniques such as steganography [8], cryptography [9], and watermarking [10] are widely used to secure digital information significantly. Digital image watermarking [11] is broadly utilized to secure digital images against illegal access, tampering/alteration and different processing attacks (e.g. compression, filtering, scaling and geometrical attacks, etc) [12]. In digital image watermarking, the watermark signal (e.g. text, image, etc) is inserted into the image (host) in a specified (algorithmic) manner and the outcome is known as the watermarked image. The watermark data can be extracted to check copyright or integrity related information during extraction [13]. Digital image watermarking can be categorized into different types [11]. Normally, image authentication and restoration are conducted by utilizing watermarking schemes of a fragile nature. The restoration data gets inserted with the fragile sequence (used for authentication purposes) to restore the altered part after the tamper detection/localization procedure [14].

Most of the watermarking schemes available in the watermarking literature are dedicated to a specific type of images (gray or color) [14–17], however, some of the schemes can be utilized for gray as well as color image types [18]. Although both types of images (gray and color) are in use by people, the color images are mostly preferred for sharing information. Larger memory space is needed to embed the authentication information (fragile watermark) for color images than for gray images. Likewise, the memory requirement to preserve the recovery information of a color image is higher (nearly three times) as compared to a gray image. There are many applications (like text data authentication, object verification, face identification, etc) in which the color information is just like additional data (which only gives an insight of the color of text/object, etc). For example, the meaning of the text information would be the same irrespective of its color. Therefore, the restoration of digital color images in a gray version can also be useful. It has an added advantage that it requires less memory space for preserving the information. Thus, more copies of recovery data can be preserved in the same memory space. It ensures better restoration (in gray version) of the tampered with image without affecting the imperceptibility of the watermarked image (color) [19].

This work presents a fragile watermarking method for the tamper detection, localization, and restoration of digital color images. This scheme efficiently detects/localizes the tampered with portion of the image. Moreover, it provides recovery of the tampered with image in the color as well as in the gray version. Therefore, it has an additional feature as compared to the many existing fragile schemes. The core contribution of the proposed work is listed pointwise as:

1. Effective tamper detection and localization with nearly 99% accuracy irrespective of the tampering sizes.
2. The randomized approach enhances the security against unauthorized access.
3. Significant self-recovery with dual restoration features improves the practicability and superiority over other existing schemes.

1.2 Literature review

In the literature of fragile watermarking, many schemes were proposed earlier to authenticate and restore the tampered with/forged images. Some of the fragile schemes [20–22] only detect and localize the tampered with portion, whereas the other schemes [23, 24] can also restore the tampered with area after the tamper localization. Some of the relevant existing schemes have been discussed in this section.

He *et al* [25] presented the fragile scheme using block neighborhood approach and non-linear mapping. The scheme had the ability of tamper detection and self-recovery. The block-wise partition of the original image was performed to embed the watermark information. The scheme used three different optimization processes to improve the quality of tamper detection and restoration. The obtained results show that the scheme was effective against different types of tampering attack and able to restore the tampered with image for tampering rate up to 60%. Chang *et al* [26] authored a fragile method using the concept of local binary pattern (LBP). The host image is block-wise divided into 3×3 size blocks for watermark insertion. The LBP operator was used to generate the authentication data, whereas the average pixel value was used to get the recovery information related to each block. The presented results are significant in terms of imperceptibility and detection accuracy. However, more analysis including visual results was needed to check the applicability of the scheme on different images in terms of restoration capability for different tampering rates. Ansari *et al* [27] presented an image watermarking method for tamper localization and restoration. The singular value decomposition (SVD) based approach divided the host image into 4×4 size blocks and SVD was applied on each block to get the singular matrix. Further, the singular matrix was used to get the authentication data that would be used to authenticate the block during the detection process. To generate the recovery information, each block was again divided into four non-overlapping 2×2 size blocks. The recovery information of each block was embedded into the other blocks using encrypted mapping procedure. The least sognificant bits (LSB) replacement process was used to embed the authentication and recovery data into the blocks. Experimental outcomes revealed that the tamper detection is nearly 99.5% accurate but the significant recovery can be achieved with up to 50% tampering rate. Singh and Agrawal [28] introduced a watermarking scheme for tamper detection and recovery of the tampered with images. The scheme performed pixel-wise tamper detection and restoration. The multi-level detection process had been employed to check the authenticity of the pixel. During restoration, the processing domain (spatial or frequency) is selected based on the type of block. The scheme achieved significant parametric results even for high tampering rate (up to 75%) but the multi-stage procedures for each pixel may increase the time complexity significantly. Singh and Singh [29] offered a self-embedding mechanism based fragile watermarking technique for the digital images in order to authenticate and recover the tampered with images. The scheme employed the concept of quantization, block-wise division and discrete cosine transform (DCT) for embedding the watermark. The embedded watermark was prepared using authentication and recovery data. Although the scheme has significant tamper localization accuracy due to the use of small-size blocks (2×2 size), it cannot be used to get significant recovery of the tampered images in the case of severe tampering. Belferdi *et al* [30] offered a self-embedding based color image watermarking technique using block-wise partition, Torus automorphism and Bayer pattern. The restoration data (color recovery information) was first reduced to gray version using Bayer pattern. Thus, the scheme reduced the watermark size and used the available embedding space for inserting three copies of the watermark. The watermark information (authentication data+recovery data) was inserted into the last 2-LSB bits of the pixel's values. The scheme provided good results upto 25% tampering rate as per the manuscript but the performance was not analyzed for severely tampered with images. Molina *et al* [31] proposed the watermarking scheme for color images to provide image authentication and self-recovery against tampering. The authentication information was obtained by XORing the neighbor blocks and the halftoning approach was used to generate the recovery data. Further, three copies of the restoration data were embedded to get effective performance in terms of self-recovery. The results are good in terms of tamper detection and restoration for moderate tampering (<50% tampering rate), but the restoration quality degraded for higher tampering rates. Al-Otum *et al* [32] recently proposed a fragile watermarking scheme for the authentication and restoration of the color images using multiple domain procedures. The scheme used the concept of block-wise division, SVD, and DCT. Two types of watermark (namely dependent and independent) data had been used for the embedding. The authentication bits were obtained using SVD and restoration bits were generated with the help of the mean value of the block. LSB bit replacement process was employed to insert the dependent watermark, whereas a DCT based approach was used to embed the content independent watermark information. The scheme has good imperceptibility and authentication ability but the restoration of tampered with images was limited to the 50% tampering rate. Sinhal *et al* [19] presented a fragile watermarking scheme for digital color images using 2-bit LSB replacement approach. A random binary sequence has been used as the watermark data that will be used to authenticate the 2×4 size blocks. The scheme used content (or block) independent authentication watermark, therefore it can effectively resist block based tampering attacks. This scheme can restore the tampered with watermarked images in color as well as gray version. To do this, the scheme embedded the recovery data of both type (color and gray). Experimental outcomes confirmed that the scheme has high tamper detection accuracy (>99%) and acceptable restoration (color and gray) ability even for severely tampered with images. However, the block size having equal rows and columns can be more effective in tamper detection, localization and image restoration.

As per the study of fragile watermarking schemes available in the literature, it can be assumed that most of the schemes do not provide dual restoration feature. Some of them even did not perform effectively against high tampering rates. This work presents an extension of our previous work [19] that can effectively perform for severe tampering attacks as well as giving dual restoration features. The randomized permutation and the random binary sequence are used for preparing the watermark. A pseudo random generator algorithm [33] has been used to get key based randomization for improved security. The scheme used blocks with equal rows and columns, thus improving the approach to get effective outcomes. The next section presents the proposed scheme in detail.

1.3 Proposed fragile watermarking scheme

The scheme proposed in this work can be categorized into different parts as watermark pre-processing, watermark embedding, watermark extraction (to authenticate the image and get the recovery data), and self-recovery of the tampered with image (color as well as gray). The proposed scheme is explained in detail in the following subsections.

1.3.1 Watermark pre-processing

The following steps are used to pre-process the watermark before embedding.

1. Select the host color image (510 × 510) and convert it into gray type (H_{gray}).
2. Divide the image H_{gray} into 3 × 3 size uniform blocks. Let the total no. of blocks be N.
3. Compute the average intensity of each block in the binary form and choose 6 MSBs (most significant bits) for each block. These 6-MSBs represents the recovery information of the corresponding block.
4. Now concatenate the recovery information of each block in a random manner (using key K_i) to get the binary sequence G_{recov} (length = $N \times 6$ bits). Where K_i represents the key used for randominzation and $i = 2, 3$ or 4.
5. Perform step 2–4 for the first channel of the host color image and obtain the Sequence R_{ch-1}.
6. Generate the key (say K_1) based random fragile sequence F_{seq} of length $N \times 6$ bits that would be used as the fragile watermark for authentication purpose.
7. Select 6 bits from F_{seq}, G_{recov} and R_{ch-1} in sequence and combine them to get 18-bit sequences W_{18-bit}.
8. Likewise, generate 18-bit sequences by combining the remaining bits of F_{seq}, G_{recov} and R_{ch-1} in a similar fashion and obtain the sequence W_{seq-1}.

Thus, the binary sequence W_{seq-1} contains the F_{seq} (for tamper detection/localization), R_{ch-1} (the recovery information of the same channel) and a copy of the recovery information of the gray version (G_{recov}). Similarly, get the sequences W_{seq-2} and W_{seq-3} for the second and third channel of the host image, respectively.

1.3.2 Watermark embedding

The embedding steps are as follows:

1. Select the first channel of the host image H_{img} and split it into 3 × 3 size blocks.
2. Choose first 3 × 3 size block and convert the pixels into 8-bit binary form.
3. Take first 18 bits from W_{seq-1} and replace the 2 lSB bits corresponding to each pixel value in a specified manner.
4. Repeat the steps 2 and 3 for each non-overlapping block to embed the W_{seq-1} sequence into the first channel.
5. Similarly, embed the sequences W_{seq-2} and W_{seq-3} into the second and the third channel of the host image.

After the completion of watermark embedding process, the watermarked image W_{img} is obtained. The watermark embedding process is shown in figure 1.1.

1.3.3 Watermark extraction

The block diagram of the watermark extraction process is shown in figure 1.2. The following steps are used for the watermark extraction process.

1. Perform block-wise division on the first channel of the received image W_{img} to divide it into 3×3 size non-overlapping blocks.
2. Select the first block and extract the 2-LSB bits corresponding to each pixel to get the 18-bit sequence EW_{18-bit}. Repeat the step for each non-overlapping 3×3 size block of the channel.
3. Select the bits from EW_{18-bit} in the same order (as used during embedding) to obtain the fragile sequence E_F_{seq}, the gray recovery data E_G_{recov1} and the recovery data of the channel E_R_{ch-1}.
4. Yield the fragile sequence F_{seq} using the same secret key (as used during embedding).
5. Compare the corresponding bits of F_{seq} and the extracted fragile sequence E_F_{seq} to detect the tampered with blocks.
6. Repeat steps 2 to 5 for the remaining channels of W_{img} to authenticate the received image and extract the recovery information.
7. Apply block neighborhood approach [25] to smoothen the authenticated image for better authentication.

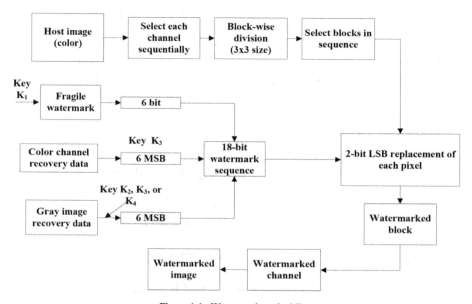

Figure 1.1. Watermark embedding

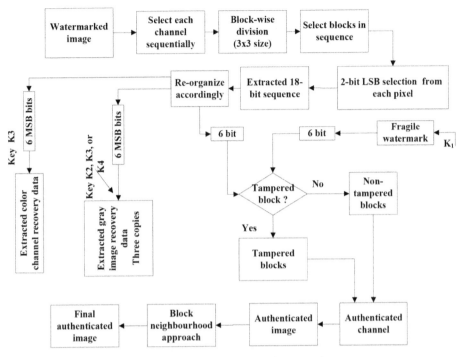

Figure 1.2. Watermark extraction process.

1.3.4 Self-recovery process

After the extraction process, if it is found that any part of the image has been tampered with then the tampered with region can be recovered with the help of the preserved recovery information. The recovery can be done in color as well as in the gray form. The steps used for the self-recovery of the tampered image are given as:

1. Divide the first channel of the authenticated image into 3×3 size blocks and select a tampered block (TB).
2. Check the mapped block (MB) (that has been used for preserving the recovery information of the tampered block TB) for tampering. The mapping can be done using the same secret key as used at the time of embedding.
3. If the mapped block MB is not tampered with then get the extracted recovery information $\boldsymbol{R}_{bits}$ (i.e. 6-bits) corresponding to block MB from $\boldsymbol{E\_R}_{ch-1}$. (It is important to note that in the case of the tampered mapped block, the corresponding recovery information cannot be used for the recovery of TB.)
4. Add 2 padding bits (e.g. 10) with the $\boldsymbol{R}_{bits}$ to generate the 8-bit binary value and convert it into a decimal number.
5. Replace each pixel value of the tampered block resultant from the previous step.
6. Follow step 2 to 5 for each tampered block of each channel of the authenticated image.
7. Apply block averaging [19] process on the result to get the final recovered image (color).

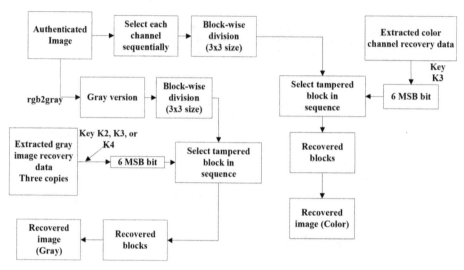

Figure 1.3. Self-recovery process (color as well as gray).

To recover the tampered with image in the gray form, the authenticated image is first converted into the gray form. Afterward, steps 1–6 are applied to get the recovered image (gray). During the gray image recovery, three copies of extracted gray recovery data E_G_{recov1}, E_G_{recov2} and E_G_{recov3} would be used. It improves the recovery results as the recovery information of each block has been preserved at three different positions (corresponding to each channel). The recovery process is also presented in figure 1.3.

1.4 Experimental results and discussion

Experimental analysis has been performed on different images (original images by authors) to test the performance of the scheme in terms of tamper detection and self-recovery. The imperceptibility parameter peak signal-to-noise ratio (PSNR) [34] has been used to test the visual quality of the watermarked and the recovered images. Figure 1.4 shows different host images, respective watermarked images, and PSNR values. The experimental outcomes show that the visual quality of the watermarked images is significantly good and the embedded information (fragile watermark and the recovery information) are completely imperceptiblie to viewers.

1.4.1 Tamper detection anaylsis

In this section, the tamper detection ability of the proposed work has been investigated by applying different types of tampering on the watermarked images. From the experimentation, it is observed that the proposed scheme is able to detect different types of tampering in an efficient manner. Further, the obtained detection results (by the proposed work) have been smoothened using the block neighborhood

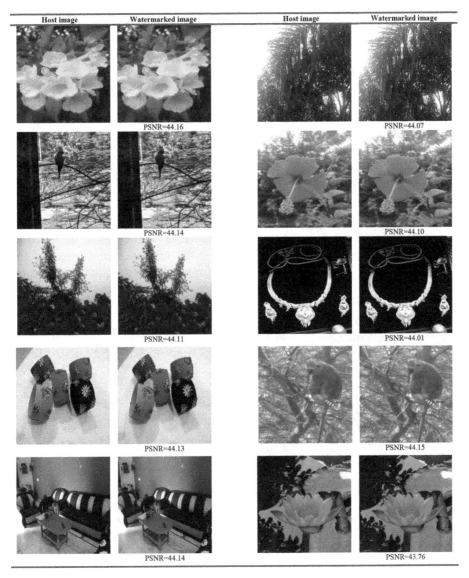

| Host image | Watermarked image | Host image | Watermarked image |

PSNR=44.16 | PSNR=44.07

PSNR=44.14 | PSNR=44.10

PSNR=44.11 | PSNR=44.01

PSNR=44.13 | PSNR=44.15

PSNR=44.14 | PSNR=43.76

Figure 1.4. Visual quality analysis for different test images.

approach. The accuracy (*Acc*) of tamper detection has been computed as per equation 1.1 given as:

$$Acc = \frac{\text{no of detected tampered blocks}}{\text{no. of total tampered blocks}} \qquad (1.1)$$

Since the tamper detection is block-wise, the compel 3 × 3 size block can be considered either tampered or non-tampered based on the detection ability. Here, even if a few pixels of a 3 × 3 size block are modified due to tampering/forgery then all 9 pixels of the block would be marked as tampered with/modified. It somehow reduces the accuracy of exact tampering detection (since the original/ non-tampered pixels are marked as tampered because of the block-wise detection process). Therefore, the small block size (3 × 3) has been selected to reduce the error because of the mentioned issue. Figure 1.5 shows the tamper detection process using experimental results that clearly explains the use of the block neighborhood process for the improvement in the tamper detection. Here, a 50% part of the watermarked image has been deleted (content removal) and then the tampered with area is authenticated using the proposed method. Similarly, figure 1.6 presents the tamper detection results for a manipulative tampering attack. Figure 1.7 depicts tamper detection results for different tampering rate (α). From the experimental outcomes, it is noticed that the accuracy of tamper detection is very high (nearly 99%) for different values of α.

As described in figure 1.7, efficient tamper detection results have been achieved for the different sizes of tampering. However, only the content removal attack has been performed to generate the above-mentioned results (as in figure 1.7). There are other different types of tampering such as copy-move, copy-paste, replacing the object, adding/removing text, or other manipulative tampering attacks, that can be used to tamper with the watermarked images. Therefore, the performance of the watermarking scheme should also be investigated against these types of manipulative attacks. Figure 1.8 represents the tamper detection results for the different manipulative attacks.

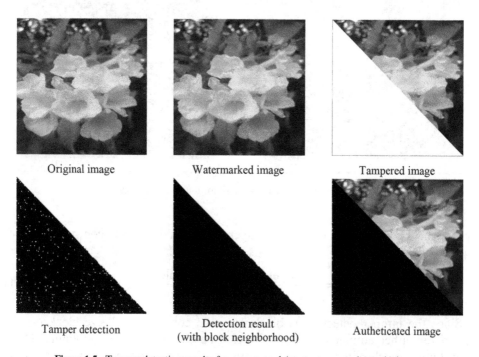

Original image   Watermarked image   Tampered image

Tamper detection   Detection result (with block neighborhood)   Autheticated image

Figure 1.5. Tamper detection results for a tampered (content removal attack) image.

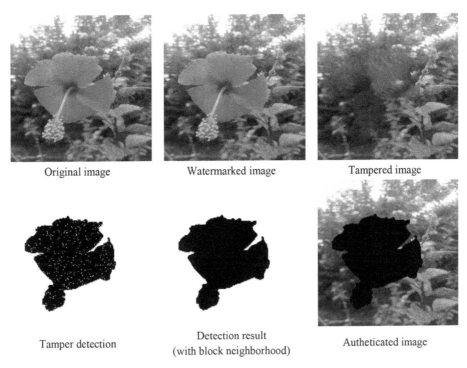

Original image	Watermarked image	Tampered image

| Tamper detection | Detection result (with block neighborhood) | Autheticated image |

Figure 1.6. Tamper detection results for a manipulative tampering attack.

As described in figure 1.8, the proposed scheme is able to detect different manipulative tampering attacks like replacing object, object removal, multiple copy, copy-move, copy-paste, text editing and other intentional forgery types. In the case of each attack, the scheme detected the tampered portion with more than 99% accuracy (except in the case of text editing, where it is nearly 96%). In terms of overall performance, the average tamper detection and localization accuracy of the proposed scheme is nearly 99%. The next section presents the self-recovery results for different types of tampered watermarked images (for different tampering rates).

1.4.2 Self-recovery of the tampered portion

In this section, the self-recovery ability of the proposed scheme has been examined against different types of tampering/manipulation attacks on the watermarked images. From the experimentation, it is observed that the proposed scheme efficiently recovers the tampered portions of the watermarked image even for a severely tampered with image. The block averaging approach further improves the quality of the recovered image. The recovery results (i.e. PSNR) have been computed with respect to the watermarked images. Figures 1.9 and 1.10 depict the experimental results for different types of manipulative tampering attacks, which shows that the self-recovery ability of the scheme is significant in both cases (color image recovery as well as gray image recovery). However, the quality of the gray

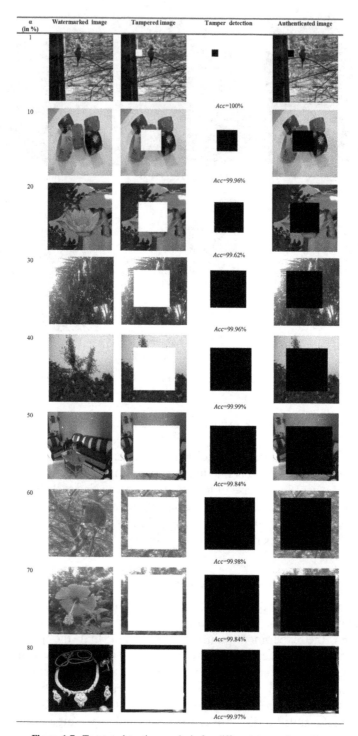

Figure 1.7. Tamper detection analysis for different tampering rates.

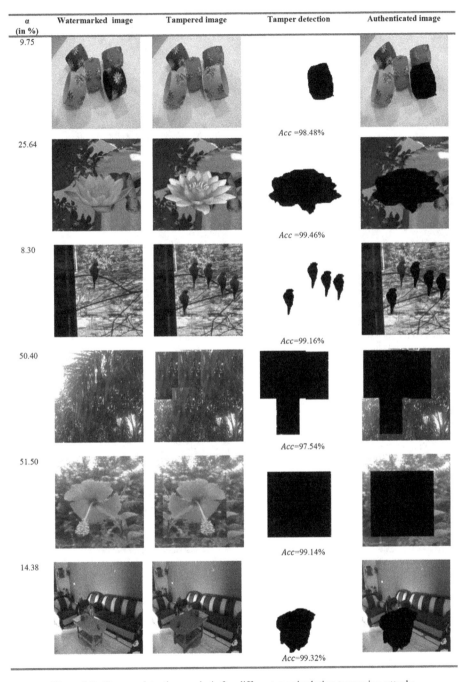

Figure 1.8. Tamper detection analysis for different manipulative tampering attacks.

image (recovered) is higher than the color image (recovered). It is because the three copies of gray image restoration data have been inserted at the time of embedding.

The recovery analysis in a detailed manner against different tampering sizes (from low to high) and types have been studied. Some of the results have been presented in

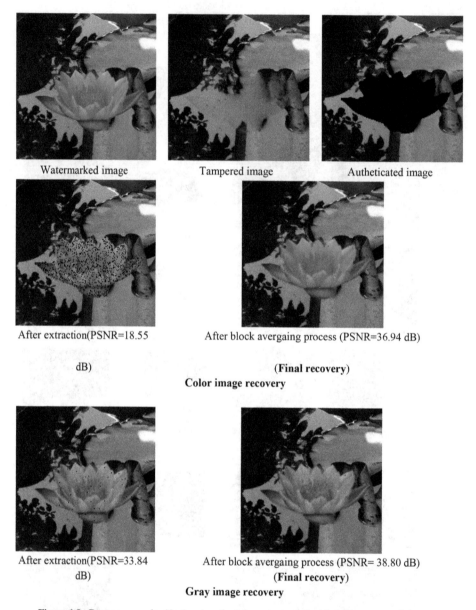

Figure 1.9. Recovery results (dual restoration) for a tampered with (object removal) image.

figure 1.11, which show an effective tamper localization and restoration for different sizes of tampering (i.e. deletion). On the other, side figure 1.12 shows the results against different types of random tampering/manipulation.

The presented results confirm that the scheme can detect, localize and recover the tampered with part of the watermarked image successfully, even in the case of high tampering rate (α). The experimental investigation reveals that the tamper localization

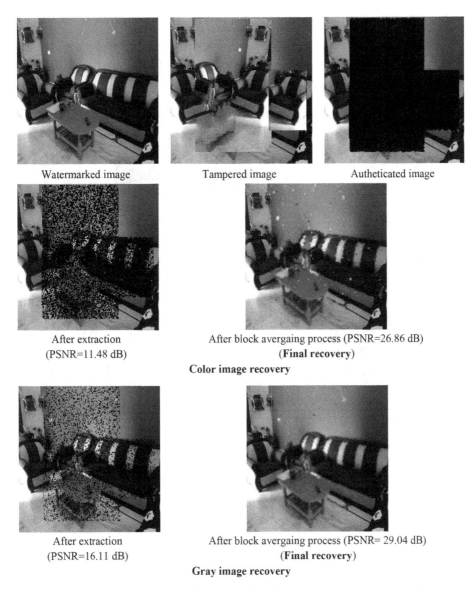

Watermarked image   Tampered image   Autheticated image

After extraction   After block avergaing process (PSNR=26.86 dB)
(PSNR=11.48 dB)   (**Final recovery**)

Color image recovery

After extraction   After block avergaing process (PSNR= 29.04 dB)
(PSNR=16.11 dB)   (**Final recovery**)

Gray image recovery

Figure 1.10. Recovery results (dual restoration) for a copy-paste tampering attack.

accuracy is nearly 99%, however, the considerable recovery of the tampered image is possible for $70 < \alpha < 80$ (in %) in the case of color image restoration. Instead, acceptable recovery can be obtained in the case of gray image restoration for $80 < \alpha < 90$ (in %). The reason for the improvement in the gray image restoration quality as compared to the color image restoration is that multiple copies (i.e. three copies) of gray image restoration data have been embedded during watermark insertion. The scheme gives highly acceptable results and can be helpful to accurately authenticate the images against forgery/manipulation. Further, if the image is found to be tampered

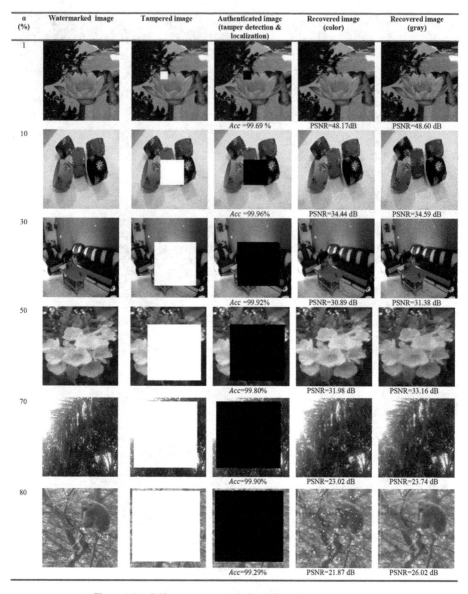

α (%)	Watermarked image	Tampered image	Authenticated image (tamper detection & localization)	Recovered image (color)	Recovered image (gray)
1			Acc =99.69 %	PSNR=48.17dB	PSNR=48.60 dB
10			Acc =99.96%	PSNR=34.44 dB	PSNR=34.59 dB
30			Acc =99.92%	PSNR=30.89 dB	PSNR=31.38 dB
50			Acc=99.80%	PSNR=31.98 dB	PSNR=33.16 dB
70			Acc=99.90%	PSNR=23.02 dB	PSNR=23.74 dB
80			Acc=99.29%	PSNR=21.87 dB	PSNR=26.02 dB

Figure 1.11. Self-recovery analysis for different tampering rates.

with then the proposed scheme is able to recover the tampered with portion even in the case of severe tampering.

Block-wise watermarking is a common phenomenon, especially in the case of fragile watermarking schemes. Likewise, the concept of block-wise watermarking has also been used in the proposed scheme. Tamper detection, localization and self-recovery are based on blocks in the proposed scheme. Therefore, the block size plays an important role in the performance of the scheme. Higher block sizes reduce the

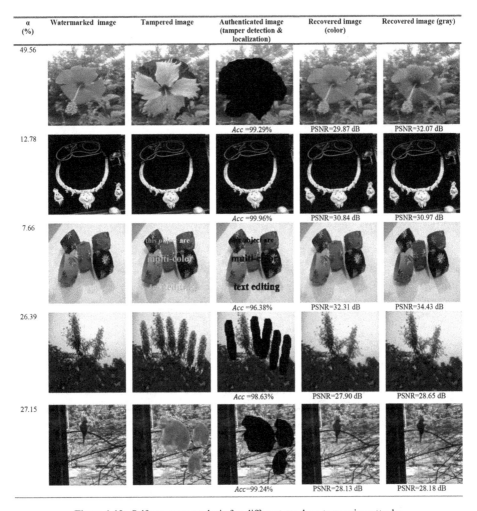

α (%)	Watermarked image	Tampered image	Authenticated image (tamper detection & localization)	Recovered image (color)	Recovered image (gray)
49.56			Acc =99.29%	PSNR=29.87 dB	PSNR=32.07 dB
12.78			Acc =99.96%	PSNR=30.84 dB	PSNR=30.97 dB
7.66			Acc =96.38%	PSNR=32.31 dB	PSNR=34.43 dB
26.39			Acc =98.63%	PSNR=27.90 dB	PSNR=28.65 dB
27.15			Acc=99.24%	PSNR=28.13 dB	PSNR=28.18 dB

Figure 1.12. Self-recovery analysis for different random tampering attacks.

authentication accuracy because even if a single pixel is tampered with/modified, the complete block would be detected as tampered with. Thus, the original part of the image is also considered as tampered with/altered (which is actually wrong). However, the higher block size gives an advantage of high watermark storing capacity. Conversely, the lower block size provides less space to embed the watermark data but reduces the chances of wrong authentication (as in the case of higher block sizes). The block size that has been selected for the proposed scheme is 3×3 (9 pixels in a block). This block size gives a fair amount of storage space while maintaining significant imperceptibility. Additionally, it decreases the possibility of wrong authentication as compared to higher block size based fragile schemes. Subjective comparison with the other existing fragile watermarking schemes has been performed and is presented in table 1.1.

Table 1.1. Subjective comparison with the existing schemes.

S. No.	Features	He *et al* [25]	Singh and Singh [29]	Belferdi *et al* [30]	Al-Otum *et al* [32]	Proposed method
1	Type of scheme	Fragile	Fragile	Fragile	Fragile	Fragile
2	Target host type	Gray	Gray and color	Color	Color	Color
3	Watermarking domain	Spatial	Transform	Spatial	Spatial + transform	Spatial
4	Extraction process	Blind	Blind	Blind	Blind	Blind
5	Embedding PSNR (in dB)	~ 44	~ 39	~ 44	~ 43	~ 44
6	Tamper localization	Yes	Yes	Yes	Yes	Yes
7	Self-recovery	Yes	Yes	Yes	Yes	Yes
8	Dual restoration	No	No	No	No	Yes
9	Restoration for severely tampered with images ($\alpha > 50\%$)	Yes	No	No	No	Yes

1.5 Conclusion

This work proposed a blind fragile watermarking scheme for color images with effective tamper detection, localization and restoration characteristics. At first, the watermark is prepared using the random binary sequence (for tamper detection and authentication), color image recovery data and the gray image recovery data. The host image is divided into uniform and non-overlapping blocks having the block size of 3×3. Afterward the watermark is inserted into the blocks by replacing last 2-LSB bits of each pixel of the blocks. Thus, an 18-bit sequence (which contains 6 bit authentication bits, 6-bit color recovery data of a different block and 6-bit gray recovery data of another block) is embedded into each block of the host image. During tamper detection, the block neighborhood approach has been used to smoothen the detection results for better authentication. Similarly, the block averaging process is adopted to improve the restoration results in terms of visual quality and parametric results. The proposed scheme gives high imperceptibility, efficient tamper detection and localiztion, and significant restoration results. Moreover, the scheme is able to restore the tampered with image in color as well as gray type. This dual restoration feature makes the scheme more versatile than the existing fragile watermarking schemes.

Acknowledgements

This work was supported by Faculty Initiation Grant of PDPM Indian Institute of Information Technology Design and Manufacturing Jabalpur, India.

References

[1] Choi S and Mokhtarian P L 2020 How attractive is it to use the internet while commuting? A work-attitude-based segmentation of Northern California commuters *Transp. Res. A* **138** 37–50

[2] Raccanello D, Burro R, Brondino M and Pasini M 2017, June Use of internet and wellbeing: a mixed-device survey *Int. Conf. in Methodologies and intelligent Systems for Technology Enhanced Learning* (Cham: Springer) pp 65–73

[3] Athanasopoulou C, Välimäki M, Koutra K, Löttyniemi E, Bertsias A, Basta M, Vgontzas A N and Lionis C 2017 Internet use, eHealth literacy and attitudes toward computer/internet among people with schizophrenia spectrum disorders: a cross-sectional study in two distant European regions *BMC Med. Inf. Decis. Making* **17** 136

[4] Kim H K and Park J 2020 Examination of the protection offered by current accessibility acts and guidelines to people with disabilities in using information technology devices *Electronics* **9** 742

[5] Deep S, Zheng X, Jolfaei A, Yu D, Ostovari P and Kashif Bashir A 2020 A survey of security and privacy issues in the Internet of Things from the layered context *Trans. Emerg. Telecommun. Technol.* e3935

[6] Mishra S, Sharma S K and Alowaidi M A 2020 Analysis of security issues of cloud-based web applications *J. Amb. Intel. Hum. Comp.* 1–12

[7] Sarkar D, Palit S, Som S and Dey K N 2020 Large scale image tamper detection and restoration *Multimedia Tools Appl.* 1–31

[8] Provos N and Honeyman P 2003 Hide and seek: an introduction to steganography *IEEE Secur. Priv.* **1** 32–44

[9] Katz J and Lindell Y 2020 *Introduction to Modern Cryptography* (Boca Raton, FL: CRC Press)

[10] Katzenbeisser S and Petitcolas F A P 2000 *Digital Watermarking* (London: Artech House) 2

[11] Potdar V M, Han S and Chang E 2005 A survey of digital image watermarking techniques *INDIN'05. 2005 3rd IEEE Int. Conf. on Industrial Informatics, 2005* (Piscataway, NJ: IEEE) pp 709–16

[12] Thapa M, Sood S K and Sharma A M 2011 Digital image watermarking technique based on different attacks *Int. J. Adv. Comp. Sci. Appl.* **2**

[13] Lai C C and Tsai C C 2010 Digital image watermarking using discrete wavelet transform and singular value decomposition *IEEE Trans. Instrum. Meas.* **59** 3060–63

[14] Zhang X and Wang S 2008 Fragile watermarking with error-free restoration capability *IEEE Trans. Multimedia* **10** 1490–99

[15] Zhang X and Wang S 2009 Fragile watermarking scheme using a hierarchical mechanism *Signal Process.* **89** 675–79

[16] Liu K C 2012 Colour image watermarking for tamper proofing and pattern-based recovery *IET Image Proc.* **6** 445–54

[17] Wang M S and Chen W C 2007 A majority-voting based watermarking scheme for color image tamper detection and recovery *Comput. Stand. Interfaces* **29** 561–70

[18] Singh D and Singh S K 2016 Effective self-embedding watermarking scheme for image tampered detection and localization with recovery capability *J. Visual Commun. Image Represent.* **38** 775–89

[19] Sinhal R, Ansari I A and Ahn C W 2020 Blind image watermarking scheme for image authentication and restoration with improved restoration features *The 9th Int. Conf. on Smart Media and Applications SMA 2020 (Jeju, Republic of Korea)* (New York: ACM)

[20] Sutcu Y, Coskun B, Sencar H T and Memon N 2007 Tamper detection based on regularity of wavelet transform coefficients *2007 IEEE Int. Conf. on Image Processing* vol 1 (Piscataway, NJ: IEEE) pp 1–397

[21] Fridrich J 1999, October Methods for tamper detection in digital images *Multimedia and Security, Workshop at ACM Multimedia* **vol 99** 29–34

[22] Fridrich J 1998 Image watermarking for tamper detection *Proc. 1998 Int. Conf. on Image Processing. ICIP98 (Cat. No. 98CB36269)* vol 2 (Piscataway, NJ: IEEE) pp 404–8

[23] Chao Y, Liu S and Liu H 2018 A novel semi-fragile watermarking algorithm with tamper localization and self-recovery *2018 IEEE 9th Int. Conf. on Software Engineering and Service Science (ICSESS)* (Piscataway, NJ: IEEE) pp 186–90

[24] Lin C H, Liu J C, Hsu W C, Wang H W, Lin W C and Li J W 2010, June Image tampering detection and recovery using dual watermarks and cyclic redundancy checks *Int. Conf. on Advanced Communication and Networking* (Berlin: Springer) pp 134–43

[25] He H, Chen F, Tai H M, Kalker T and Zhang J 2011 Performance analysis of a block-neighborhood-based self-recovery fragile watermarking scheme *IEEE Trans. Inf. Forensics Secur.* **7** 185–96

[26] Chang J D, Chen B H and Tsai C S 2013 LBP-based fragile watermarking scheme for image tamper detection and recovery *2013 Int. Symp. on Next-Generation Electronics* (Piscataway, NJ: IEEE) pp 173–6

[27] Ansari I A, Pant M and Ahn C W 2016 SVD based fragile watermarking scheme for tamper localization and self-recovery *Int. J. Mach. Learn. Cybern.* **7** 1225–39

[28] Singh P and Agarwal S 2016 An efficient fragile watermarking scheme with multilevel tamper detection and recovery based on dynamic domain selection *Multimedia Tools Appl.* **75** 8165–94

[29] Singh D and Singh S K 2017 DCT based efficient fragile watermarking scheme for image authentication and restoration *Multimedia Tools Appl.* **76** 953–77

[30] Belferdi W, Behloul A and Noui L 2019 A bayer pattern-based fragile watermarking scheme for color image tamper detection and restoration *Multidimension. Syst. Signal Process.* **30** 1093–112

[31] Molina J, Ponomaryov V, Reyes R, Sadovnychiy S and Cruz C 2020 Watermarking framework for authentication and self-recovery of tampered colour images *IEEE Lat. Am. Trans.* **18** 631–38

[32] Al-Otum H M and Ibrahim M Color image watermarking for content authentication and self-restoration applications based on a dual-domain approach *Multimedia Tools Appl.* 1–26

[33] Saito M and Matsumoto M 2008 SIMD-oriented fast Mersenne Twister: a 128-bit pseudorandom number generator *Monte Carlo and Quasi-Monte Carlo Methods 2006* (Berlin: Springer) pp 607–22

[34] Huynh-Thu Q and Ghanbari M 2008 Scope of validity of PSNR in image/video quality assessment *Electron. Lett.* **44** 800–1

IOP Publishing

Advanced Security Solutions for Multimedia

Irshad Ahmad Ansari and Varun Bajaj

Chapter 2

Secure, robust and imperceptible image watermarking scheme based on sharp frequency localized contourlet transform

Esmaeil Najafi

In this chapter, using sharp frequency localized contourlet transform (SFLCT) we propose an imperceptible, robust and secure image watermarking procedure. After considering in detail, we apply SFLCT on both watermark and cover images. The advantage of different downsampling rates of the SFLCT helps us to derive acceptable results of the watermarking properties. Employing various downsampling rates of the SFLCT to the cover work and watermark image enables us to choose a watermark image size as large as possible. We describe a method for near optimization of the strength factors. The experimental setup of the procedure is performed and its imperceptibility and robustness are experimented with under different attacks for a dataset of test images. Comparison to other schemes is given and we test the security of the scheme against ambiguity, sensitivity analysis and copy attacks.

2.1 Introduction

Human life is moving to be more digitized and necessarily we need to define our life metrics in the digital world. One of the important controversial issues in society is ownership and then ownership rights and proof of ownership are of important interest in the digital world. Multimedia producers can utilize the digital water-marking to control the distribution flow of their products and recognize unauthorized usages. Then, digital watermarking can be used to determine the ownership right of digital productions and has applications such as authentication, ownership identification, secret communication, medical applications, copy and copyright protection [1, 2]. This protection is performed by inserting information about the owner inside the product in such a way that is invisible and very slightly degrades the visual appearance of the product and also is resistant against operations that may be

doi:10.1088/978-0-7503-3735-9ch2   2-1

legally or illegally done on the product. The information is the watermark and the product is the cover work.

Any watermarking system includes two separate procedures: the first process is the embedding procedure that the watermark should be placed into the cover work and the result is watermarked data. The second operation is the extraction or detection process, which detects the hidden watermark from the watermarked cover work. The transmitter of the data performs the embedding process and after receiving the data, the receiver side implements the detection process to extract the watermark.

Any watermarking scheme should undertake properties like imperceptibility, robustness, capacity and security. Embedding the watermark degrades the quality of the multimedia. This decreasing of the quality is an imperceptibility property of the process and its value is calculated by peak signal-to-noise ratio (PSNR). A scheme is robust or resistant if it is able to preserve the watermark against multimedia degradations. This feature is application-dependent and depending on which application is used, the scheme will be resistant under special attacks. The capacity requirement measures how much of the data which are embedded as watermark inside the selected multimedia and has an inverse relationship with the imperceptibility.

The security property of a watermarking procedure is related to its ability to preserve the watermark against intentional tampering. An operation, in which an opponent wants to prevent a watermark from serving its intended purpose, is the intentional tampering or hostile attack. Security and robustness sometimes are the same since some alterations on the watermarked work can be implemented for both removing the watermark or legal handling. However, in many issues they are completely different. Any watermarking scheme has its own applications and an adversary attacks the scheme with respect to those applications. Then, the security or robustness of the schemes are related to their applications.

In this chapter, we discuss watermarking of images and a watermarking scheme with its properties is proposed. Every watermarking technique needs a transform to map the cover work (host image) to a frequency space, imbed the watermark and remap the watermarked frequency magnitudes to the origin space to derive the watermarked work.

Contourlet transform (CT) is a two-dimensional non-separable transform, which for the multiscale decomposition uses the Laplacian pyramid [3] and for the directional decomposition utilizes directional filter banks (DFBs) [4]. Discrete wavelet transform (DWT) is a particular case of the CT when we choose just three directions in the directional filter bank of the CT. In the digital watermarking we aim to benefit from the directional feature of the CT where can detect the contours of the images in many directions and resolutions, whereas, this can happen in DWT just in horizontal, vertical and diagonal directions. Although CT represents the images with smooth contours in many directions, its filters cannot disjoint the frequencies in the frequency domain. In other words, its frequency domain is not localized sharply and a significant number of them are placed outside of the desired support. These misplaced components reduce the efficiency of CT in catching the edges of the images.

Next generation of CT is introduced in [5] where the sharp frequency localized contourlet transform (SFLCT) is presented, in which the filters are modified and the aliasing problem is considerably resolved. Then SFLCT decomposes the high-pass and low-pass frequencies much better than the other transforms like CT or DWT.

In the watermarking techniques, we look for transforms, where applying them can upgrade the requirements of the scheme. Some schemes use more than one transform and combine them [6–11]. In [18], the authors use invariant wavelet transform and singular value decomposition (SVD) to add the watermark to the original image. In [19], one level integer wavelet transform (IWT) is implemented on the host image and then SVD is applied on the subbands of IWT as well as on the watermark image. The scheme in [20] uses DWT and SVD on the host image and employs sparse codding to tackle the security problems. A leakage in a transform can make the scheme useless. The schemes, which employ the SVD, may lose the security property and are exposed against ambiguity attacks. In the SVD based schemes the watermark is nearly independent of the cover work or secret keys. The problem solution is increasing the dependency between the watermark and the host image along with preserving the other properties of the watermarking scheme [12, 18, 19]. Another problem of using SVD is its large secret keys, which the receiver part needs in detection as side information [12, 19]. When working on large databases, managing this high volume of secret keys is a problem. On the other hand, in the informed detections, secret keys improve the robustness and security of the scheme. Using them is therefore unavoidable, but we can manage their measures.

We use SFLCT as a transform in our represented watermarking scheme. Since this transform has different downsampling rates, we can use it to choose the watermark as large as possible along with preserving the other requirements. To obtain reliable results, any watermarking scheme should be examined on a large volume of work and watermark images and the mean of the results should be reported. Then we choose 50 couples of cover works and watermark images of the same size for implementation. In addition, strengths factors are used in the embedding of the watermark. We choose these coefficients such that we get the optimal acceptable values for imperceptibility and robustness of the technique.

This chapter is arranged as follows. In section 2.2, we consider the properties and construction of the SFLCT. In section 2.3, the proposed scheme is discussed in detail and the embedding and detection algorithms and selection of the strength factors are indicated. Section 2.4 collects all of the examinations on the properties of the represented watermarking technique, and especially, comparison to the other methods and security of the scheme are tested against some security attacks.

2.2 The properties of SFLCT

The SFLCT introduced in [5] is the next generation of the CT in which the non-localization problem of the original one is solved. CT uses the Laplacian pyramid [3] and the DFBs. Examinations show that the low-pass and high-pass filters of the CT are not perfect where the aliasing of the frequency domain leads . In other words, as we can see in figure 2.1(b), the separation of the frequencies is not exact and some of

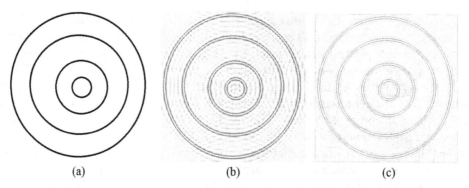

(a)   (b)   (c)

Figure 2.1. Different between frequency decomposition. (a) Original image. (b) CT and its non-localization frequency components. (c) SFLCT and localized frequency components.

the low frequencies components are mixed with the high frequencies. This mixture makes the representation of the edges unclear in the spatial domain [13].

To remove the non-localization problem, instead of the Laplacian pyramid, a new multiscale pyramid is introduced which employs modified low-pass and high-pass filters for all of the multiscale levels. In this new computation, first the domain $\omega = (\omega_1, \omega_2)$ of low-pass filters $L_i(\omega)$, $i = 0,1$ are limited with the modification of the passbands and stopbands components such that the non-localization components are eliminated. In this way, the waste components of the low-pass frequencies are not allowed (figure 2.1(c)). After deriving the modified low-pass filters, we can obtain the high-pass filters $D_i(\omega)$ from the following condition

$$|L_i(\omega)|^2 + |D_i(\omega)|^2 = 1, \qquad i = 1, 2$$

In the implementation of this new SFLCT, we can choose three different down-sampling rates $d = 1, \frac{3}{2}, 2$. This is a useful property of the SFLCT and each choice of this rate produces various sizes of the subbands. Using this property, we can choose different sizes of the watermark image for our watermarking.

2.3 The proposed SFLCT watermarking scheme

In this section, we consider a watermarking scheme based on SFLCT. When we apply SFLCT on an image, the frequency components including approximation and details are obtained. Since filter banks of SFLCT are directional, we can choose to detect the edges in many directions in all of the decomposition levels. However, observations show that we have no more enhancement in robustness or impercept-ibility by choosing number of directions more than four. Then choosing four directions prevents extra computations. Small changes in high level of decomposi-tions make large changes in the pixel numbers of the image. Hence, we decompose the original image in two levels. On the other hand, watermark and original images are in the same size if we choose one-level decomposition of the watermark image and allowing downsampling rate $d = 1$ and downsampling rate $d = 2$ for decom-position of original image. When the two original images x and watermark images w

Table 2.1. Embedding procedure of the proposed watermarking scheme.

Step 1: Decompose x in two levels with $d = 2$ and w in one level with $d = 1$ and derive the following components:

$$(A, D) = SFLCT(x), \quad (A_w, D_w) = SFLCT(w)$$

Step 2: Embed the components of the watermark decomposition inside the original ones using strengths factors α_A and α_D as follows:

$$A^w = A + \alpha_A A_w, \quad D^w = D + \alpha_D D_w$$

Step 3: Drive the watermarked image x^w using inverse SFLCT in two levels with $d = 2$:

$$x^w = SFLCT^{-1}(A^w, D^w)$$

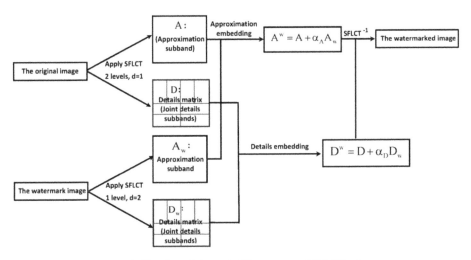

Figure 2.2. The flow of the embedding process of SFLCT scheme.

are decomposed, we insert some components of the watermark decomposition in some components of the original image decomposition according to the embedding procedure in table 2.1. Figure 2.2 shows the flow of the embedding process.

In table 2.1, A and A_w are the approximation components of the original and watermark images, respectively. For the detailed components, we join all of them as they appear in the decomposition and derive the matrices D and D_w. In this embedding process, the watermark depends on both original and watermark images which is a crucial point in the security property.

When a sender watermarks an original image x by using table 2.1, x^w is ready for distribution or sending to the receiver part for decoding thorough a channel.

Table 2.2. Detection procedure of the proposed watermarking scheme.

Step 1: Decompose $\hat{w}$ in two levels with $d = 2$ and derive the following components:

$$(\hat{A}^w, \hat{D}^w) = SFLCT(\hat{x}^w)$$

Step 2: Extract the noisy approximation subband $\hat{A}_w$ using the secret keys α_A and A as follows:

$$\hat{A}_w = \frac{1}{\alpha_A}(\hat{A}^w - A)$$

Step 3: Extract the noisy details subbands $\hat{D}_w$ using the secret keys α_D and D as follows:

$$\hat{D}_w = \frac{1}{\alpha_D}(\hat{D}^w - D)$$

Step 4: Apply inverse SFLCT on $\hat{A}_w$ and $\hat{D}_w$ in one level and $d = 1$ to detect the noisy watermark:

$$\hat{w} = SFLCT^{-1}(\hat{A}_w, \hat{D}_w)$$

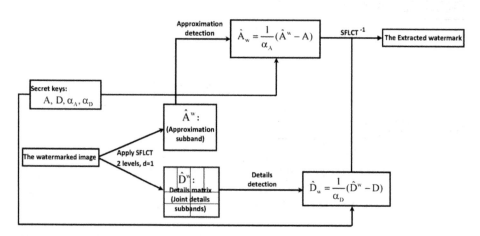

Figure 2.3. The detection flow of the SFLCT scheme.

However, the channel may be degraded or an adversary may attacked the watermarked image x^w and the receiver part is delivered an altered watermarked image $\hat{x}^w$. Using the received $\hat{x}^w$, properties of the channel and what is sent from the encoder side (secret keys A, D, α_A and α_D) we always have some auxiliary information in the decoder side that assists the watermark extraction. The extraction process is the reverse of the embedding process and extracts the degraded watermark $\hat{w}$. Table 2.2 and figure 2.3 represent the steps of the detection procedure.

2.3.1 Computing strength factors

Before discussing about the evaluating strength factors, some definitions are required. If x is the host image and x^w is its watermarked version, then PSNR computes the similarity between x and x^w is obtained by the following relation:

$$PSNR = 20 \log_{10}\left(\frac{Max\{x(i, j)\}}{\sqrt{MSE}}\right), \ MSE = \frac{1}{M \times N}\sum_{i=1}^{N}\sum_{j=1}^{M}(x(i, j) - x^w(i, j))$$

Here, M and N are the dimensions of the image. We choose normalized correlation (NC) as a criterion for robustness that is computed as

$$NC = \frac{\displaystyle\sum_{i=1}^{N}\sum_{j=1}^{N}\left(w(i, j) - \mu_w\right)\left(\hat{w}(i, j) - \mu_{\hat{w}}\right)}{\sqrt{\displaystyle\sum_{i=1}^{N}\sum_{j=1}^{N}\left(w(i, j) - \mu_w\right)^2}\sqrt{\displaystyle\sum_{i=1}^{N}\sum_{j=1}^{N}\left(\hat{w}(i, j) - \mu_{\hat{w}}\right)^2}}$$

In this equation, w and $\hat{w}$ are the original and detected watermark images, respectively, and μ_w and $\mu_{\hat{w}}$ are their mean of the pixel values.

Strength factors have important roles in both robustness and imperceptibility of the scheme. For the robustness, we need to choose an attack to examine its variation when we vary the values of α_A and α_D. The Gaussian white noise alters nearly all of the pixels of an image. On the other hand, among all attacks, robustness under noise addition attacks is a challenge for watermarking systems in the literature. The Gaussian noise inherently decreases the correlation coefficients and if we know that a scheme is resistant against Gaussian noise, it helps to ensure that the scheme is resistant to most of the other attacks. Therefore, we choose Gaussian white noise with small variance $V = 0.001$ and try to nearly optimize the robustness.

Clearly, imperceptibility and robustness are decreasing and increasing functions, respectively, with respect to α_A and α_D. Furthermore, these two factors are independent of each other and we need to consider a method that selects values in such a way that the yielded PSNR and NC values are acceptable. If we choose a good enough value for PSNR for some choices of α_A and α_D, then the value derived for NC will be imposed and vice versa. Then, we specify minimum acceptable values of 42 for PSNR and 0.92 for NC and try to solve the following maximization problem:

$$\text{Maximise } \min\left\{\frac{NC}{0.92}, \frac{PSNR}{42}\right\}$$

$$\text{Subject to } \quad \alpha_A > 0, \quad \alpha_D > 0, \quad NC \geqslant 0.92, \quad PSNR \geqslant 42$$

A numerical solution for this problem is derived by plotting the surface of the subject function in certain intervals of α_A and α_D and determining its maximum, as is shown in figure 2.4. With this method, the maximum occurs for the values $\alpha_A = 0.016$ and $\alpha_D = 0.07$ and we get $PSNR = 42.56$ and $NC = 0.9401$.

2.4 Implementations and results of the proposed SFLCT scheme

In this section, we describe the examination of the proposed watermarking technique on a dataset of test images and consider its imperceptibilty, robustness, capacity and security in a variety of situations. Since quantities of NC and PSNR for different images have slightly different values, then we examine our scheme on a dataset that has 50 different popular original and watermark test images of the same size, 512×512, and we perform all of our examinations on them and report the mean of the quantities derived for NC and PSNR. Some of these test images are shown in figure 2.5. We use MATLAB software and some of its built-in functions for simulation of the proposed watermarking scheme.

After we run our scheme on 50 different host and watermark images for various values of strength factors, we derive PSNR values. Then we add Gaussian white noise with $V = 0.001$ to the watermarked images, apply detection procedure and derive NC values. Using figure 2.4, when we found the best values of the strength factors, we implement our scheme with the specified values $\alpha_A = 0.016$ and $\alpha_D = 0.07$ for the next examinations. With these values we derive $PSNR = 42.56$ and $NC = 0.9779$. Since SFLCT is not a shift-invariant transform, embedding the watermark changes other subbands of the host image, which do not include any parts of the watermark and then our detection is not perfect.

2.4.1 Robustness of the proposed SFLCT scheme

In this subsection, we report the robustness property results of the SFLCT scheme. After watermarking the original image, we put the watermarked image under different image processing and geometrical variations. These degrading actions weaken the detection process of extracting the perfect watermark. Since the attacked watermarked image is in hand, we can use some auxiliary information about the kind of the attack. On the other hand, we have received secret keys of the detection

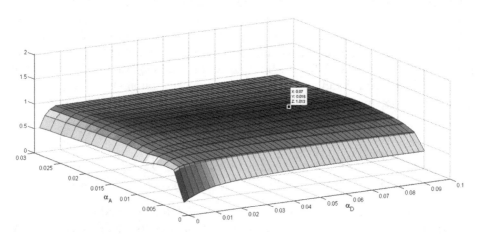

Figure 2.4. The surface of the subject function of the maximization problem and its maximum point. $X = \alpha_D$, $Y = \alpha_A$, $Z = \min\left\{\dfrac{NC}{0.92}, \dfrac{PSNR}{42}\right\}$.

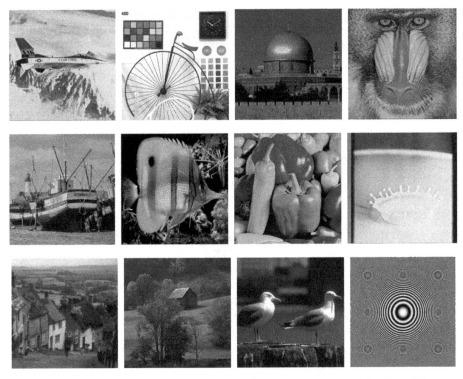

Figure 2.5. A number of our used original and watermark test images of size 512 × 512.

Table 2.3. The mean NC values for noise addition attacks.

Density/ variance	Gaussian noise	Salt and pepper noise	Speckle noise
0.001	0.9401	0.9494	0.9495
0.005	0.9342	0.9489	0.9495
0.01	0.9275	0.9484	0.9495
0.05	0.8955	0.9439	0.9492

process and we notice that the secret keys are equivalent with the original image, since according to the Kerckhoffs' principle 'the opponent knows the selected algorithm but not the private key'. Applying this information, we extract the watermarks of our dataset and report the mean NC values of each attack for different parameters.

Results for noise attacks (Gaussian, salt and pepper, speckle) which are added with different densities or variances are reported in table 2.3. These attacks may be added in many operations for images such as during their acquisitions by sensors or their transmissions.

We examine the Gaussian, median and Wiener filtering attacks that are used in noise reduction processing. It is considered in [14] that, if the added watermark is independent of the host image, or both the host image and the embedded watermark

Table 2.4. The mean NC values for filtering attacks.

Block size	Gaussian filtering	Median filtering	Wiener filtering
3 × 3	0.9669	0.9696	0.9493
5 × 5	0.9669	0.9674	0.9490
7 × 7	0.9669	0.9663	0.9488

Table 2.5. The mean NC values for JPEG and wavelet compressions and sharpening attack.

Quality	JPEG compression attack	Rate	Wavelet compression attack	Strength	Sharpening attack
90	0.9478	20	0.9429	2	0.9225
80	0.9472	30	0.9419	3	0.9091
70	0.9469	40	0.9414	4	0.8974
50	0.9461	50	0.9408	6	0.8783
30	0.9442	70	0.9390	8	0.8635
20	0.9451	80	0.9384	10	0.8520

are received from a normal distribution with zero mean, and or linear correlation is used as the detection statistic, then, Wiener filtering attack optimally removes the watermark. Table 2.4 shows the mean NC results of the filtering attacks.

The compressions are routine image processing applications in transmitting the data. We considered JPEG and wavelet compressions on the watermarked images. Our watermarking scheme remains robust against image compressions as the mean values of NC are shown in table 2.5. Another attack that we investigated is a sharpening attack for which we observe the mean NC values in table 2.5.

The other category of operations on images are geometrical scaling and rotation attacks. The scaling attack, especially in shrinking, changes the bit values of the images and can be used as a removal attack. The robustness under this operation with various rates is considered and the results are presented in table 2.6. Rotation operation may also be used as an attack. We rotate the watermarked images to different angles, then rotate back and implement the detection process. Table 2.6 observes the obtained mean NC values. Other geometrical attacks including cutting rows or columns, shearing and histogram equalization are considered and the mean NC values are shown in table 2.7.

2.4.2 The security examination of the proposed scheme

In this subsection, we examine the security of the proposed scheme under three security attacks. The ambiguity attack, copy attack and sensitivity analysis attack are discussed and it is shown that the proposed SLFCT watermarking scheme is secure against these attacks.

Table 2.6. The mean NC values for different scaling and rotation operations.

Ratio	Scaling operation	Rotation degree	Rotation operation
0.5 × 0.5	0.9661	2	0.9538
0.25 × 0.5	0.9655	45	0.9560
2 × 0.5	0.9664	110	0.9567
2 × 2	0.9669	−80	0.9561
4 × 0.25	0.9660	−110	0.9568

Table 2.7. The mean NC values of cutting, shearing and histogram equalization attacks.

Cut rows, columns	Cutting attack	Shearing factors	Shearing attack	Level number	Histogram equalization
(10,10)	0.8685	(0.2,0.2)	0.9671	264	0.9463
(10,15)	0.8487	(0.2,0.5)	0.9669	128	0.9438
(10,20)	0.8295	(0.5,0.2)	0.9669	64	0.9368
(15,15)	0.8221	(0.5,0.5)	0.9667	–	–
20 rows	0.8469	(1,0.5)	0.9659	–	–
20 columns	0.8788	(3,3)	0.9662	–	–

2.4.2.1 Security against ambiguity attacks

An adversary uses an ambiguity attack to pretend that his/her own watermark is embedded in a watermarked image and claims the ownership. In this attack, the adversary chooses a fake watermark w_f, and then embeds the watermark using our embedding process and derives rewatermarked image x_f^w. Hence, makes his/her own secret keys A_f and D_f and in the extraction process uses them to extract his/her watermark and claims the ownership. To defend our ownership, the implementations show that if in the detection process of w_f, we use the main secret keys A and D, in the extracted image w_f^e a footprint of our main watermark w can be seen, and the mean NC between w and the w_f^e is 0.7062. Figure 2.6 shows the flow of the ambiguity attack.

2.4.2.2 Security against sensitivity analysis attack

Described in [15–17], when the adversary has access to the detection process, he/she can try to remove the watermark by adding some noises and moving the watermarked image to the edge of the detection region such that the NC value for extracted watermark is still acceptable. Then, using the detector and adding patterns tries to move the attacked watermarked image inside the detection region and acquire the watermarking pattern of the detection. This is a sensitivity analysis attack, which is used for unauthorized removal of a watermark. Yielding the watermarking pattern that the embedder adds on the cover work is equivalent to deriving a normal diagonal vector to the boundary of the detection region, as is shown in figure 2.7.

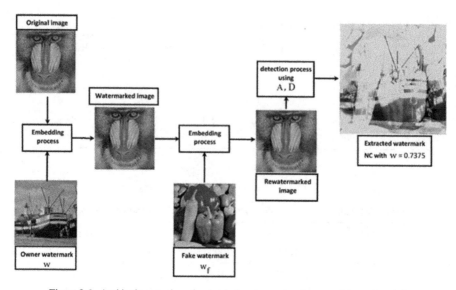

Figure 2.6. Ambiguity attack and extracted watermark using secret keys A and D.

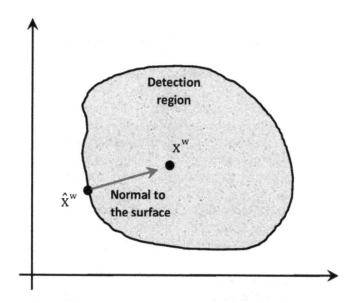

Figure 2.7. Detection region and directional normal vector.

To examine our watermarking scheme against sensitivity analysis, we gradually add gray pixels to the watermarked image x^w until we get $\hat{x}^w$ with $NC(w, \hat{w}) = 0.700090$. To approximate the directional normal vector to the boundary of the detection region, we turn to adding Gaussian white noise with very small variance $V = 0.00001$ to the $\hat{x}^w$. If the result has an NC value above 0.70, then we add noise pattern to the estimated normal vector. Otherwise, we neglect it. As we iterate this procedure, the normalized

Figure 2.8. Security of the scheme against copy attack. (a) Original image; (b) watermark image; (c) non-watermarked image; (d) detected watermark with Wiener filter; (e) detected watermark with median filter.

estimated vector is tending to the watermark pattern if the watermarking scheme satisfies some conditions. We implement this attack on our watermarking scheme and after 100 000 iterations for estimating the pattern, the best result is

$$NC(x^w, \hat{x}^w + \text{Est. Pattern}) = 0.706390$$

This shows that our watermarking scheme is not satisfied in the conditions of the sensitivity attack.

2.4.2.3 Security against copy attack

When an adversary tries to copy a watermark pattern from a watermarked image x^w to an unwatermarked image, the copy attack that takes place is an unauthorized embedding. In this attack, the adversary attempts to remove the watermark pattern $\hat{p}$ using some filtering or noise removal attacks to derive an acceptable approximation $\hat{x}$ of the host image x. Then by the subtraction

$$\hat{p} = x^w - \hat{x}$$

and adding the estimated pattern $\hat{p}$ to a unwatermarked image c, tries to obtain the watermarked image c^w. We employ median and Wiener filters as noise removals, and using the extraction process on c^w, we try to detect the watermark w. As we show in figure 2.8, our proposed scheme is robust against this security attack.

2.5 Comparative analysis of the proposed scheme

In this section, we compare our scheme to the other recent similar schemes. In [20], the authors use sparse coding, a procedure that relates the watermark image to the host

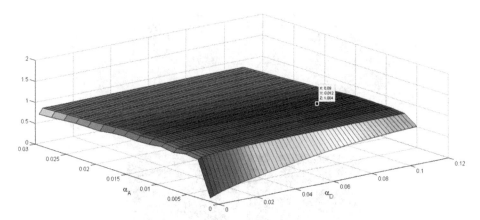

Figure 2.9. Choosing nearly optimal strength factors in comparison with the other methods.

Table 2.8. The comparison of the imperceptibility with recent procedures (mean of six test images PSNR).

Method in [19]	Method in [18]	Our proposed scheme
42.94	41.81	43.47

image and encodes it. After sparse coding, they apply DWT and SVD on the host image to insert the watermark image of size 256×256. Also in [19], the authors propose an SVD-based watermarking scheme in which the unitary matrices of the SVD of the watermark image are secret keys and the diagonal matrix is embedded in the embedding process. The original image is decomposed using integer wavelet transform (IWT) and to overcome the false positive problem, a secret key is extracted from the watermarked image of size 256×256. In [18], the authors use invariant wavelet transform and decompose the host image. Then, they apply SVD on blocks of approximation subband and imbed the bits of the 32×32 binary watermark into the singular vectors with the help of an artificial bee colony algorithm.

The experimental results of these methods are implemented on a small number of test images. So, to compare the schemes in the same conditions, we reset the strength factors of our scheme according to their used test images by the method stated in subsection 2.3.1. In this manner, we derive the new values $\alpha_A = 0.012$ and $\alpha_D = 0.09$ (figure 2.9) and we get $PSNR = 43.47$ and $NC = 0.9835$. In addition, we choose the size of the watermark as in the methods [19, 20]. With these new settings, we compare the imperceptibility of our scheme with the other methods in table 2.8, which shows the superiority of our scheme. Table 2.9 represents the comparison of the robustness of the schemes against some attacks.

2.6 Conclusion

In this chapter, we introduced a new watermarking scheme using sharp frequency localized contourlet transform (SFLCT). Utilizing special properties of the SFLCT like sharp frequency localization and different downsampling rate, our proposed

Table 2.9. Robustness comparison of the proposed scheme.

Attack	Scheme in [20]	Scheme in [19]	Proposed scheme
Gaussian noise, $V = 0.001$		**0.9810**	0.9752
Gaussian noise, $V = 0.01$	0.9681	0.9712	**0.9726**
Gaussian noise, $V = 0.1$	0.8619	0.9594	**0.9633**
Salt and pepper noise, $D = 0.05$		0.9736	**0.9753**
Salt and pepper noise, $D = 0.01$	0.9823	**0.9841**	0.9761
Salt and pepper noise, $D = 0.1$	0.9113	0.9220	**0.9742**
Speckle noise, $D = 0.01$	**0.9838**	0.9903	0.9763
Speckle noise, $D = 0.1$	0.9541	0.9578	**0.9762**
Scaling 0.5×2	0.9652	**0.9808**	0.9800
Scaling 0.25×4		0.9667	**0.9800**
JPEG $Q = 50$	**0.9852**	0.9811	0.9759
JPEG $Q = 75$		**0.9819**	0.9760
Median filtering 3×3	**0.9817**	0.9800	0.9805
Median filtering 2×2		**0.9802**	0.9799
Rotation $d = 45$	0.9763	0.9779	**0.9794**
Rotation $d = 270$	0.9867	**0.9884**	0.9818
Shearing $(1,0.2)$		0.9315	**0.9800**

scheme shows acceptable imperceptibility and high robustness against several attacks. We considered the effects of the strength factors on NC and PSNR and derived their values larger than the minimum expected values. To examine the resistance of the scheme, we investigated several attacks like noise addition, filtering and geometrical attacks on our dataset and reported the NC values of the procedure for each of them. About the security of the process, we analyzed the scheme against three security attacks where the obtained results show its security.

References

[1] Morimoto N 1999 Digital watermarking technology with practical applications *Multimedia Inform. Technol.* **4** 107–11

[2] Wu H T and Cheung Y M 2010 Reversible watermarking by modulation and security enhancement *IEEE Trans. Instrum. Meas.* **59** 221–8

[3] Jahne B 2013 *Digital Image Processing* (Berlin: Springer Science & Business Media)

[4] Do M N and Vetterli M 2001 Pyramidal directional filter banks and curvelets *Proc. of the 2001 Int. Conf. on Image Processing (Thessaloniki)* vol 3 158–61

[5] Lu Y and Do M N 2006 A new contourlet transform with sharp frequency localization *Proc. of the 2006 IEEE International Conference on Image Processing* (Atlanta, GA: IEEE) pp 1629–32

[6] Poonam A S M 2018 A DWT-SVD based robust digital watermarking for digital images *Procedia Comput. Sci.* **132** 1441–8

[7] Makbol N M and Khoo B E 2014 A new robust and secure digital image watermarking scheme based on the integer wavelet transform and singular value decomposition *Digit. Signal Process.* **33** 134–47

[8] Makbol N M and Khoo B E 2013 Robust blind image watermarking scheme based on redundant discrete wavelet transform and singular value decomposition *AEU Int. J. Electron. Commun.* **67** 102–12

[9] Chakraborty S *et al* 2017 Comparative approach between singular value decomposition and randomized singular value decomposition-based watermarking *Intelligent Techniques in Signal Processing for Multimedia Security* (Cham: Springer) pp 133–49

[10] Abdallah H A *et al* 2014 Homomorphic image watermarking with a singular value decomposition algorithm *Inf. Process. Manag.* **50** 909–23

[11] Ansari I, Aand and Pant M 2016 Multipurpose image watermarking in the domain of DWT based on SVD and ABC *Pattern Recognit. Lett.* **94** 228–36

[12] Najafi E 2019 Hybrid secure and robust image watermarking scheme based on SVD and sharp frequency localized contourlet transform *J. Inform. Secur. Appl.* **44** 144–56

[13] Bamberger R H and Smith M J T 1992 A filter bank for the directional decomposition of images: theory and design *IEEE Trans. Signal Proc.* **40** 882–93

[14] Su J K and Girod B 1999 On the imperceptibility and robustness of digital fingerprints *Proc. IEEE Int. Conf. Multimedia Computing and Systems* **2** 530–5

[15] Cox I J and Linnartz J-P M G 1997 Public watermarks and resistance to tampering *Proc. of Int. Conf. on Image Processing* 3 pp 0_3–0_6

[16] Kalker T, Linnartz J P and van Dijk M 1998 Watermark estimation through detector analysis *Proc. 1998 Int. Conf. on Image Processing* vol 1 ICIP98 (Cat. No.98CB36269) pp 425–9

[17] Linnartz J P M G and van Dijk M 1998 Analysis of the sensitivity attack against electronic watermarks in images *Information Hiding. IH 1998Lecture Notes in Computer Science, vol 1525* ed D Aucsmith (Berlin: Springer)

[18] Ali M, Ahn C W, Pant M and Siarry P 2015 An image watermarking scheme in wavelet domain with optimized compensation of singular value decomposition via artificial bee colony *Inf. Sci.* **301** 44–60

[19] Makbol N, Bee E K, Taha H R and Loukhaoukha K 2017 A new reliable optimized image watermarking scheme based on the integer wavelet transform and singular value decomposition for copyright protection *Inf. Sci.* **417** 381–400

[20] Tareef A and Al-Ani A 2015 A highly secure oblivious sparse codingbased watermarking system for ownership verification *Expert Syst. Appl.* **42** 2224–33

Chapter 3

Content watermarking and data hiding in multimedia security

Jay Gohil, Jay Patel and Manan Shah

With the wake of modernity, the access and reach of several forms of media, generally termed as multimedia, have increased to massive levels. The introduction of cheap and fast internet, presence of computationally powerful devices on everyone's palm, and increase in the integration of IoT in our lives, have together paved way for the rise of multimedia's importance in our daily lives. However, with such a level of interconnectivity comes several threats such as malicious activity, unauthorized access, illegal reproduction of content and alterations to the content (spoiling its integrity). This has led to the introduction of multimedia security techniques that help prevent and/or eradicate such issues. This chapter aims at providing a synopsis or summary about two mainstream multimedia security techniques, namely, content watermarking and data hiding. Content watermarking is the procedure of implanting a special message in multimedia in such a manner that it (message or watermark) is extractable for identification intent. Data hiding (specifically steganography), on the other hand, is a method that conceals or protects the data itself to prevent unauthorized use. The chapter provides a thorough understanding of the topics, along with their history, classification, areas of application, advancements occurring in the last few decades and citation of recent research work conducted in a tabulated manner. Upon completion of the chapter, the reader will be thoroughly equipped with comprehensive knowledge of the topics and be able to apply these concepts in real world scenarios.

3.1 Introduction

Multimedia, as the name suggests, is the combination of the various types and forms of media, and includes several media components (as portrayed in figure 3.1). It can be referred to as computer-controlled integration of this content which stores, transmits, and processes each information type in a digital manner. It can also

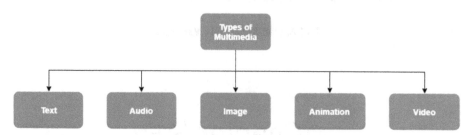

Figure 3.1. Several forms of multimedia.

interact with users via data entry, speech recognition, interactive display, and video apprehension. Its main characteristic is to serve several types of media in order to offer utility and content, and its primary system consists of IO tools, several applications and external storage devices [1].

With the advancements in information technology, multimedia equipment is progressing in the direction of efficient energy utilization and a remarkably smart path of sustaining a variety of information utilities [2]. This has occurred through a series of evolutionary improvements. This, in a nutshell, is shown in figure 3.2 [3], outlining the evolution of the multimedia applications. Along with the advancements, the reach and level of usage by humans has grown by massive proportions. For instance, Google performs 2 million queries, FaceBook receives 685 thousand posts, Twitter executes 100 thousand tweets and 2Dlength of media is uploaded on YouTube in a single minute [4]!

In the contemporary world, the multimedia technologies are far reaching throughout several domains, including interactive television, digital libraries and video conferencing. Multimedia can be partitioned into three categories, viz., information systems, remote representation systems and entertainment systems. The applications of multimedia are also diverse (due to introduction of coding and better user experience), and include supervision networks, digital education, e-newsletter, media distribution systems, remote IoT tools and immersive VR games. Most of these implementations are predominantly based upon utilizing wireless networks to obtain data and multimedia systems. Also, it is in part due to the presence of such communication channels, that advancements in multimedia sharing are becoming easier and increasing in number day by day.

When it comes to conventional data, the volume of multimedia information is comparatively enormous (its magnitude is quite unimaginable in several ways). A major part of this information is very sensitive and should not be placed in the wrong hands during transmission, to avoid instances such as mischievous data usage, replication and hacking [5]. Therefore, safety of this information transferred across the internet is the primary issue facing the current generation.

The three main threat domains that are hanging over any multimedia system are: confidentiality, integrity and availability, i.e., confidentiality of the information from unauthorized individuals, integrity of data from illicit alteration, and availability of authentic data. In most of the cases related to multimedia attacks, the attack is undertaken with bad intention, with a few done to check the security of multimedia.

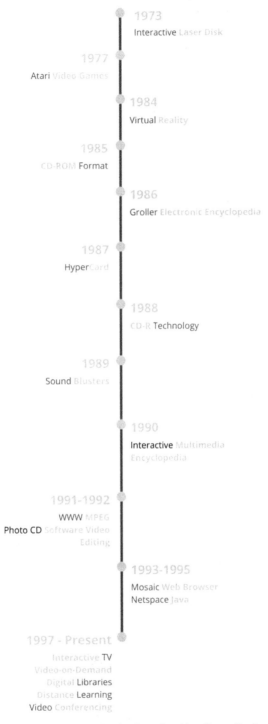

Figure 3.2. Comprehensive timeline of multimedia applications.

As a result of most attacks commenced for stealing data, the major challenges that are faced during multimedia content transmission, are safety, fair information usage and swift transmission of data when needed.

As an outcome to this need for security in the multimedia domain, an enormous amount of interest has been shown by researchers in the field, which was followed by various proposed security techniques that helped in prevention of misappropriation, prohibited stealing and distortion of multimedia. As an outcome of this quick boom in the amount of research work done in the domain, the term known as 'multimedia security' was born. In simple terms, multimedia security can be referred to as a method or set of methods that are used for protection purposes pertaining to multimedia content.

The major methodologies through which the security of multimedia is ensured, include data hiding (focused on steganography), content watermarking and cryptography. Cryptography is a standard approach in the multimedia content protection, as the multimedia contents in this approach are encrypted with an encryption key (known by issuer and receiver of the content) by the issuer, and is transmitted to the receiver over internet. Although, thus can be a hectic method to use, due to the computational need and time taken due to the involvement of encryption and decryption at the issuer's and receiver's end, respectively.

Thus, in this chapter, we take a deep look at data hiding (steganography) and content watermarking, which need not be encrypted at all and are very feasible for transmission and access to an individual. Content watermarking is the procedure of implanting a special message in multimedia in a manner so that it (message or watermark) is extractable for identification intent at a later stage (for purposes like flow control and inhibition of reproduction). This method is mainly used in scenarios where the access to content is not the main priority, but the identification of the individual with an illegal copy as well as the origin of reproduced content is given more focus. Therefore, content watermarking is broadly applied in authentication, copyright safeguard, circulation trailing and accredited accessibility.

Data hiding, on the other hand, is a process concerned with hiding or protecting the data itself (specifically called steganography), unlike watermarking where the data is open to access to content by any individual with its possession. The data is written and/or stored in a way that is secret (or gibberish) to an unauthorized individual, but to the specific end user, makes perfect sense. This method is mainly used when the access to the contents of the media is the major priority, rather than tracing of the illegal or reproduced data (which would be of no use as even the copied data is unreadable). Hence, data hiding is chiefly used in circumstances of classified information transmission and secret communications, and is generally used by secret services, government agencies and structured organizations.

The purpose of this chapter is to offer a concise outline of multimedia security, typical issues associated with it, and various techniques that are currently being used in order to tackle them. A standard outline about the information on digital watermarking and steganography is portrayed in the chapter, along-with its history. In addition, common challenges and their resolutions are mentioned as well.

The arrangement of the forthcoming sections is in the following manner. The next section provides deep knowledge of content watermarking, its methods and review on a few methodologies based on research work conducted in the last few decades. Section 3.3 follows the same content, except for data hiding, specifically steganography. Finally, section 3.4 provides a summary and overview on the information mentioned in the entire chapter.

3.2 Content watermarking in multimedia security

3.2.1 Introduction

When it comes to securing multimedia, the most prominently used technique in the current age is content watermarking. Digital watermarking has been the go-to methodology in several applications pertaining to securing multimedia of any format (text, audio, video, etc). In a nutshell, it refers to the method of embedding a message or information in a piece of multimedia data without altering or destroying its quality or content. It embeds a known set of information that aids in the identification of the rightful owner of the data. Due to its feasible approach and varied applications, it is a widely utilized method that protects intellectual properties (like imagery, music, songs and movies) from illegal copying.

The term 'digital watermarking' was conceived in 1992 when three individuals from Monash University Physics Department met for lunch, viz., G Rankin G, A Tirkel and E C Osborne. Upon constant persuasion of Osborne to Tirkel about doing something with his code, they came up with an idea for concealing code/message in medical pictures in order to keep every patient's identity safe. Within 10 min of emergence of the idea, the group could easily come up with 50 other applications. They realized that the idea could revolutionize entire industries struggling with security related issues of their media data [6]. Within months of the emergence of the idea, Rankin effectively implanted maximum-length-sequences in picture data, and extracted the implanted sequences from the same picture in the span of the following month. This was followed by submission of a manuscript at DICTA'93, followed by acceptance in August/September 1993. The paper was presented at the last conference in Sydney later in the year, and acted as the beginning of era where content watermarking became a prime method of securing intellectual properties and preventing its illegal reproduction.

The working and ideology of watermarking is simple. The digital watermark is (generally and frequently) permanently embedded into a digital file, which can then be extracted with the help of predetermined operations for obtaining insights on the status of the data (whether it is copied/original, or legal/illegal). It is concealed in data in a manner that makes it indistinguishable from original data as well as resistant to operations or attacks conducted to isolate the watermark from the original digital file. Hence, the distribution of multimedia becomes fluent as the work is protected while being permanently marked to prevent prohibited activities.

The workflow of digital multimedia watermarking is broadly divided onto two parts, implanting and extraction process. The implanting process consists of inserting copyright information inside the host multimedia with the help of certain methodologies like cryptography, probability theory, network technology, algorithm design, stochastic theory, etc; (which is demonstrated in a simplified manner in figure 3.3). The procedure of extraction consists of back-tracking or decrypting the process carried out in implanting the process to extract the embedded message; useful for figuring out the rightful owner of the multimedia. The simplified demonstration of the same is shown in figure 3.4 as well.

There are several types of watermarking techniques, and they can be classified based on several criteria including robustness, domain, perceptivity, host data and data extraction. Based on robustness, we have fragile (easily manipulated method), semi-fragile (resistant to some specific attacks) and robust methods (unaffected by all attacks). Based on perceptivity (with respect to humans), we have visible (like a broadcasting logo) and invisible watermarking techniques (like steganography). We have image, audio, video and text watermarking techniques when it comes to methods classified upon host data. However, by far the most important classification is based upon domain, which consists of spatial (like least significant bit (LSB) and spread spectrum) and frequency domain techniques (discrete wavelet transform (DWT),

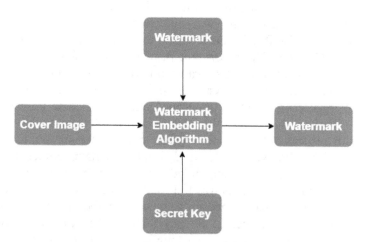

Figure 3.3. Embedding process of watermark in content watermarking.

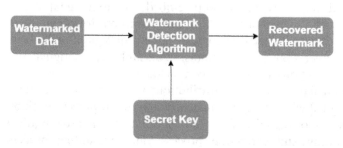

Figure 3.4. Extraction process of watermark in content watermarking.

discrete cosine transform (DCT), discrete Fourier transform (DFT), and singular value decomposition (SVD)). These classifications are summarized in figure 3.5.

The implementation of these techniques or methods, which often boils down to decision of choice between domains, is mostly dependent on field of application. For spatial domain, the pixel values of the original picture are modified in order to implant the watermark. However, for frequency domain, the watermark is implanted by transforming the data in a certain manner rather than modifying the content itself. There are several aspects where the spatial domain method triumphs (like computational cost and time) while frequency domain technique gains an upper hand in other aspects (like robustness). Thus, it is very necessary to understand the benefits and drawbacks of both methods (portrayed in table 3.1).

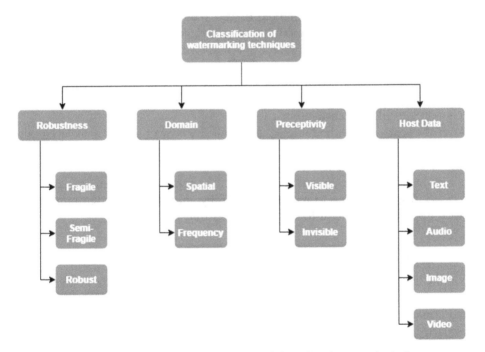

Figure 3.5. Classification of watermarking techniques based on several criteria.

Table 3.1. Contrast among spatial domain and frequency domain methods.

Features	Spatial domain technique	Frequency domain technique
Computational cost	Low	High
Robustness	Low	High
Perpetual quality	High control	Low control
Computational time	Low	High
Capacity	High	Low
Application field	Authentication	Copyright protection

There are a multitude of applications in several domains for content water-marking, but we can compress the number down to a few, based on their common outcomes. The most common application is copyright protection, which is used in order to prevent infringement of intellectual properties. Other applications include fingerprinting (to track the distribution source of illegal copies), broadcast monitoring (to verify if the advertisements are broadcast as per the contract), data authentication (to identify any form of tampering with data during transfer process), and covert communication (to share information in asecret manner, generally used by the military).

Moreover, it is always wise to know common forms of attacks (intentional or un-intentional) that can affect the watermark object in several forms. The most common form of attack is inference attack, which occurs due to the addition of additional noise into the watermarked object, reducing the watermark's effective-ness. Lossy compression, re-modulation, averaging, de-noising, collusion and quantization are some of its common examples. Other applications include removal attacks (for intentionally removing the watermark), geometric attacks (to affect the content of media by cropping, rotating or flipping it), security attacks (for modifying the watermark though invalid or estimate methods) and cryptographic attacks (using methods like exhaustive burst force).

Over the years, the methodology and complexity of watermarking techniques has advanced to exceptional levels. The applications now reach almost every form of digital multimedia and possess explicit techniques specifically dedicated to them. The next section cites recent advancements in the content watermarking techniques dedicated to specific forms of media, followed by another section that tabulates the focused approaches brought forward in the last few decades.

3.2.2 Content watermarking technique reviews

Lin and Chang [7] proposed a semi-fragile content watermarking technique focused on images of type JPEG in May of 2000. The technique allows lossy-compression based implanted pictures up-to a certain extent while rejecting mischievous actions. Its security is accomplished with the help of a confidential mathematical function that regulates the embedding process of the signature or watermark.

The authenticator in the technique relies on two 'in-variant' features of DCT co-efficient (prior and post-compression of the image), that are deterministic, and remove the need for probability-based decision making. The first property portrays that coefficient(s) could be precisely re-assembled once a satisfactory level of compression is reached (even upon modifications in a DCT coefficient), while the second property is among a pair of coefficients in prior and post-image compression. The technique thus utilizes the second property to create a signature or watermark, and the first property to embed it in the image. As a result, the said authenticator is able to detect tarnished pieces' location in a data file, and recover them by replacement with approximated pieces of data from the original file. It also accepts an increase in brightness of the image within acceptable range, apart from the acceptance in the compression process (which assures inhabitancy of incorrect alarms). There is little to no reduction in the implanted image's quality as per experimental observations as well. In finality, the technique has shown feasible application capacity in the real world by tackling several issues in image watermarking like compression and filter-change.

Voloshynovskiy *et al* [8] presented a novel non-systematic method that can be implemented with various watermarking approaches. They mentioned that the process of embedding can leave visible marks in the image, especially near the flat regions due to relative predictability. Thus, to prevent such alterations from taking place, the watermark's strength needs to be decreased, but that can open up the data to malicious attacks due to decrease in its robustness and resistance to manipulation. As a solution to this problem, the presented method utilizes calculation of NVF (noise visibility function). It identifies coarse and perimeter sections of image where the watermark can be implanted without any issue of visible distortion in the image. To do the same, detailed formulas with fast computation time for embedding and extraction process, are put forward. The proposed solution assumes the implanted data as noise (utilizing a classical 'maximum posteriori probability' image de-noising method for evaluation) which in turn helps in formulation of a 'texture-masking-function' that decides the optimal regions along-with optimal strength of embedment there. The experimental analysis has proved that the visibility of the distortion has drastically reduced with the successful implementation of the approach, while maintaining the strength of the watermark, making it resilient to various attacks.

Seok *et al* [9] put forward a new watermarking method for audio files that provided resistance against illegal and unauthorized copy of digital audio files. The technique contained a 'psychoacoustic model' of MPEG coded audio files, to ensure that the quality of the audio is not altered or degraded from the former host file in any manner. The implanting procedure in the technique exploited the masking effect of the human auditory system and accomplished near transparency of the watermark after it was embedded in the digital audio file, with focus on maximizing the strength of watermark while keeping it under limitation of reducing the distortions to maximum extent. The extraction process of the technique includes application of whitening (that removes correlation in the signal with linear prediction filtering method) or de-correlation before correlation, even without access to the original audio file. The experimental results portrayed that the presented method is resilient to conventional attacks (like mix down, amplitude compression and data compression) and exhibits no form of audio distortion compared to the original audio file.

Su *et al* [10] suggested a watermarking method for video files, based on two crucial approaches, viz., content synchronized placement and statistical invisibility. Their study argued upon the importance of statistical invisibility in preventing statistical collusion of watermarks in video files, while using a 'content-dependent' and 'spatially localized' watermarking technique. They introduced spatial locations (a new watermark footprint) for aggregating the watermark in data file. As a result of the approach, watermark strength is concentrated in sub-frames of data with desirable properties (where the sub-frame regions are synchronized using optical data instead of structured data). They also demonstrated that the watermark footprints selected using criteria in the proposed approach (namely low average interpolation noise), have better robustness for geometric distortions. The method has shown distinct capability of being embedded and extracted in multimedia using frame-based algorithms for optimum performance. In finality, the experimental observations have proved the effectiveness of the algorithm in video watermarking, while maintaining statistical invisibility (of watermark) to reduce collusions in the data.

Lubin *et al* [11] discussed the role of watermarking as an instrument to combat replication of copyrighted movies. However, in order to be effective, it must possess specific features. The technique must be undetectable in the high-definition motion picture, thus being invisible to the viewers of the data. The watermark in the technique must also be reliably extracted from the source in difficult circumstance like cam-corded, compressed and internet distributed copy of the data. And finally, it must be resistant to malicious and un-authorized removal of watermark. The study argued that no such technique existed before that satisfied all the necessities of visibility, robustness and security. The presented solution meets all the three requirements, with integrated robustness, imperceptibility (by humans) due to low 'spatiotemporal frequency watermark', and an embedding technique that makes the malicious attacks excessively expensive to undertake (even when the attacker has knowledge of the technique). The suggested technique was tested with a high-definition anamorphic lens source displayed in a theatre. Upon evaluation of results, the watermark was declared to be invisible to the naked eye, while being resistant to several alterations that include low-pass filtering of data, addition of noise, geo-metric shifts in alignment, and quality modifications in brightness and contrast.

There is no limit to the amount of work undertaken in this domain due to its practical applicability, which is in part the reason why research work is still ongoing to date. Thus, in order to cover most of the work done in the recent decades, the next sub-section is dedicated to mentioning the same in a tabulated fashion.

3.2.3 Table pertaining to research work on content watermarking in multimedia security

Table 3.2. Summary of recent research studies related to content watermarking in multimedia.

Study	Dataset(s)	Proposed methodology/ algorithms	References
Reversible image watermarking	Random and typical image sets	Reverse watermarking with interpolation technique	[31]
Image adaptive watermarking	Random and typical image sets	Wavelet domain singular value decomposition	[32]
Image watermarking	Clown image	DCT watermarking using subsampling	[33]
Digital image watermarking	'Lena' and 'Photographer' image	DWT and SVD	[34]
Text document watermarking	Random and typical English language image sets	Edge direction histograms	[35]

Electronic text documents watermarking	Random and typical text document sets	Spread-spectrum and Bose–Chaudhuri–Hocquenghem error correction technique	[36]
Wireless video communication watermark detection	Random and typical video sequence	Force even watermarking (FEW) [an error recognition and localisation system]	[37]
Efficiently self-synchronized audio watermarking	Two (16-bit) audio signals of about 15 s	Self-synchronized watermarking [implantation into low frequency coefficients in DWT]	[38]
Audio watermarking	16 bits signed stereo audios sampled at 44.1 kHz [Rock, Jazz, and Classical music]	Modified patchwork algorithm (MPA)	[39]
Time-domain audio watermarking	Random and typical audio sample	Robust and high-quality watermarking with low-frequency amplitude modification	[40]

3.2.4 Inference

The section has evidently mentioned the applications, approaches and importance of content watermarking in the security of multimedia. It has emerged from a mere idea at Monash University's Physics department to a widespread utilized approach of protecting data in digital format. Various approaches have been proposed that deal with one or more of security aspects including robustness, human perception, fragility, computational costs and quality of the multimedia content. Several techniques have been proposed throughout the decades that have solved several issues like prevention of illegal copying of data, manipulation in the content of data, removal of watermark in the data and protection against malicious attacks in the data. As an outcome of such feasibility and effectiveness, content watermarking has now become the standard strategy in protecting copyrighted content.

3.3 Data hiding in multimedia security

3.3.1 Background

Data hiding has immerged from secrete writing methodology applied thousands of years ago (and mentioned by several historians), and is now interconnected with every aspect of our day-to-day lives. It was devised in the form of pictographs in the ancient Egyptian culture, where it was intentionally used for symbolic representation of historical timelines for particular lords or kings. In Chinese culture, the messages used to be first written onto silk and then rolled into a block, and finally sealed with wax, in order to transmit administrative and army secrets. As the civilizations evolved, people started using more sophisticated data hiding and encryption techniques for increased security of the content. Figure 3.6 outlines the prominent advancements over the centuries (up to 1985 AD) [12].

After the digital information revolution and advancements in broadcast services, the transmission process for multimedia among network clients has achieved boundless heights. Due to amplified access and rapid transfer of multimedia files like audio, video, image, pdf, etc, security measures like the ownership safeguards, validation, prevention of illicit alteration and access control have come into the picture. As a resolution to quench these necessities, several techniques have been brought forward, where implantation of sensitive data in multimedia components in a manner that makes it challenging for anyone to discover the message and send it through multimedia communication channels to other clients. This technique(s) is useful for achieving supplementary functionalities, enhancing performance, increase robustness, imperceptibility, and can hide large number of bits [13]. In simple words, data hiding methods aim to conceal the presence of secret messages/data embedded in the complete multimedia file [14, 15], creating hurdles for an attacker to find the position of secret data in files components.

Data hiding methods are distributed under various categories, but the standard classification depends on type of multimedia source. In this categorization, data hiding can be distributed among two major types, namely, perceptual multimedia (like binary image, color picture, motion picture, sound and 3-D arts; acting as primary source) and text and executable codes [16]. It is to be noted that this section focuses on all the mentioned sources except executable codes. If we further classify data hiding, it includes encryption, decryption, steganography and watermarking. As we have already mentioned, the shortcomings of encryption–decryption in previous sections, and have thoroughly discussed content watermarking in the last section, the current section is dedicated to steganography.

In steganography, secret information is hidden in the image/video file which makes it difficult for an attacker to predict whether the data is being transmitted or not with the naked eye, unlike in cryptography (encryption–decryption), where the secret data is disarranged with the normal data (that results in cipher text, while allowing an attacker to guess the existence of secret data and perform the decryption algorithm on it). Its structure is distributed among four processes. First, the multimedia components that will be used to hide the data are selected. Then, the message which is sensitive (and needs to remain hidden) is selected. Third, a proper algorithm or function that fits best for the application is selected (and is later used for implanting and extraction purposes). Lastly, the key that can be used for authentication or to hide and extract data is devised. It is in part of this process and flow of technique, why steganography is also known as the art and science of communication in a manner that conceals the presence of secret information [17, 18].

One thing to be noted here is that the secret data is hidden utilizing (at-most) three least significant bits (LSBs) deformation, and when LSB bits go above four, distortion of the image occurs. Now, although steganography was highly secure, the distortion in the multimedia source after the extraction process means that the user will not get the original image, which is a matter of sensitivity in fields like the military, medicine, and the arts [19]. Therefore, new data hiding methods were

Figure 3.6. Data hiding (steganography) timeline.

introduced to tackle this, and are now known as reversible data hiding techniques (where the original image also gets recovered with the extracted secret data) [20, 21]. This reversible data hiding can be accomplished in two main ways, viz., alteration of the difference value between neighboring pixels based on local characteristics of original images [22] and alteration of the histogram of original image by considering the global characteristics [23].

Moreover, with the introduction of such a huge amount of techniques in solving data hiding or multimedia security in general, there need to be certain methods and evaluation matrices that help in comparison and evaluation of these techniques by finding their performance and efficiency. Its standard evaluation parameters include capacity and peak signal-to-noise ratio (PSNR). The PSNR helps in evaluating how well the watermarked image (image obtained after data embedment) looks compared to the former picture (where the PSNR value and watermarked content quality are directly proportional to each other) [24, 25]. The capacity, on the other hand, indicates the storage size of the secret information (where the capacity value and number of distortions in the marked content are proportional to each other, and thus, indirectly proportional to the PSNR score). These two factors, thus, have a crucial role to play in deciding the effectiveness of the techniques in play, to articulate a novel and operative technique, one needs to have a feasible balance between these two factors in order for it to become as effective as possible.

Having said that, there has been an enormous level of advancements in data hiding techniques or steganography in general. Like content watermarking, the applications now extend to wider fields and are more complex, yet more effective than ever. The next sub-section cites such advancements in the data hiding domain, followed by another sub-section with tabulated citation of research work done in the last few decades.

3.3.2 Data hiding technique reviews

Gurunathan and Rajagopalan [26] proposed a method that can embed the secret information in the picture in a manner that inhibits the capability for anyone to detect the presence of information over the image. This method uses the standard LSB replacement along-with Cuckoo Search (CS) to find an ideal replacement matrix to modify every block's message. This method is distributed among the five phases: firstly, message encryption in which CS algorithm is used for selecting the optimal matrix and using that matrix to convert the secrete message; the second is the image pre-processing where a picture is distributed over various 8×8 pixel blocks (after this, quantized DCT coefficients are obtained upon passing through DCT and quantization table); the third phase/stage includes implanting of the secret message, where the former encrypted message is substituted with later quantized DCT coefficients; once this secret message gets embedded, the fourth phase or the JPEG entropy coding occurs, where all blocks are compressed using Run-Length coding (or Huffman coding), followed by picture generation that contains the quantization table. In the final stage, the picture with its replacement matrix are transmitted. Then, for the extraction purpose, a reverse algorithm is applied and extraction of secret data from every block's various DCT coefficients is performed. After the evaluation of method was held, it yielded PSNR greater than 33 dB and achieved a capacity of 72 bits, which outperformed other methods (like JPEG and JQTM) in terms of picture quality, implanting capacity and safety standards.

Muhammad *et al* [27] presented a secured image framework based on the stego-key adaptive LSB substitution method along with multi-level cryptography. For stego-key and secret information encryption, it utilizes a two-level encryption algorithm (TLEA) and multi-level encryption algorithm (MLEA). This framework is based on four algorithms. Firstly, TLEA is implemented for the encryption of the secret key, followed by second algorithm, where the secrete data is encrypted using MLEA which uses the encrypted secret key. The aforementioned two methods act as a barrier for secret data extraction by attackers, thus resulting in increase of robustness of the method. Then the encrypted data is embedded (on red channel' LSB and secret information encryption basis) into green/blue channel, which results into stegopictures. Then, finally, extraction of the secret information from stegopictures is performed using an extraction algorithm. After the evaluation on 50 experimental pictures, it produced PSNR of 45 dB, NCC of 0.95, RMSE of 0.28 and SSIM of 0.955, outperforming other methods like CLSB, SCC, and ST-FMM. This proved that the proposed method maintained uniformity among safety, computational complication and picture quality.

Adelsbach *et al* [28] proposed a fingerprint casting method that achieved broadcast message fingerprinting and combined decryption in a confidential manner, where an attacker cannot separate or prevent them to execute simultaneously. This method is a mixture of fingerprint scheme, broadcast encryption approach and an (Chameleon cipher referenced) encryption scheme. The proposed method utilizes the merits of both methods, while reducing the demerits. This method offers renewability, privacy and traceability for encryption of transmission (with the assumption for presence of collusion-resistant watermarks). The method provides a proper safeguard that builds a solid wall against malicious users and their illegal activities. Here, traceability is achieved by fingerprinting the receiver's key table that embeds the fingerprint into the content during decryption. Renewability is achieved by a broadcast encryption scheme which generates the new session keys after every encryption as an input to the Chameleon scheme. Transmission is performed by distribution of the number of copies. In this method, fingerprint embedding (FE) is done at transmitter and receiver side. In transmitter-side FE, a message is secured by minor amalgamation of encryption and fingerprint imposed by the source. The efficiency of this method is calculated using computation expenses, broadcast overhead and receiver storage capacity. In terms of outcomes, transmission overhead is moderate, storage size is 1 Mbyte and computation cost is also moderately neutral (not high).

Puteaux *et al* [29] put forward a Paillier cryptosystem based on data hiding in encrypted images (DHEI) method. Here, homomorphic properties are used to multiply pixel blocks and message bits, while images' pre-processing is done before encryption; this becomes an LSB replacement. During the process, the former image is distributed into blocks (where the pixel is 8 bits encoded). Also, using Paillier cryptosystem, a summation in the clear domain is reflected using multiplication in the encrypted domain, which results into substitution of the block's LSB with 0. Now, the encrypted message is divided into several LSBs (equal to zero), while Paillier encryption approach is used to encrypt message blocks. Then, by executing a multiplication modulus, message encrypted blocks are implanted into a single block of the picture. Thereafter, during the decoding phase, Paillier decryption function (using a private key) is executed on every encrypted picture's pixel block, which results in decrypted pictures. Then, in order to extract the former picture(s), a post-processing algorithm is applied, followed by extraction of secret information present in the pixel's LSB. The experiments in the research were performed keeping PSNR and SSIM as key parameters, which turned out to be larger than 50 dB and close to 1, with expansion rate of 2 and payload of 1 BPP. Hence, this method is stated to be highly secured and does not expand with high rate (proving its feasibility). Moreover, the difference between former and generated pictures turned out to be negligible.

Rabie and Kamel [30] proposed a novel DCT approach based on steganography for coloured image and achieved tremendous implanting capability. To achieving better perceptibility and capacity, the secret information is implanted to the high-frequency DCT areas, followed by smooth regions. In this method, the first image is separated into equally-sized and non-coinciding MxMregions, where 2D-DCT is executed for every region. Then, using an embedding function, a high frequency region of each DCT block (in the picture) is assessed. Thereafter, secret image pixels are then embedded in the region of high frequency by replacing the pixel from the secret image, followed by transmission to the receiver. This implanting process is reiterated for the original picture's DCT blocks, followed by reverse order extraction process. For evaluation of the performance, several tests were performed that scored 14.07 BPP (bits per pixel) and 20.31 BPP for capacity and 34.7 dB and 26.0 dB for PSNR pertaining to 16×16 and 256×256 resolutions, respectively. These results convey that the method has maximum storage size without hampering the perceptibility under 20 dB.

3.3.3 Table pertaining to research work on data hiding in multimedia security

Table 3.3. Summary of recent research studies related to data hiding in multimedia.

Study	Dataset(s)	Proposed methodology/ algorithms	References
Information hiding scheme	Four grayscale (GS) test images	Concept of magic cube matrix	[41]
PDF file-based steganography	38 secrete text characters and a random PDF file	Chinese remainder theorem	[42]
Reversible steganography method	Six 512×512 GS pictures	Bivariate linear box-spline interpolation	[43]

Secure steganography scheme	Image dataset	Weighted matrix approach through DCT	[44]
Reversible data hiding scheme based on super-pixel	Kodak, CID, USC-SIPI, STARE and ISIC disease picture dataset	Cellular Automata (CA) and DCT	[45]
Data hiding (steganography method)	CVG-UGR image dataset	Cover image representation using number theory (Fibonacci series)	[46]
Separable and reversible data hiding	Miscellaneous, Kodak and BowsBase image datasets	Parametric binary tree labelling scheme (PBTL)	[47]
Reversible DHEI	Publically available, standard grayscale image dataset	Redundant space transfer (RST) scheme	[48]
Separable and reversible DHEI	Publically available, standard grayscale image dataset	Adaptive embedding strategy with block selection (or stream-cipher and block permutation)	[49]
Reversible DHEI	BOSSbase, BOWS-2 and UCID image dataset	Multi-MSB (most significant bit) prediction and Huffman coding	[50]
Reversible data hiding for HEVC	Motion picture sequence of people on street, traffic, basketball drive, kimono1, BQ mall, party scene, basketball pass, BQ square, race horses	Rivest Cipher 4 (RC4) algorithm	[51]
Reversible data hiding algorithm for H.264/AVC videos	Video sequences of city, news, foreman, coastguard, car-phone, mobile, container and salesman	Histogram shifting of motion vector	[52]

3.3.4 Inference

Data hiding has evolved drastically throughout the ages and has transformed from a secret writing technique used in ancient times to an advanced content protection mechanism used around the globe. Several techniques pertaining to data hiding technique exist, wherein the conventional (and mentioned in this section) one is steganography. All the approaches offer distinct compromise between sturdiness, imperceptibility, volume, reliability and confidentiality; while solving the issues or advancing the methods used in the previously proposed techniques. Despite the presence of various methodologies, data hiding has become the go-to technique as far as securing the contents of the media in the communication process is concerned.

3.4 Conclusion

The chapter has shed light on the prevalent techniques used in the entertainment industry for the protection of multimedia files including text, PDF, audio, image and motion pictures (video). The focus has been upon data hiding (mainly steganography) and content watermarking for data protection and prevention of illegal reproduction, respectively. The chapter discusses introduction, working and enumeration of the processes involved in the beginning, in a brief and crisp manner. This is followed by a brief citation of the history of these techniques along with the reason behind their emergence.

Several processes (like embedding an extraction in content watermarking) are mentioned along with workflow diagrams to help the reader better understand them. The classification of the techniques based upon several parameters has been mentioned as well. Major applications that are made possible due to these techniques are cited with viable information. These aspects cover the fundamental understanding of the concept in the reader's mind.

Then, to give the reader a fresh perspective of the advancements in the contemporary world, summaries of research work done in the past few decades is mentioned, which is followed by tabulation of several research papers and articles published in esteemed publications, providing a brief overview of the current scenario of the techniques and extent of importance they have reached. The chapter attempts to equip every reader to comprehend and gain familiarity with the general aspects of multimedia protection offered by content watermarking and data hiding.

Acknowledgments

The authors are grateful to Department of Information and Communication Technology and Department of Chemical Engineering, School of Technology, Pandit Deendayal Petroleum University for the permission to publish this research.

References

[1] Qiao L 1998 Multimedia security and copyright protection *Technical Report, University of Illinois at Urbana-Champaign, USA*

[2] Kim Y, Park N and Won D 2007 Privacy-enhanced adult certification method for multimedia contents on mobile RFID environments *2007 IEEE Int. Symp. on Consumer Electronics* 1–4

[3] Sait A R W, Uthayakumar J, Shankar K and Kumar K S 2019 Introduction to multimedia tools and applications *Handbook of Multimedia Information Security: Techniques and Applications* (Cham: Springer) pp 3–14

[4] Zhang K, Liang X, Shen X and Lu R 2014 Exploiting multimedia services in mobile social networks from security and privacy perspectives *IEEE Commun. Mag.* **52** 58–65

[5] Rani M M S, Germine Mary G and Rosemary Euphrasia K 2015 Multilevel multimedia security by integrating visual cryptography and steganography techniques *Adv. Intell. Syst. Comput.* 403–12

[6] Tirkel A 2009 Watermark origins *Academia Article* 1 https://academia.edu/5670500/Watermark_Origins

[7] Lin C-Y and Chang S-F 2000 Semifragile watermarking for authenticating JPEG visual content *Proc. Security and Watermarking of Multimedia Contents II* **3971** 140–51

[8] Voloshynovskiy S, Herrigel A, Baumgaertner N and Pun T 2000 A stochastic approach to content adaptive digital image watermarking *Information Hiding* (Lecture Notes on Computer Science vol 1768) (Berlin: Springer) pp 211–36

[9] Seok J, Hong J and Kim J 2002 A novel audio watermarking algorithm for copyright protection of digital audio *ETRI J.* **24** 181–9

[10] Su K, Kundur D and Hatzinakos D 2001 A content dependent spatially localized video watermark for resistance to collusion and interpolation attacks *Proc. 2001 Int. Conf. on Image Processing (Cat. No.01CH37205)* 818–21

[11] Lubin J, Bloom J A and Cheng H 2003 Robust content-dependent high-fidelity watermark for tracking in digital cinema *Security and Watermarking of Multimedia Contents V* 536–45

[12] Raggo M and Hosmer C 2013 History of secret writing *Data Hiding* (London: Newnes) pp 1–17

[13] Wu M and Liu B 2003 Introduction *Multimedia Data Hiding* (Berlin: Springer) pp 1–11

[14] Wang R-Z, Lin C-F and Lin J-C 2000 Hiding data in images by optimal moderately-significant-bit replacement *Electron. Lett.* **36** 2069–70

[15] Hussain M, Abdul Wahab A W, Ho A T S, Javed N and Jung K-H 2017 A data hiding scheme using parity-bit pixel value differencing and improved rightmost digit replacement *Signal Process. Image Commun.* **50** 44–57

[16] Ashour A S and Dey N 2016 Security of multimedia contents: a brief *Intelligent Techniques in Signal Processing for Multimedia Security* (Berlin: Springer) pp 3–14

[17] Cheddad A, Condell J, Curran K and Mc Kevitt P 2010 Digital image steganography: survey and analysis of current methods *Signal Process.* **90** 727–52

[18] Cox I J, Miller M L, Bloom J A, Fridrich J and Kalker T 2008 *Digital Watermarking and Steganography* (Amsterdam: Elsevier) pp 1–2

[19] Kim P-H, Yoon E-J, Ryu K-W and Jung K-H 2019 Data-hiding scheme using multidirectional pixel-value differencing on colour images *Secur. Commun. Netw.* **2019** 1–11

[20] Zhicheng N, Yun-Qing S, Ansari N and Wei S 2006 Reversible data hiding *IEEE Trans. Circuits Syst. Video Technol.* **16** 354–62

[21] Huang L-C, Tseng L-Y and Hwang M-S 2013 A reversible data hiding method by histogram shifting in high quality medical images *J. Syst. Softw.* **86** 716–27

[22] Li X, Li B, Yang B and Zeng T 2013 General framework to histogram-shifting-based reversible data hiding *IEEE Trans. Image Process.* **22** 2181–91

[23] Chen Y-H, Huang H-C and Lin C-C 2015 Block-based reversible data hiding with multi-round estimation and difference alteration *Multimedia Tools Appl.* **75** 13679–704

[24] Xiaolong Li W Z and XinluGui B Y 2013 A novel reversible data hiding scheme based on two-dimensional difference-histogram modification *IEEE Trans. Inf. Forensics Secur.* **8** 1091–100

[25] Huang H-C and Fang W-C 2010 Techniques and applications of intelligent multimedia data hiding *Telecommun. Syst.* **44** 241–51

[26] Gurunathan K and Rajagopalan S P 2019 A stegano—visual cryptography technique for multimedia security *Multimedia Tools Appl.* **79** 3893–911

[27] Muhammad K, Ahmad J, Rehman N U, Jan Z and Sajjad M 2016 CISSKA-LSB: color image steganography using stego key-directed adaptive LSB substitution method *Multimedia Tools Appl.* **76** 8597–626

[28] Adelsbach A, Huber U and Sadeghi A-R 2007 Fingercasting–joint fingerprinting and decryption of broadcast messages *Transactions on Data Hiding and Multimedia Security II* 1–34

[29] Puteaux P, Vialle M and Puech W 2020 Homomorphic encryption-based LSB substitution for high capacity data hiding in the encrypted domain *IEEE Access* **8** 108655–63

[30] Rabie T and Kamel I 2016 High-capacity steganography: a global-adaptive-region discrete cosine transform approach *Multimedia Tools Appl.* **76** 6473–93

[31] Lixin Luo Z C, Ming Chen X Z and Xiong Z 2010 Reversible image watermarking using interpolation technique *IEEE Trans. Inf. Forensics Secur.* **5** 187–93

[32] Bao P and Ma X 2005 Image adaptive watermarking using wavelet domain singular value decomposition *IEEE Trans. Circuits Syst. Video Technol.* **15** 96–102

[33] Chu W C 2003 DCT-based image watermarking using subsampling *IEEE Trans. Multimedia* **5** 34–8

[34] Lai C-C and Tsai C-C 2010 Digital image watermarking using discrete wavelet transform and singular value decomposition *IEEE Trans. Instrum. Meas.* **59** 3060–3

[35] Kim Y-W and Oh I-S 2004 Watermarking text document images using edge direction histograms *Pattern Recognit. Lett.* **25** 1243–51

[36] Alattar A M and Alattar O M 2004 Watermarking electronic text documents containing justified paragraphs and irregular line spacing *Proc. Security, Steganography, and Watermarking of Multimedia Contents VI* **5306** 685–95

[37] Minghua Chen Y H and Lagendijk R L 2005 A fragile watermark error detection scheme for wireless video communications *IEEE Trans. Multimedia* **7** 201–11

[38] Wu S, Huang J, Huang D and Shi Y Q 2005 Efficiently self-synchronized audio watermarking for assured audio data transmission *IEEE Trans. Broadcast.* **51** 69–76

[39] In-Kwon Y and HyoungJoong K 2003 Modified patchwork algorithm: a novel audio watermarking scheme *IEEE Trans. Speech Audio Process.* **11** 381–6

[40] Wen-Nung L and Li-Chun C 2006 Robust and high-quality time-domain audio watermarking based on low-frequency amplitude modification *IEEE Trans. Multimedia* **8** 46–59

[41] Wu Q, Zhu C, Li J-J, Chang C-C and Wang Z-H 2016 A magic cube based information hiding scheme of large payload *J. Inform. Secur. Appl.* **26** 1–7

[42] Ekodeck S G R and Ndoundam R 2016 PDF steganography based on Chinese remainder theorem *J. Inform. Secur. Appl.* **29** 1–15

[43] Benhfid A, Ameur E B and Taouil Y 2020 Reversible steganographic method based on interpolation by bivariate linear box-spline on the three directional mesh *J. King Saud Univ.—Comp. Inform. Sci.* **32** 850–9

[44] Chowdhuri P, Jana B and Giri D 2018 Secured steganographic scheme for highly compressed color image using weighted matrix through DCT *Int. J. Comp. Appl.* 1–12

[45] Singh P K, Jana B and Datta K 2020 Superpixel based robust reversible data hiding scheme exploiting Arnold transform with DCT and CA *J. King Saud Univer.—Comp. Inform. Sci.* 1–19

[46] Rehman A, Saba T, Mahmood T, Mehmood Z, Shah M and Anjum A 2018 Data hiding technique in steganography for information security using number theory *J. Inf. Sci.* **45** 767–78

[47] Yi S and Zhou Y 2019 Separable and reversible data hiding in encrypted images using parametric binary tree labeling *IEEE Trans. Multimedia* **21** 51–64

[48] Liu Z-L and Pun C-M 2018 Reversible data-hiding in encrypted images by redundant space transfer *Inf. Sci.* **433–434** 188–203

[49] Qin C, Zhang W, Cao F, Zhang X and Chang C-C 2018 Separable reversible data hiding in encrypted images via adaptive embedding strategy with block selection *Signal Process.* **153** 109–22

[50] Yin Z, Xiang Y and Zhang X 2020 Reversible data hiding in encrypted images based on multi-MSB prediction and Huffman coding *IEEE Trans. Multimedia,* **22** 874–84

[51] Long M, Peng F and Li H- 2017 Separable reversible data hiding and encryption for HEVC video *J. Real-Time Image Process.* **14** 171–82

[52] Niu K, Yang X and Zhang Y 2017 A novel video reversible data hiding algorithm using motion vector for H.264/AVC *Tsinghua Sci. Technol.* **22** 489–98

Chapter 4

Recent advances in reversible watermarking in an encrypted domain

Hanzhou Wu

Reversible watermarking (RW) in encrypted domain has been a hot spot in recent years, since it allows both the raw cover content and the secret message to be perfectly retrieved at the data receiver side. Meanwhile, the semantic information of the cover can be protected. The cover can be any media object, making it quite suitable for cloud media data management and authentication. RW algorithms in encrypted domain can be roughly categorized into two types: reserving (data embedding) room before encryption and reserving (data embedding) room after encryption. The former can provide the relatively better rate-distortion performance, but may need more side information so as to realize RW in the encrypted domain. The latter can reduce the side information, but often provides a relatively lower data embedding capacity. Along these two lines, in this chapter, we are to review the state-of-the-art RW methods in the encrypted domain. By analyzing these methods in terms of the rate-distortion performance, we discuss the research trends of RW in encrypted domain. This chapter is intended as a tutorial introducing recent advances in media watermarking in the encrypted domain.

4.1 Introduction

As a special means of information hiding [1], *reversible watermarking (RW)* [2], typically also named *reversible data hiding (RDH)* [3] or *lossless data embedding (LDE)* [4], allows both the hidden information and the raw cover content to be reconstructed without error at the data decoder side. As shown in figure 4.1, RW can be modeled as a communication task. A data encoder embeds a secret message into a digital object (also called *cover/host*) without significantly distorting the object content. The digital object could be an arbitrary multimedia file such as a digital image. The resulting *marked* object containing hidden information will be sent to the desired decoder, who can derive the decoding procedure with the secret key to

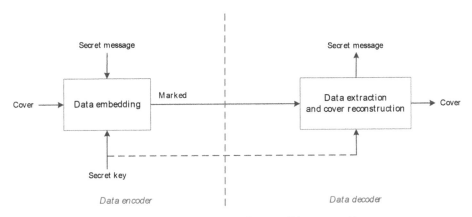

Figure 4.1. General framework for reversible watermarking.

perfectly retrieve the hidden information. However, unlike other watermarking systems [5–7], RW further allows the data decoder to recover the original cover content, which is quite useful for sensitive applications such as medical imagery and cloud data management.

In RW, in most cases, when a marked object was previously altered, the data decoder may not fully retrieve the embedded information. It implies that, RW is typically fragile [8]. As RW inserts extra data into a cover, it is required that the insertion should not impair the use of the cover. It leads a RW system to be often evaluated by rate-distortion performance. This means that, for a fixed level of distortion, it would be quite desirable to embed as many message bits as possible. In other words, it is expected to reduce the introduced distortion as much as possible for a fixed length of the secret message. Additionally, it is necessary that the computational complexity for an RW system should be kept low so that it can be helpful for deployment in practice.

With the aforementioned point of view, a lot of advanced RW systems have been reported in the literature in the past two decades. Early RW algorithms such as [4, 9, 10] are based on lossless compression. The core idea behind them can be briefly explained as follows. First, the well-selected noise-like component of the cover is losslessly compressed to generate a compressed code. Then, the compressed code together with the secret message are used to substitute the well-selected noise-like content. In this way, RW can be realized. Obviously, the embedded secret message and the original noise-like content can be easily reconstructed by the data decoder. However, since the entropy of the noise-like component is usually very high, the compression ratio will be low, meaning that, even though the introduced distortion due to data embedding is low, the maximum embeddable size of the secret message (defined as *capacity*) is low as well, which is not superior in terms of rate-distortion performance evaluation.

Ni *et al* [3] present a novel algorithm called *histogram shifting (HS)* to RW. The HS method was originally designed for grayscale images. The method uses a histogram directly determined from the given cover image to carry the secret message. The basic idea can be described as follows. First of all, a pair of peak-zero bins are selected from the histogram based on the payload to be embedded. Then, by shifting the histogram bins between the peak bin and the zero bin along the corresponding direction, additional space can be created. Finally, by shifting the peak bin to the created empty space, the secret message can be successfully embedded in a reversible manner. The maximum embeddable payload size equals the frequency of the peak bin. Obviously, by applying multiple peak bins, more message bits can be embedded. Therefore, comparing with lossless compression (LC), HS has the ability to not only provide relatively higher capacity, but also introduce relatively lower distortion. However, using the histogram determined from the raw cover for RW does not take into account the correlations between adjacent cover elements, which limits the data embedding capacity. To this end, many RW methods [11–15] adopt a prediction-error histogram, rather than the original histogram, to reversibly embed the secret message. The core steps can be described as follows. First, a well-designed predictor is used to predict the cover elements such that a prediction-error histogram (PEH) can be produced. Then, by processing the PEH with the HS operation or variants [13–16] (e.g., prediction-error expansion (PEE) [14]), a secret message can be embedded. Since PEH is often Gaussian-like, by using the central bins (that have high occurrence) for RW, a higher capacity or lower distortion can be achieved. It can be said to a certain extent that mainstream RW works are based on HS (or variants) and prediction errors. In addition, other methods such as difference expansion [17, 18], integer wavelet transform (IWT) [19], and pixel value ordering (PVO) [20–22] are also proposed to provide superior performance.

Regardless of the rate-distortion performance of the above-mentioned arts, they are actually all designed for plaintexts. This means that, anyone may access the semantic information without the permission of the content owner, which is not suited to sensitive applications requiring the cover content to be kept secretly. Imagining such a realistic scenario, a user hopes to send a digital image to the cloud for storage. They may not want to share the visual content of the image with anyone else unless someone has obtained the permission from the user. To this end, before sending the image to the cloud platform, the user encrypts the content of the image as noise-like. However, the cloud administrator needs to manage a lots of encrypted images due to the larger number of end users. To this end, the cloud administrator may insert additional data such as source information into the encrypted images so that by retrieving the hidden data from the marked and encrypted image, the entire image database can be well managed. Obviously, the insertion should be lossless, namely, both the original encrypted image and the inserted data can be recovered without any error since the administrator has no right to permanently distort the encrypted image. Therefore, it is straightforward to consider RW as the effective means to address the above problem since RW has the property allowing both the hidden data and the cover to be fully restored, which motivates scholars to study RW in an encrypted domain.

Embedding data in the encrypted domain without any preprocessing is not optimal to the practical use because the entropy for the encrypted data is maximized and simply modifying the encrypted data may not allow the original cover content to be correctly decrypted. We therefore need take into account the impact caused by encryption in order to design a superior RW algorithm. Along this direction, increasing RW works suitable for encrypted domain have been proposed in recent years, e.g., [23–29]. Similar to previous works, these arts are actually still trying to mine the redundant component of the cover so that the additional information can be successfully embedded, e.g., reserving data embedding space before encryption [27], using spatial correlations between pixels for cover recovery [24].

This chapter will review advanced RW methods designed for an encrypted domain. The structure is organized as follows. First, we introduce the necessary preliminaries. Then, we will review the state of the art and provide analysis. Finally, we conclude this chapter. It is intended as a tutorial introducing recent advances in media watermarking.

4.2 Preliminaries

4.2.1 Cover source and formats

There is no limitation to the cover source, meaning that, the cover can be naturally captured, computer-aided designed, manually generated and so on. Since media objects are widely distributed over social networks and necessary to be protected, they have become the most commonly used cover for RW. For example, up to now, a digital image is one of the most important cover-types for RW due to the ease of modification. Therefore, in this chapter, unless mentioned, we mainly consider digital image as the cover object. On the one hand, many existing RW methods are originally designed for images, indicating that, most state-of-the-art methods can be properly summarized. On the other hand, similar to other covers, digital image has different formats, e.g., an image can be stored as uncompressed or compressed, which means that image based RW methods can be properly extended to other covers by making adjustments accordingly, thus providing good generalization ability. For example, an image can be compressed with the JPEG (Joint Photographic Experts Group) standard. For RW, the secret data can be embedded in the discrete cosine transform (DCT) domain, namely, coefficients in the DCT domain will be used to carry the secret data. Thus, one may easily extend the data embedding operation to a given video sequence by exploiting the (quantized) DCT coefficients for RW as well. However, it should be admitted that, as different cover objects always have their own statistical characteristics, when designing an advanced RW system, one has to further take into account the impact caused by the cover object itself [30].

4.2.2 Encryption methods

Encrypting the cover should allow the secret information to be fully embedded in the encrypted content and enable both the secret information and the original non-encrypted cover to be perfectly restored. Therefore, prior to encryption, the cover may be preprocessed to reserve room for the subsequent data embedding procedure since directly encrypting the cover results in the maximum entropy. Regardless of the cover-preprocessing procedure to be well designed, a straightforward idea to encrypt the (processed) cover is applying a secure cryptographic algorithm such as

Advanced Encryption Standard (AES) [23]. Another simple but effective encryption approach is directly applying the bit-wise XOR (Exclusive-OR) operation to the cover elements, which has been widely used in many existing works [24–26]. For example, let $x_{i,j}$ represent a pixel value located at the ith row and jth column in a grayscale image. And assuming that, $x_{i,j}$ is stored with 8 bits, meaning that, $x_{i,j}$ can be written as a binary string $\{x_{i,j,0}, x_{i,j,1}, ..., x_{i,j,7}\}$, where $x_{i,j,k} \in \{0, 1\}$, $\forall\, 0 \leqslant k \leqslant 7$, and $x_{i,j} = \sum_{k=0}^{7} x_{i,j,k} \cdot 2^k$. The bit-wise XOR encryption applied to $x_{i,j}$ is described as:

$$y_{i,j,k} = x_{i,j,k} \oplus r_{i,j,k}, \; 0 \leqslant k \leqslant 7. \tag{4.1}$$

where $\oplus$ means the XOR operator and $r_{i,j,k} \in \{0, 1\}$, $k \in [0, 7]$ is produced with a key. In this way, $x_{i,j}$ can be encrypted as $y_{i,j} = \sum_{k=0}^{7} y_{i,j,k} \cdot 2^k$. By applying equation (4.1) for all pixels, we can generate the corresponding encrypted image. It is possible that one may only encrypt a part of bits of a pixel. For example, since the image content is mainly affected by the higher bit planes, we can only encrypt the higher bit planes and keep the lower ones unchanged. The resultant encrypted image may not reveal information about the original image content since the low bit planes are noise-like. Additionally, one may also simply permute the cover elements for content protection [8]. An advantage is that, permuting the cover elements allows us to use the aforementioned HS operation or variants to embed the secret data since permutation does not change the histogram directly determined from the raw cover. However, the capacity (of data embedding) is subjected to the frequency values of used histogram bins. Recently, homomorphic encryption [31] has also been utilized for encryption of the cover.

4.2.3 Evaluation metrics

An RW algorithm can be often measured by the rate-distortion performance, security and computational complexity [8]. The term 'rate' means the size of embedded data (usually in bits). The term 'distortion' measures the difference between the (raw) cover and the directly decrypted cover that may contain hidden information. For digital images, the peak signal-to-noise ratio (PSNR, dB) is often used as the distortion measurement. For example, let $X = \{x_{i,j} | 1 \leqslant i \leqslant N, 1 \leqslant j \leqslant M\}$ and $Y = \{y_{i,j} | 1 \leqslant i \leqslant N, 1 \leqslant j \leqslant M\}$ be any two grayscale images sized $N \times M$ that all pixel values are in the range [0, 255]. The PSNR is defined as:

$$\text{PSNR} = 10 \log_{10} \frac{255^2}{\text{MSE}} \tag{4.2}$$

where

$$\text{MSE} = \frac{1}{NM} \sum_{i=1}^{N} \sum_{j=1}^{M} (x_{i,j} - y_{i,j})^2. \tag{4.3}$$

Generally, a higher PSNR corresponds to a better image quality. Throughout this chapter, unless mentioned, in default, we consider PSNR for quantitative analysis of image quality. In this way, in terms of rate-distortion performance, it is expected to embed as many secret bits as possible for a pre-fixed PSNR. The equivalent task is to keep the PSNR as high as possible for a fixed size of the payload. For security, on the one hand, the cover-encryption procedure should not leak any semantic information of the cover. On the other hand, for data extraction, it should be impossible to easily retrieve the embedded information for an attacker, implying that the attacker should not be able to access the data embedding parameters. In addition, from the point of practical usage, it is very necessary to keep the overall computational complexity low. Currently, most advanced RW systems in encrypted domain are mainly trying to improve rate-distortion performance.

4.2.4 Auxiliary data

In RW, to ensure reversibility, there may be auxiliary data to be self-embedded. The auxiliary data can be a secret key, the data embedding parameters and/or so-called location map [11, 12]. For instance, a data receiver (decoder) has to first find the marked elements and then reconstruct the hidden information from the marked elements, which requires the data receiver and the data hider (encoder) to share the secret key and embedding parameters. Though these auxiliary data can be shared in advance between the data encoder and the data decoder via a third secure channel independent of the marked object, it is quite effective to hide the auxiliary data in the given cover so that there is no need to apply for additional resource. In addition, directly modifying the cover may introduce underflow problem or overflow problem, e.g., by HS, a grayscale image pixel may be changed from '0' to '−1' or from '255' to '256' if each pixel value is stored with 8 bits. In this case, one (the data hider) has to pre-adjust some cover elements to avoid the underflow/overflow problem, leading the hider to first construct a location map and then self-embed it to the cover for full cover reconstruction at the data receiver side. For more details about the location map, we refer the reader to [13].

For RW in encrypted domain, the detailed construction of auxiliary data is dependent on the designer. Regardless of the method to construct the auxiliary data, the self-embedding procedure of auxiliary data for many works can be roughly described as follows. The cover elements are partitioned into two (disjoint) element-sets. One element-set will be used for carrying the auxiliary data and the other one will carry the additional data. A common method is to replace the noise-like components of the first set with the auxiliary data, and then construct the corresponding side information. For example, in many image based RW systems, the LSBs of some pixels are identified and replaced with the auxiliary data. In this way, the auxiliary data can be embedded. Then, the original LSBs of these pixels will be recorded as side information to be considered as a part of the additional data, which should be carried by the other pixels. Accordingly, at the receiver side, one has to first reconstruct the auxiliary data from some pixels and then use the auxiliary data to fully retrieve the additional data (including the side information). Thus, the original cover content can be further reconstructed according to the side information and other necessary auxiliary operations. Notice that, here, the additional data not only includes the secret information that will be embedded by the data hider, but also may include side information. For compactness, we consider auxiliary data and side information as equivalent to each other.

4.3 State-of-the-art methods

4.3.1 General framework

Before detailing the review and analysis, we first describe the general framework for RW in an encrypted domain. For simplicity, we here consider the cover object as a digital image unless otherwise stated. We follow the scenario mentioned in the Introduction section. As shown in figure 4.2, a given cover image may be preprocessed (defined as '*Phase-I preprocessing*') before image encryption. The Phase-I preprocessing can produce either a modified version of the cover or side information used for the subsequent procedure. Then, by applying image encryption, we can obtain an encrypted image, from which, generally, we cannot find the plain information of the cover image. The encrypted image is then uploaded to the cloud for, e.g., saving storage space. For data embedding, the encrypted image may be preprocessed again (defined as '*Phase-II preprocessing*') such that the additional data can be inserted into the encrypted content. In this way, a marked image can be finally generated for management or other purposes. It is noted that the Phase-I preprocessing and Phase-II preprocessing are optional. Furthermore, a secret key should be used for image encryption and decryption. Another secret key is also necessary for data embedding and extraction. In this way, given the marked image, the additional data as well as the cover can be fully reconstructed according to the two keys.

It can be seen that, we do not show the detailed use of the two secret keys in figure 4.2. The reason is that different RW algorithms actually have different mechanisms in extracting the inserted data and recovering the raw cover, which may reduce the generalization ability if we detail the use of the secret keys in figure 4.2. For example, it can be observed from figure 4.2 that there may exist interaction between data extraction and image recovery. It implies that, though in some cases, the embedded data can be extracted only according to the data extraction key, and the plain information of the cover may be near-perfectly reconstructed with only the

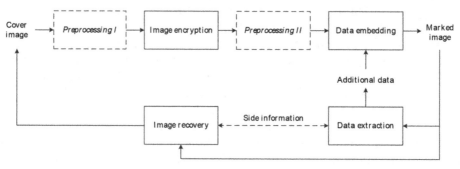

Figure 4.2. General framework for RW in encrypted domain.

decryption key, there should also exist cases that, e.g., the data extraction key and the image decryption key are needed as a whole to fully retrieve the original cover [23–26].

As mentioned previously, prior to data embedding, one has to reserve room to carry the additional data. It can be done during Phase-I preprocessing or Phase-II preprocessing. For those methods that directly embed data in the encrypted domain without any intuitive preprocessing procedure, one can consider it as a special case of the Phase-II preprocessing. In this way, all RW methods in encrypted domain can be categorized into two types: reserving (data-embedding) room after encryption (Phase-II) and reserving (data-embedding) room before encryption (Phase-I). In terms of data embedding positions, many advanced methods use the spatial grayscale values of image pixels to carry the additional data, which is due to the reason that grayscale images are quite easy to be modified and can accommodate more bits comparing with other types of images. JPEG images have also attracted lots of attention as they are the most popular image format over social networks. Different from grayscale images, the DCT coefficients are the cover elements for RW in JPEG images in most cases. Palette images have also received increasing concern from researchers [8] because they are popular in social networks as well, e.g., animated images over social networks are belonging to palette images. In the following, for better presentation, we review the existing arts in terms of embedding-room reservation.

4.3.2 Reserving room after encryption

Reserving room for RW after encryption is intuitive as there is no need to directly handle the plaintext. Figure 4.3 shows the sketch for RW in an encrypted domain based on reserving room after encryption. It involves three roles including the content owner, the data hider and the data receiver. The entire process can be

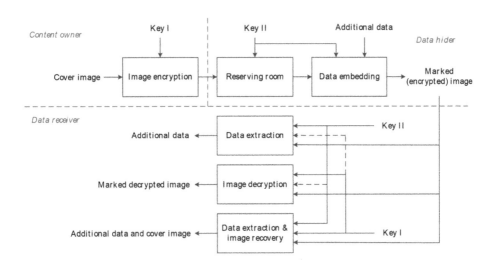

Figure 4.3. Sketch for RW in encrypted domain by reserving room after encryption.

described as follows. First of all, the content owner uses a secret key (defined as 'Key I') to produce an encrypted image, which will be sent to the data hider that may serve as the data manager in the cloud. Then, the data hider inserts the additional data into the encrypted image content by mining the embeddable (encrypted) elements according to a secret key (defined as 'Key II'). It results in a marked and encrypted image, which should be further conveyed to the data receiver. However, the data receiver can be either the data hider (manager) or the content owner. This indicates that the subsequent procedure is dependent on the role of data receiver, namely, it relies on the key(s) held by the data receiver. In detail, as shown in figure 4.3, if the data receiver holds Key I only, he may be able to recover a decrypted image containing hidden information, named as 'marked decrypted image'. If he only holds Key II, he may perfectly retrieve the embedded data. If the data receiver has both keys, he can not only recover the original cover, but also can perfectly retrieve the embedded data. We sometimes call 'Key I' as the encryption key, and 'Key II' as the embedding key. For compactness, we may also call them the decryption key and the extraction key, respectively. That means, the decryption key is equivalent to the encryption key. And, the extraction key is equivalent to the embedding key. The reason is that, the decryption key and the extraction key can be derived from the encryption key and the data embedding key, respectively.

Based on the above analysis, advanced works have been introduced in the past years. The first method was probably proposed by [23]. In the method, according to an encryption key, an image was first encrypted by AES. The resultant encrypted image is then embedded by replacing an encrypted bit with the secret bit according to the embedding key. Notice that, there is no need to require that the bits to be modified should be the LSBs (least significant bits) of pixels. Thus, a marked encrypted image can be generated. For the data receiver, he can directly extract all marked bits to constitute the entire secret data. However, to recover the raw image content, the receiver has to analyze the local complexity of pixels so as to identify the original values of the bits that were altered for data embedding. It can be said that, here, the data receiver holds both the encryption key and the embedding key since he cannot identify all modified bits in a low computational complexity without the embedding key.

Zhang [24] improved the method in [23] in terms of two aspects. The first one is to replace the encryption method with the simple bit-wise XOR operation, which can speed up the encryption process as there is no need to collect bit-blocks for encryption at each time. Second, by partitioning an encrypted image into multiple disjoint blocks each carrying a secret bit, the embedded data can be reconstructed with a lower error rate during the decryption processing. Its significant advantage comparing with [23] is: a single bit is carried by multiple randomly selected encrypted pixels in a block, rather than only one bit of some pixel, which leads the secret bit being more likely reconstructed because modifying multiple randomly selected pixels will significantly distort the spatial correlations between pixels in the block, allowing the spatial local complexity difference between embedding '0' and embedding '1' to be significantly large which can benefit data extraction a lot.

Obviously, the image recovery can be finished after all secret bits have been identified. To reduce the error rate of data extraction, the authors in [25] use the spatial correlations between adjacent blocks to further enlarge the local complexity difference between 'embedding 0' and 'embedding 1'.

To extract the embedded secret information, the methods in [24, 25] require that the data receiver should have both 'Key I' and 'Key II', which is not applicable in the case where the data receiver cannot interact with the content owner. To tackle this problem, Zhang [26] further introduces a *separable* RW algorithm in the encrypted domain. The algorithm encrypts the cover image also with the bit-wise XOR operation. However, instead of collecting pixel blocks, the LSBs of some pixels in the encrypted image are collected to constitute a cover bit-vector, which will be then divided disjoint short bit-vectors. Each short bit-vector will be compressed to reserve the data-embedding space for carrying the additional bits with bit replacement. Thus, the data receiver can directly retrieve the secret data by reading bits from the marked encrypted image only with the data extraction key. With only the decryption key, the data receiver can also generate an image quite close to the original cover image, which means that, the distortion between the original cover image and the generated image is small. It can be seen that there is no need to share any side information between the content owner and the data receiver when the data receiver does not decrypt the image.

However, there are two aspects to be improved for the method in [26]. First, directly compressing the LSBs of the encrypted pixels has a relatively low embedding capacity because the entropy of the encrypted LSBs is maximized. Second, the spatial correlations between the LSBs of pixels (in the plain domain) are not strong, meaning that exploiting the correlations between LSBs of pixels for image recovery may be not perfect, i.e., it leads to an error rate of content recovery. To this end, Zhang *et al* [32] reduce the error rate by using high-layer bits of encrypted pixels for data embedding. Qian *et al* [33] propose a prediction based RW algorithm with distributed source coding (DSC), which exploits high significant bits for data embedding. It can not only provide the higher capacity, but also reduce the error probability. This is due to the reason that high significant bits can be accurately predicted from the adjacent ones. We here refer the reader to [34–36] for more prediction based RW works designed for the encrypted spatial domain.

RW in the encrypted JPEG domain has also been studied in the literature. A straightforward idea is to extend the main idea of RW in the encrypted spatial domain to encrypted JPEG domain by making adjustments accordingly. For example, one may select the most suitable cover elements (that can be either encrypted DCT coefficients or other components) in the encrypted JPEG stream to carry the additional data, while allowing the plaintext to be fully recovered by considering block correlations or structural characteristics. Some representative works can be found in [37, 38].

In terms of rate-distortion evaluation, reserving room after encryption cannot provide a high capacity because the data hider has no knowledge about the plaintext and therefore cannot capture enough redundant space for carrying additional data. For example, one can use almost all pixels in a non-encrypted image for RW, which, however, is not realistic to encrypted images. The reason limiting the capacity is due to the requirement of reversibility. On the other hand, the introduced distortion depends on the data embedding operation. If the secret bits are carried by the LSBs of pixels, the introduced distortion will be low since the LSBs are noise-like and therefore will not introduce noticeable artifacts. However, if the higher bit planes are embedded, the directly decrypted image will have a significantly higher distortion compared to the original image content. Fortunately, by exploiting the spatial correlations between cover pixels, the distortion can be reduced during image recovery. It can be said to a certain extent that most works are designed along this line, e.g., prediction based works.

4.3.3 Reserving room before encryption

Reserving room for RW before encryption requires the content owner to preprocess the cover content. The target of preprocessing is to losslessly compress the cover content so that enough space can be vacated for carrying additional data. Figure 4.4 shows the sketch for RW in the encrypted domain by reserving room before encryption. It can be seen that the overall flowchart is similar to figure 4.3. The entire procedure can be described as follows. The content owner first preprocesses the cover image to vacate embedding room for the data hider. During the preprocessing, some necessary auxiliary data may be collected to be sent to the data hider. The auxiliary data, usually also called side information, will tell the data hider where to embed the secret data. Such side information should be shared with the data hider via a secure channel. For example, the side information may be self-embedded into the cover by LSB substitution such that the data hider can read the side information before data embedding. Once the preprocessing is completed, the content owner encrypts the resultant preprocessed image to produce the encrypted image, which will be thereafter sent to the data hider, e.g., via a cloud application

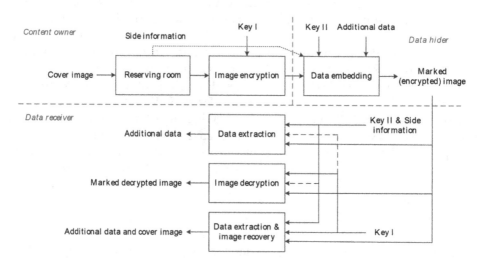

Figure 4.4. Sketch for RW in encrypted domain by reserving room before encryption.

programming interface (API). Since the embedding space has been vacated by the content owner, the data hider can directly embed secret data into the vacated room. In this way, a marked encrypted image can be finally generated. When the data receiver receives the marked encrypted image, the subsequent operation depends on his identity. That is, if the receiver holds 'Key II' and side information, he may be able to fully extract the embedded data. If he only holds 'Key I', a rough version of the original cover image can be obtained. If the receiver holds two keys and side information, he will be able to reconstruct both the hidden information and the original cover content without any error.

A lot of RW works in encrypted domain can be categorized into this type since it can realize the better rate-distortion performance. A simple and intuitive idea is to losslessly compress the LSBs of all pixels to produce a compressed code, whose length is less than the total number of pixels such that the compressed code can be used to replace a part of the raw LSBs and the remaining LSBs can be emptied to accommodate the additional bits in the encrypted domain. In this case, it requires the content owner to tell the vacated LSBs to the data hider, i.e., there should exist side information shared between the content owner and the data hider. However, regardless of the detailed process, it can be inferred that the embedding capacity is low since losslessly compressing LSBs cannot reserve sufficient room for data embedding because of the near-maximum entropy. It is therefore straightforward to use other operations to create room for data embedding. Motivated by this idea, in 2013, Ma *et al* [28] applied a traditional RW operation designed for an image in the plain domain before its encryption to vacate room for RW in the encrypted domain. In the method, the LSBs of some pixels are reversibly embedded into the noise-like components of other pixels by using a conventional RW method [40] so that the vacated LSBs can be used to insert additional data. The reported experimental results demonstrate that the work will not produce any error in data extraction and image recovery. Moreover, it can embed more than 0.4 bits per pixel (bpp), which is a significant improvement compared to methods by reserving room after encryption. And, the PSNRs for different test images are often above 40 dB, which shows superior performance. Notice that here the PSNR is computed between the marked decrypted image and the raw cover image. As reported in reference [27], patch-level sparse representation can be used to compress the lower bit planes for capacity improvement, which demonstrates that, for the same level of distortion, more secret bits can be carried comparing with the method in [28].

As mentioned previously, prediction based operation can benefit the data embedding. Motivated by this technical perspective, Zhang *et al* [39] estimate some cover pixels before image encryption so that, in the encrypted domain, the estimated errors of cover pixels can be reversibly shifted to carry secret data. In terms of rate-distortion performance, it indeed outperforms methods that vacate room after encryption. However, the embedding capacity is relatively low. It is necessary to design a more accurate prediction mechanism and advanced embedding operation to improve the performance. Inspired by this perspective, in order to embed a large amount of information, Puteaux and Puech [41] present a RW method based on most significant bit (MSB) prediction. Their simulation results show that the method can not only provide high capacity, but also keep the image distortion (for the decrypted image) low, which has demonstrated its superiority. For more related prediction based RW systems in the encrypted domain, one can refer to [42–45].

The above methods use symmetric algorithms such as AES for encryption. In recent years, public-key encryption has also been applied to RW in an encrypted domain. For example, Chen *et al* [46] first propose an RW method with the Paillier homomorphic encryption [47]. In this method, by using the public key, the content owner can generate the encrypted image that will be sent to the data hider. By embedding the secret data with the public key, the data hider can produce a marked encrypted image that can allow the data receiver to retrieve the embedded data according to the corresponding key. Though the method provides good rate-distortion performance, a weakness is, it transforms a pixel to two parts that are encrypted to generate two cipher-texts [48], which requires high transmission resource. Another method that directly embeds data in the encryption domain can be found in [49]. As preprocessing the image before encryption has the ability to provide better performance, increasing arts are first preprocessing the image to reserve room for embedding, and then encrypting the image by public-key encryption, e.g., [31, 48, 50]. In brief summary, using a public-key system, particularly with probabilistic and homomorphic properties, avoids the involved parties sharing the same key, which is quite desirable for high-level secure signal processing (SSP).

4.3.4 Challenges and opportunities

On the one hand, many applications such as cloud data management can benefit a lot from advanced RW technologies in the encrypted domain. On the other hand, there are also challenges to be addressed and opportunities to be seized. We discuss some challenges and opportunities below.

First, many conventional works are originally designed for digital images. However, diverse covers are widely distributed over social networks, such as texts, videos and audios. From the perspective of large-scale usage, it is necessary to design RW algorithms suited to various cover objects. For example, increasing works have been proposed for H.264/AVC video sequences [51, 52], audio signals [53], 3D mesh models [54], and vector graphics [55]. It can be therefore inferred that, one direction (or say opportunity) of RW in the encrypted domain in the future is to design general approaches independent of cover types or introduce novel RW approaches designed for particular cover objects.

Second, though the primary goal of encryption is to prevent the cover plaintext from being leaked, the encryption operation also has impact on the data embedding performance. In other words, in order to provide the superior rate-distortion performance, we have to design well the encryption operation and the embedding operation. For example, Wu *et al* [8] use permutation to encrypt the pixel matrix so as to preserve the histogram, which can be used for data embedding with a high capacity by the data hider. If they simply encrypt the pixel matrix with standard encryption, e.g., AES, the performance will decline significantly. Therefore, in terms of rate-distortion optimization, how to vacate more space for embedding while protecting the privacy of the given cover is the core.

Third, in terms of security, the cover content should be protected, which can be done by the encryption algorithm. On the other hand, according to Kerckhoffs's principle, one has to ensure that any illegal decoder cannot determine the embedded information from the encrypted and marked object. It requires that the embedding procedure should be controlled by a key so that recovering the embedded data becomes a probabilistically impossible task for the illegal decoder. Additionally, many RW systems only consider the rate-distortion evaluation, which may be not enough for particular covers. For example, RW in an encrypted video sequence not only distorts the visual quality, but also will affect the bit rate of the resulting video file. How to well preserve various statistical features for a specific cover during embedding is an important and challenging problem.

Finally, from the information-theoretic view, given the cover, we expect to compute the maximum embeddable payload size under distortion constraint. In other words, given a fixed payload size, it is necessary to determine the minimum distortion introduced by data embedding. Moreover, how to design an advanced RW system approaching the bound(s) is equally important. On the one hand, one may extend the theoretical results in the plaintext domain to the encrypted domain, by making adjustments accordingly. On the other hand, when multi-objective optimization is introduced (e.g., preserving various statistical features), finding information-theoretic bound(s) becomes a challenging task, needing further studies.

4.4 Conclusion

RW in an encrypted domain has become a quite active research field in the past years, which is due to: (a) RW enables us to embed data into a media object without permanent distortion; (b) many users store encrypted media files by an outsourced manner; (c) a data manager needs to manage a huge number of encrypted files and inserts data to every encrypted file for better management. In this chapter, we have reviewed recent state-of-the-art RW algorithms in the encrypted domain. Most RW works are originally designed for images and their ideas can be extended to various types of covers by making adjustments accordingly. Since the entropy of encrypted content has been near-maximized, many works reserve room before encryption so that enough space can be used for accommodating additional data. We have also discussed the challenges and opportunities. It is believed that RW in the encrypted domain will move rapidly ahead in the near future even though there are some challenging problems to be addressed.

Acknowledgements

This work was partly supported by the National Natural Science Foundation of China (NSFC) under grant number 61902235, and also supported by the Shanghai 'Chenguang' Project under grant number 19CG46.

References

[1] Petitcolas F A P, Anderson R J and Kuhn M G 1999 Information hiding—a survey *Proc. IEEE* **87** 1062–78

[2] Wu H and Zhang X 2020 Game-theoretic analysis to parameterized reversible watermarking *IETE Tech. Rev.*

[3] Ni Z, Shi Y, Ansari N and Su W 2003 Reversible data hiding *IEEE Trans. Circuits Syst. Video Technol.* 16 354–62

[4] Fridrich J, Goljan M and Du R 2002 Lossless data embedding—new paradigm in digital watermarking *EURASIP J. Adv. Signal Process.* **2** 185–96

[5] Liu X, Lin C and Yuan S 2016 Blind dual watermarking for color images' authentication and copyright protection *IEEE Trans. Circuits Syst. Video Technol.* **28** 1047–55

[6] Lu C and Liao H 2001 Multipurpose watermarking for image authentication and protection *IEEE Trans. Image Process.* **10** 1579–92

[7] Bas P, Chassery J and Macq B 2002 Geometrically invariant watermarking using feature points *IEEE Trans. Image Process.* **11** 1014–28

[8] Wu H, Shi Y, Wang H and Zhou L 2017 Separable reversible data hiding for encrypted palette images with color partitioning and flipping verification *IEEE Trans. Circuits Syst. Video Technol.* **27** 1620–31

[9] Fridrich J, Goljan M and Du R 2001 Invertible authentication *Proc. SPIE* 4314 197–208

[10] Celik M, Sharma G and Tekalp A 2006 Lossless watermarking for image authentication: a new framework and an implementation *IEEE Trans. Image Process.* **15** 1042–9

[11] Wu H, Wang H and Shi Y 2016 PPE-based reversible data hiding *Proc. ACM Workshop Inf. Hiding Multimed. Security* pp 187–8

[12] Wu H, Wang H and Shi Y 2016 Dynamic content selection-and-prediction framework applied to reversible data hiding *Proc. IEEE Workshop Inf. Forensics Security* pp 1–6

[13] Sachnev V, Kim H J, Nam J, Suresh and Shi Y 2009 Reversible watermarking algorithm using sorting and prediction *IEEE Trans. Circuits Syst. Video Technol.* **19** 989–99

[14] Li X, Yang B and Zeng T 2011 Efficient reversible watermarking based on adaptive prediction-error expansion and pixel selection *IEEE Trans. Image Process.* **20** 3524–33

[15] Wu H T and Huang J 2012 Reversible image watermarking on prediction errors by efficient histogram modification *Signal Process.* **92** 3000–9

[16] Li X, Li B, Yang B and Zeng T 2013 General framework to histogram-shifting-based reversible data hiding *IEEE Trans. Image Process.* **22** 2181–91

[17] Tian J 2003 Reversible data hiding using a difference expansion *IEEE Trans. Circuits Syst. Video Technol.* **13** 890–6

[18] Hu Y, Lee H K and Li J 2009 DE-based reversible data hiding with improved overflow location map *IEEE Trans. Circuits Syst. Video Technol.* **19** 250–60

[19] Alattar A M 2004 Reversible watermark using the difference expansion of a generalized integer transform *IEEE Trans. Image Process.* **13** 1147–56

[20] Qu X and Kim H J 2015 Pixel-based pixel value ordering predictor for high-fidelity reversible data hiding *Signal Process.* **111** 249–60

[21] Wang X, Ding J and Pei Q 2015 A novel reversible image data hiding scheme based on pixel value ordering and dynamic pixel block partition *Inf. Sci.* **310** 16–35

[22] Zhou K, Ding Y and Bi W 2021 High-capacity PVO-based reversible data hiding scheme using changeable step size *Multimed. Tools Applic.* **80** 1123–41

[23] Puesh W, Chaumont M and Strauss O 2008 A reversible data hiding method for encrypted images *Proc. Electronic Imaging, Security, Forensics, Steganography, and Watermarking of Multimedia Contents* X **6819** 534–42

[24] Zhang X 2011 Reversible data hiding in encrypted image *IEEE Signal Process Lett.* **18** 255–8

[25] Hong W, Chen T S and Wu H Y 2012 An improved reversible data hiding in encrypted images using side match *IEEE Signal Process Lett.* **19** 199–202

[26] Zhang X 2012 Separable reversible data hiding in encrypted image *IEEE Trans. Inf. Forensics Security* **7** 826–32

[27] Cao X, Du L, Wei X, Meng D and Guo X 2016 High capacity reversible data hiding in encrypted images by patch-level sparse representation *IEEE Trans. Cybern* **46** 1132–43

[28] Ma K, Zhang W, Zhao X, Yu N and Li F 2013 Reversible data hiding in encrypted images by reserving room before encryption *IEEE Trans. Inf. Forensics Security* **8** 553–62

[29] Qian Z, Zhang X and Wang S 2014 Reversible data hiding in encrypted JPEG bitstream *IEEE Trans. Multimed* **16** 1486–91

[30] Wu H, Wang W, Dong J and Wang H 2019 New graph-theoretic approach to social steganography *Proc. IS&T Electronic Imaging, Media Watermarking, Security and Forensics* pp 5391–7

[31] Xiang S and Luo X 2017 Reversible data hiding in homomorphic encrypted domain by mirroring ciphertext group *IEEE Trans. Circuits Syst. Video Technol.* **28** 3099–110

[32] Zhang X, Qian Z, Feng G and Ren Y 2014 Efficient reversible data hiding in encrypted images *J. Vis. Commun. Image* R **25** 322–8

[33] Qian Z and Zhang X 2016 Reversible data hiding in encrypted images with distributed source encoding *IEEE Trans. Circuits Syst. Video Technol.* **26** 636–46

[34] Huang F, Huang J and Shi Y 2016 New framework for reversible data hiding in encrypted domain *IEEE Trans. Inf. Forensics Security* **11** 2777–89

[35] Guan B and Xu D 2020 An efficient high-capacity reversible data hiding scheme for encrypted images *J. Vis. Commun. Image* R **66** 102744

[36] Wu H and Sun W 2014 High-capacity reversible data hiding in encrypted images by prediction error *Signal Process.* **104** 387–400

[37] Qian Z, Xu H, Luo X and Zhang X 2019 New framework of reversible data hiding in encrypted JPEG bitstreams *IEEE Trans. Circuits Syst. Video Technol.* **29** 351–62

[38] Qian Z, Zhou H, Zhang X and Zhang W 2018 Separable reversible data hiding in encrypted JPEG bitstreams *IEEE Trans. Depend. Secure Computing* **15** 1055–67

[39] Zhang W, Ma K and Yu N 2014 Reversibility improved data hiding in encrypted images *Signal Process.* **94** 118–27

[40] Luo X, Chen Z, Chen M, Zeng X and Xiong Z 2010 Reversible image watermarking using interpolation technique *IEEE Trans. Inf. Forensics Security* **5** 187–93

[41] Puteaux P and Puech W 2018 An efficient MSB prediction-based method for high-capacity reversible data hiding in encrypted images *IEEE Trans. Inf. Forensics Security* **13** 1670–81

[42] Yu M, Liu Y, Sun H, Yao H and Qiao T 2020 Adaptive and separable multiary reversible data hiding in encryption domain, *EURASIP J. Image Video Process* **16** 15

[43] Wu H, Yang Z, Cheung Y, Xu L and Tang S 2019 High-capacity reversible data hiding in encrypted images by bit plane partition and MSB prediction *IEEE Access* **7** 62361–71

[44] Puteaux P, Trinel D and Puech W 2016 High-capacity data hiding in encrypted images using MSB prediction *IEEE Int. Conf. Image Process. Theory, Tools & Appl.* pp 1–6

[45] Yin Z, Xiang Y and Zhang X 2020 Reversible data hiding in encrypted images based on multi-msb prediction and Huffman coding *IEEE Trans. Multimed.* **22** 874–84

[46] Chen Y, Shiu C and Horng G 2014 Encrypted signal-based reversible data hiding with public key cryptosystem *J. Vis. Commun. Image* R **25** 1164–70

[47] Paillier P 1999 Public-key cryptosystems based on composite degree residuosity classes *Int. Conf. Theory & Appl. Cryptographic Techniques* pp 223–38

[48] Shiu C, Chen Y and Hong W 2015 Encrypted image-based reversible data hiding with public key cryptography from difference expansion *Signal Process. Image Commun.* **39** 226–33

[49] Xiang S and Luo X 2017 Efficient reversible data hiding in encrypted image with public key cryptosystem *EURASIP J. Adv. Signal Process.* **59** 13

[50] Zhang X, Long J, Wang Z and Cheng H 2016 Lossless and reversible data hiding in encrypted images with public-key cryptography *IEEE Trans. Circuits Syst. Video Technol.* **26** 1622–31

[51] Xu D and Wang R 2014 Efficient reversible data hiding in encrypted H.264/AVC videos *J. Electron. Imaging* **23** 1–14

[52] Xu D, Wang R and Shi Y 2013 Reversible data hiding in encrypted H.264/AVC video streams *Int. Workshop Digital Watermarking* pp 141–52

[53] Qiu J, Lin Y and Wu J 2015 Reversible data hiding for encrypted audios by high order smoothness *Int. Workshop Digital Watermarking* pp 350–64

[54] Jiang R, Zhou H, Zhang W and Yu N 2018 Reversible data hiding in encrypted three-dimensional mesh models *IEEE Trans. Multimed* **20** 55–67

[55] Peng F, Lin Z, Zhang X and Long M 2019 Reversible data hiding in encrypted 2D vector graphics based on reversible mapping model for real numbers *IEEE Trans. Inf. Forensics Security* **14** 2400–11

IOP Publishing

Advanced Security Solutions for Multimedia

Irshad Ahmad Ansari and Varun Bajaj

Chapter 5

An analysis of deep steganography and steganalysis

Mahdie Abazar, Peyman Masjedi, Ali Ghorbani, Mohammad Taheri and Seyed Mostafa FakhrAhmad

Steganography is a technology that aims to hide secret information in a cover. On the other hand, a steganalysis tries to detect existence of a secret message in digital media. With the propagation of technology, the security of information has become a crucial concern. Images are widespread as media in communications. This is why image steganography and steganalysis have attracted increased attention. Steganography deals with hiding information via fewer possible changes and produces the stego file (the cover file that carries the secret information). Steganalysis is a binary classification tool to separate clean from stego files. In recent years, steganography and steganalysis have progressed by the advancement of deep learning and convolutional neural networks (CNNs). By growing CNNs, steganalysis has tended to use them to achieve better classification. Also, generative adversarial network (GAN) and encoder–decoder structure have attracted much attention in new steganography approaches. This chapter presents a general outline of deep learning image steganography and steganalysis structures that were recently proposed.

5.1 Introduction

With the advance in the development of information technology and digital communication on the internet, the need for security is increased to protect data and communication. The amount of digital data has grown in the web and digital communications; hence, much attention has been paid recently to data security (integrity and privacy). For secure transmission, information may be encrypted or hidden in a cover. But encrypted information attracts people's attention and motivates them to decode. As another way of intangible information transfer and information protection, steganography was introduced.

Steganography is the art of covering secret information in common carriers. The type of carriers can be any media such as a file, video, image, or voice recording. Image steganography attracts more interest than others. Hiding the information into the complex areas of an image reduces the risk of visibility and changes in statistical properties. The clean image and corresponding steganographic image are named cover and stego, respectively. Figure 5.1 shows all steps in image steganography. The stego image is produced by hiding secret information in the cover image. The receiver, at the other side, extracts this information from stego.

As the simplest method of image steganography, the least significant bit (LSB) technique was proposed in [1]. In this technique, the LSB bits of the cover image's pixels are replaced with the secret message bits. After that, matrix embedding is proposed and researched widely [2–9]. Matrix embedding could conceal a secret message in a cover with lower changes than LSB. Also, syndrome trellis code (STC) is a state-of-the-art embedding algorithm proposed by Fridrich et al [10] and is incorporated in many steganography algorithms. Steganography schemes are followed by more complicated algorithms to have more security. In the next step, finding the embedding location is considered as an essential factor to prevent the statistical analysis attack. Therefore, researchers focused on finding the best pixels of a cover for embedding. To achieve this goal, some popular algorithms are proposed, like WOW [11] and S-UNIWARD [12].

The process of distinguishing the stego image from a clean image (represented as a binary classification) is named image steganalysis. Previous traditional steganalysis approaches, spatial rich model (SRM) [13] and its selection-channel awareness version [14] was proposed by Fridrich et al. It provides various hand-crafted features to be used by a binary classifier. They have focused on the statistical properties of stego and cover hand-crafted features. Fridrich and Kodovský proposed ensemble classifiers (ECs) [15] to improve performance for the high-dimensional feature set.

The classical steganalysis techniques' performance was not considerable for the huge datasets with complex instances. Hence, deep neural networks (e.g., CNNs) were applied on complicated instances and large datasets successfully. Globally, CNN is the most widely used neural network for image datasets; also, it is used for image steganalysis, and it provides a hopeful framework with good performance.

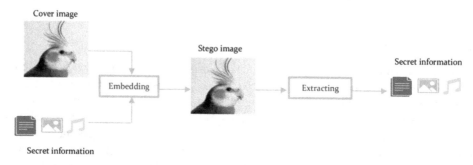

Figure 5.1. Steps in image steganography.

Although CNN decreased the number of feature dimensions by extracting image features and dimension reduction [16], using CNN models instead of classical ones increased computational complexity and memory usage caused by the huge amount of training data and model parameters. Steganalysis consists of three steps: preprocessing, feature extraction, and classification. In traditional steganalysis, each step performs individually, but in deep steganalysis, all steps are integrated in one architecture. In section 5.2, the overall process of deep-learning-based steganalysis is explained.

5.2 Deep learning

Deep learning is a machine learning model based on the artificial neural network. Hinton *et al* [17] proposed an unsupervised pretraining method to optimize the initial weights for the network. Several frameworks of deep learning, such as CNNs [18], deep belief networks (DBNs) [19], and recurrent neural networks (RNNs), have been used to improve performance in computer vision (CV), natural language processing (NLP) and speech recognition.

Lately, deep learning achieved significant results on classification, and image classification attracts much attention due to the redundancy of data in images and its applications in the worldwide web (internet). This progress has affected image steganalysis and steganography and their development. CNN is the most useful deep learning framework for image classification. A deep learning steganalysis technique provides automatic feature extraction and classification steps together in an architecture. The steganalysis technique based on CNNs has obtained amazing performance. To classify an image in CNN-based steganalysis it should be firstly tuned by a set of training images with associated labels. Each image is fed to CNN as an input vector, and in training, CNN tries to learn the different class distribution.

As mentioned before, the traditional steganalysis technique consists of three main steps: preprocessing, feature extraction, classification. Deep learning-based steganalysis, specifically a CNN-based method, is very similar to traditional steganalysis in steps. It brings together all three steps in one architecture; in the first step, it uses some preprocessing filters in order to achieve a noise residual view of the image. The convolutional layer is used in the second step for feature extraction. This layer may contain convolution layer, batch normalization layer, activation function, and pooling. Finally, a fully connected and soft-max layer is used for the classification task. All steps will be explained in detail. In figure 5.2, the traditional process and deep learning process are shown.

One or more high-pass filters are used in the preprocessing step. SRM high-pass filters are the most useful filter for preprocessing in CNN-based steganalysis. These filters transform the input image into a noise residual component. Using the high-pass filter before CNN layers causes faster convergence and improves the perform-ance. In CNN, the model may not use any fixed filter and the filter is learnt [20]. Finally, filters are used to remove redundant content in the image. A sample high-pass filter used in steganalysis is presented in figure 5.3. The most popular high-pass filter is a 5×5 KV-Kernel.

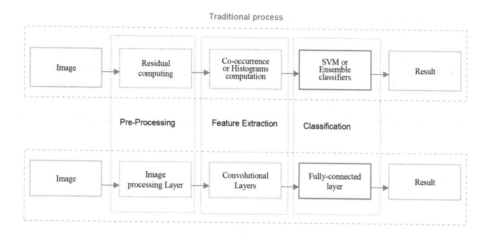

Traditional process

Deep learning process

Figure 5.2. Traditional and deep learning steganalaysis.

$$\frac{1}{4}\begin{bmatrix} 0 & 0 & 0 & 0 & 0 \\ 0 & -1 & 2 & -1 & 0 \\ 0 & 2 & -4 & 2 & 0 \\ 0 & -1 & 2 & -1 & 0 \\ 0 & 0 & 0 & 0 & 0 \end{bmatrix} \quad \frac{1}{12}\begin{bmatrix} -1 & 2 & -2 & 2 & -1 \\ 2 & -6 & 8 & -6 & 2 \\ -2 & 8 & -12 & 8 & -2 \\ 2 & -6 & 8 & -6 & 2 \\ -1 & 2 & -2 & 2 & -1 \end{bmatrix} \quad \frac{1}{2}\begin{bmatrix} 0 & 0 & 0 & 0 & 0 \\ 0 & 0 & 0 & 0 & 0 \\ 0 & 1 & -2 & 1 & 0 \\ 0 & 0 & 0 & 0 & 0 \\ 0 & 0 & 0 & 0 & 0 \end{bmatrix}$$

Figure 5.3. A sample high-pass filter used in steganalysis.

The feature extraction step usually contains convolution layer, normalization layer, activation function, and pooling layer. The convolution module is composed of neurons as the computing unit to generate the feature map from the noise residual. In some steganalysis, batch normalization is used to normalize the feature map and applies an activation function such as ReLU [21], TanH [22] to achieve nonlinearity. Pooling is used to reduce the feature map dimensionality. Average and max pooling are the types of pooling most often used. The average pooling layer averages the feature map's value, and the max pooling layer takes the max value of the feature map according to the filter size. Hence, dimensional reduction appears in both scenarios. The third step is the classification that uses some fully connected and SoftMax layers to classify the image. In figure 5.4 typical CNN structure for steganalysis is depicted.

The same as steganalysis, the progress of deep learning has opened a novel field in image steganography. Researchers tend to use the capacity of learning abilities of neural networks to build strong steganography models. Using GAN [23] in state-of-the-art steganography has been a huge success. GAN is used in different image-related research, including image steganography, which is introduced as steganography generative adversarial networks (SGANs). In total, GAN consists of a generator network and a discriminator network. The generator produces fake images to trick the

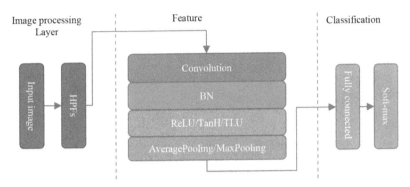

Figure 5.4. Typical CNN for steganalysis.

discriminator by simulating object distribution, and the discriminator aims to differentiate between fake and real images.

In the past few years, the auto-encoder deep learning structure also attracted many studies. The auto-encoder was first proposed for use as nonlinear representation learning that finds interesting feature representations. The auto-encoder contains two major components: first, an encoder that mapped input data from original space to latent space, and second, a decoder that reconstructs the input data from the new features in the latent space.

The variational auto-encoder (VAE) is a generative model that is inspired by auto-encoder. The idea is to learn a distribution in the latent space corresponding to the input data instead of a latent vector for each instance. It creates the latent variables by sampling from the latent distribution. Thus, there is a probabilistic relationship between the input and the latent variable. This is why, unlike the simple auto-encoder, VAE is a more powered model from the viewpoint of generalization.

In GAN, generator (G) and discriminator (D) would be trained simultaneously in a zero-sum game. G tries to generate a fake image from near the real image distribution, while D tries to detect whether the input image is real or fake. After generating the fake image, it is given to D to determine its label. If D recognized the image as fake, the result would be fed back to G to generate a better fake image according to the feedback. Also, the discriminator is trained with these real and fake images at the same time. This process will be continued until G can generate proper images.

There are some GAN structures used in steganography. In one schema, the discriminator is a steganalysis that determines the clean and stego image. In some other schemas, the discriminator is used to distinguish the fake image from the real image. In another schema, both previous steganalysis and discriminator networks are used. Also, there are some types of generators in SGAN. Some of them generate the cover image (from a noise) used for embedding a secret message. Here, a steganographic algorithm is used to produce the stego sample. In this structure, the generator tries to generate a suitable cover to be more undetectable after the embedding process. In the other structure, the generator takes the secret message and noise, then directly generates the stego image. In this structure, the embedding

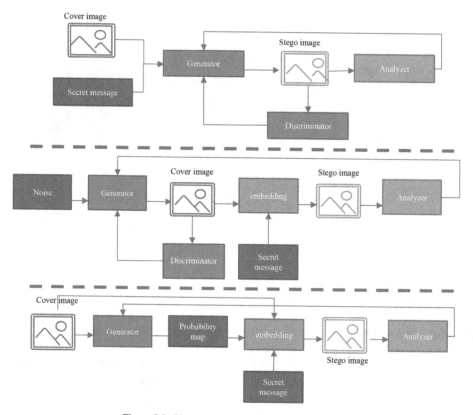

Figure 5.5. Three common architectures of SGAN.

algorithm is embedded in the generator. In these two structures, both discriminator and steganalysis may be incorporated to make the generator output more real and secure. Some other work uses the generator for producing the modification map of the input image for embedding. In this structure, the image is given to the generator to achieve the modification map. The modification map represents the change probability of pixels. An embedding algorithm is then needed to take the modification map and embed the secret message to produce the stego image. The most common structures of SGANs are shown in figure 5.5.

5.2.1 Steganalysis

The steganography method is divided into spatial and transform domains. Therefore, steganalysis also has these two domains. The secret information is embedded inside the image by changing pixel values, which affects an image's statistical characteristic. This subsection focuses on deep learning-based steganalysis research and its contributions. The steganalysis learns and extracts the features for a training data set. Then, the extracted features of images are given to a binary classifier to determine the image label (stego or cover).

The first CNN image steganalysis in the spatial domain was proposed by Tan and Li in 2014 [24], which used a stack of auto-encoders training. In the preprocessing step, a high-pass filter is applied to increase the noise of modified zones. This network has three convolution layers; so it is not deep enough. They used the sigmoid activation function. Its fully connected layer is too large, and the network is too slow. Their proposed model achieved better performance than the subtractive pixel adjacency matrix (SPAM) [25], but it was still lower than SRMs [13].

In 2015, Qian *et al* [26] proposed the first CNN network for steganalysis with supervised learning, called Qian-Net. Qian-Net achieved comparable results to the state of the art of classical steganalysis and SRM [13]. Also, they proved that transfer learning is helpful for detecting low embedding rate steganographic images [27]. They used a 5×5 high-pass filter (KV-filter) for the preprocessing step that helped network training to be convergent. The feature extraction step of Qian-Net consisted of five groups of convolutional layers. A particular activation function named Gaussian activation function was used in that research. Gaussian activation can identify the stego signal and cover signal from the prediction error values. They also used the average pooling layer. The classification part of Qian-Net consists of three fully connected layers and a SoftMax layer. Figure 5.6 shows the architecture of the Qian-Net.

In 2016, Pibre *et al* [28] tested 40 designs of Qian's work and achieved better performance than SRM in two new neural networks. The best one had two convolutional layers, and another one was a fully connected neural network including two layers. Salomon *et al* [29] introduced another deep learning framework for steganalysis that uses only two convolutional layers. They used large filters and then produced high-level features (256 features for 512×512 input images).

In 2016, Xu *et al* [30] proposed a CNN image steganalysis, called Xu-Net, which gained competitive performance in competition with SRM. XU-Net used five groups of convolutional layers, the same as Qian-Net. In the first convolutional group, an absolute ABS activation layer was applied after the convolution layer to avoid overfitting. The batch normalization appeared in each convolutional layer to prevent getting involved with local minima, which prevents the network from finding the optimal parameters for feature mapping. TanH activation function is

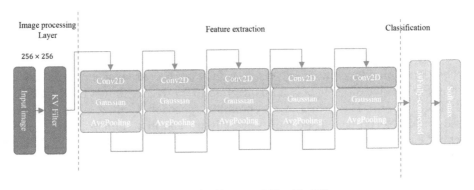

Figure 5.6. Architecture of Qian-Net [27].

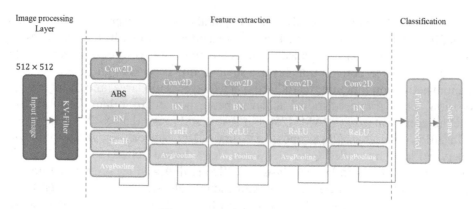

Figure 5.7. Architecture of Xu-Net.

used in the first two groups of convolutional layers, and ReLU is used in the last three groups of convolutional layers to improve statistical modeling and avoid overfitting. The average pooling layers are also used in all groups of Xu-Net. They used a 1 × 1 convolution layer in the last layer. Figure 5.7 shows the total architecture of Xu-Net.

In other research, Xu *et al* [31] extended their network [30] and added one more group of convolutional layers. They enhance the kernel size of max-pooling for the last two pooling layers from 5 × 5 to 7 × 7. The proposed network tries to introduce ensemble learning and could improve detection accuracy.

Wu *et al* [32] proposed a novel normalization method. Their method is called share normalization (SN), and is used to share statistics during the network's training and testing. The preprocessing step contains the high-pass filter for extracting the noise on the input image. In addition, for controlling the dynamic range of the input feature maps, a truncation layer (TLU) is used. The feature extraction step consists of several processing units (convolutional layer, SN layer, ReLU, and average pooling layer) that are used to extract effective features for image steganalysis. The classification step maps the features into 'stego' or 'cover' labels. Their proposed steganalysis model improved performance compared with previous methods.

Ye *et al* [33] introduced a novel steganalysis CNN approach, called Ye-Net, with selection channel information and data augmentation techniques. They used a set of high-pass filters for preprocessing a novel activation function named truncation linear unit (TLU) and eight convolution layers. They also used the ReLU activation function after all convolutional layers. The fully connected layer and SoftMax are used in the classification step. The architecture of Ye-Net is shown in figure 5.8.

In 2018, Li *et al* [34] proposed an ensemble approach by three parallel subnets based on Xu-Net in spatial domain steganalysis. The first subnet used 16 Gabor filters [35], the second subnet used 16 filters of linear-SRM [13], and the third subnet used 14 filters of nonlinear SRM [13]. They used Xu-Net as a base model and changed its activation function in second and fourth convolution groups; TanH, ReLU and sigmoid [21] are used parallelly in second and fourth convolution groups.

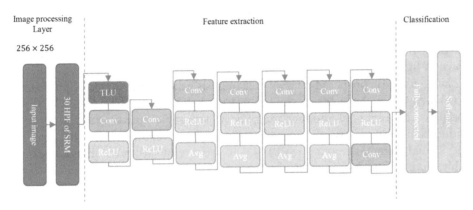

Figure 5.8. Architecture of Ye-Net.

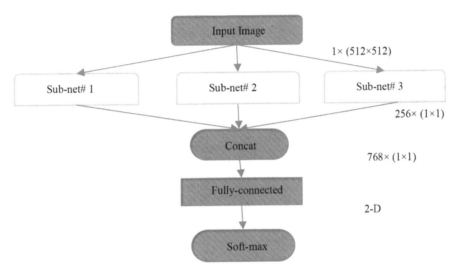

Figure 5.9. Architecture of ResT-Net.

The training process in this model contains two steps. In the first step, all three subnets are trained separately, and in the second step, the subnets' outputs are fed to a fully connected layer for training (the subnet parameters stay frozen). As the result shows, this model achieved a better result than Xu-Net on S-UNIWARD [12], HILL [36] and CMD-HILL [37] steganography algorithms. However, they used a deeper and wider network that is slower than its base model Xu-Net. The architecture of ResT-Net is shown in figure 5.9.

Yedroudj *et al* [38] proposed a CNN framework for steganalysis. They unified the best characteristic of Xu-Net [30] and Ye-Net [33] and used BOSSbase [39] and BOWS2 [40] datasets to train their model. A set of filters are applied in the preprocessing step, the same as Ye-Net. They used batch normalization, ABS layers, and five groups of convolutional layers, the same as Xu-Net. Augmentation is used to increase data by resizing, rotation, cropping, and interpolation operations. In the classification step, three fully connected layers and a SoftMax layer are used that increased model complexity and made it slow. They showed that their model improved the result of Xu-Net and Ye-Net. The architecture of Yedroudj-Net is shown in figure 5.10.

Zhang *et al* [41] proposed a CNN steganalysis called Zhu-Net that optimizes the kernel weights in the preprocessing step to enhance embedding noise. It applied separable convolutional modules (depthwise separable convolutions [42]) to get residue channel and spatial correlations to improve feature extraction, and then used spatial pyramid pooling (SPP) [43] to work with arbitrary image sizes. The architecture of Zhu-Net is shown in figure 5.11.

In [44], Jicang Lu introduced an improved content-adaptive steganalysis by pre-classification and feature selection to enhance performances. K-means is used for clustering images based on texture and complexities. They selected optimal features from each cluster and improved overall performances.

In 2019 Bromand *et al* [20] introduced deep residual steganalysis with 12 convolutional blocks called SR-Net. This network did not use any filters in the preprocessing step. SR-Net consists of four different types of layers. The convolution

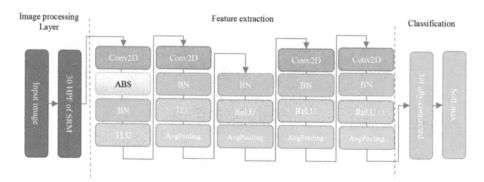

Figure 5.10. Architecture of Yedroudj-Net.

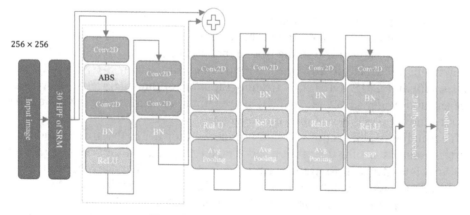

Figure 5.11. Architecture of Zhu-Net.

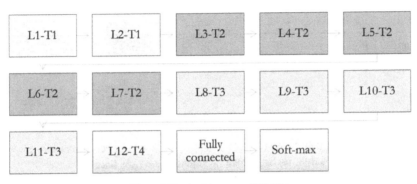

Figure 5.12. Architecture of SR-Net.

layer and batch normalization layer are in all layers. They also used the ReLU in type 1, average pooling layer in type 2, and global average pooling layer in types 3 and 4. They achieved good performances in JPEG and spatial domain, but the network is so deep and very slow as expected. The architecture of SR-Net is shown in figure 5.12.

Table 5.1 [45] shows the comparison of the illustrious steganalysis methods.

In 2020, Abazar *et al* [46] proposed an efficient ensemble framework based on Xu-Net. Their framework contains three main parts: clustering, training base-learners, and ensemble of classifiers. In the first part, they clustered images by using K-means algorithm. Next, they fed to each base-learner (Xu-Net), corresponding clustered data from part one. For the last part, they proposed a weighting algorithm to set a weight for each base-learner. The classification step used two reasoning methods to ensemble the results: single winner and weighted vote. They showed that their framework could reduce the training time and memory space and improved the detection accuracy slightly compared to the base model Xu-Net.

Another ensemble steganalysis was proposed by Abazar *et al* in 2020 [47]. The main idea of this method is to select the proper base models for classifying each image. They used a binary relevance (BR) method to achieve this aim. For binary classification, they used Fisher linear discriminant (FLD) in binary relevance to obtain if a base-learner is proper for the given image or not. After training all the base learners, the BR is trained in two different modes. They designed three ensemble strategies based on BR training modes, and for the final classification, 'majority vote' and 'weighted vote' was used.

Table 5.2 shows the error rates of some popular steganalysis methods for detecting three steganographic algorithms.

5.2.2 Steganography

By growing CNN-based steganalysis, traditional steganography methods have been faced with major security problems. Traditional steganography algorithms were based on some hand-crafted methods that could be learned by new steganalysis tools based on learning methods. To solve this issue, deep learning has opened a new field in steganography. This subsection explains the deep-learning-based steganography

Table 5.1. Comparison of different steganalysis algorithms.

Algorithms	Pros	Cons
Tan-Net [24]	• First CNN-based steganalysis • Comparable to SPAM	• Three Conv layers (not deep enough) • Used large fully connected layer and Avg pooling (slower)
Qian-Net [26]	• Better than SPAM • Designed Gaussian activation function • Used high-pass filter (KV-filter) layer	• The performance of SRM is better than Qian-Net • High-pass filter is necessary to converge in their network
Xu-Net [30]	• Xu-Net better than SRM • Used batch normalization, ABS layer and avg polling	• Not deep enough
Xu-Net [31]	• Used 7 × 7 pooling and six groups of convolution • Ensemble of Xu-Net	• Slow training
Ye-Net [33]	• First CNN-based steganalysis with selection channel information and data augmentation	• Slow training
Yedroudj-Net [38]	• Combined useful characteristics of Xu-Net(used BN & ABS layers) and Ye-Net(a set of HPF) • Better than Xu-Net and Ye-Net	• Used three fully connected layers to increase model complexity but made it slower conversion
ReSt-Net [34]	• Ensembled Xu-Net and achieve better performance than Xu-Net • Used Gabor, SRM linear and SRM nonlinear filters	• Wider and deeper structure • Slower training
SR-Net [20]	• Deep residual framework • Work well for both JPEG and spatial domain	• Very slow as compare to Xu-Net
Zhu-Net [41]	• Tow separable blocks of convolutional layers • Used SPP	• Larger Conv kernel size may lead the model to under-fitting

schemes, which belong to the two major deep learning fields: GAN and encoder–decoder. A simple encoder–decoder architecture is shown in figure 5.13.

Hayes *et al* [48] proposed a three-party game, Alice, Bob, and Eve. They used GANs for image steganography, and their method is one of the first applications of

Table 5.2. Error rate comparison of different steganalysis algorithms.

Steganalysis	Image size	WOW	S-UNIWARD	HILL
Spatial rich model (SRM)	512 × 512	20.08	20.47	24.53
Xu-Net	512 × 512		19.76	20.76
ReST-Net	512 × 512		14.56	18.34
Spatial rich model (SRM)	256 × 266	25.5	24.7	
Qian-Net	256 × 266	29.3	30.9	
Ye-Net	256 × 266	23.2	31.2	
Yedroudj-Net	256 × 266	14.1	22.8	
Zhu-Net	256 × 266	11.8	15.3	15.2
SR-Net	256 × 266	8.93	10.23	14.4

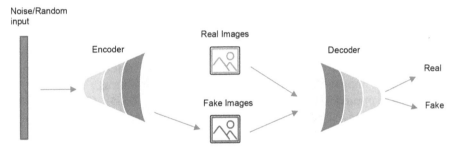

Figure 5.13. Simple encoder–decoder architecture.

GAN in steganography. In HayesGAN, three neural networks are used as Alic, Bob, and Eve. Alice is trained to hide secret information in the cover and generate stego images. Bob is trained to extracted hidden information of stego, and Eve is the steganalysis part as the discriminator.

Volkhonskiy *et al* [49] proposed another GAN-based steganography method called SGAN. SGAN contains three neural networks: A generator (G), a discriminator (D), and a steganalysis classifier (S). In this structure, G generates the cover image suitable for embedding secret information by using standard steganographic algorithms like STC. D tries to distinguish the generated cover image from the realistic images and, S determines if an image carries the secret information. The experimental result shows that SGAN can generate better images than real ones that cannot be detected by steganalyzers easily, but generated images in this way will attract human sight easily.

Shi *et al* [50] proposed SSGAN (secure steganography based on GAN) based on WGAN [51]. The stego image has a more realistic image than similar work (SGAN), and the speed of network training is enhanced. These models increased the steganalysis error rate. The competition between Qian-Net and Generator has improved to generate the stego image and makes the model more robust in steganography.

Hu *et al* [52] introduced a steganography method in that the noise, which consists of the secret information, is fed into the generator. In this work, the stego image can be generated without any modification of the cover image. The quality and security level of the stego image increased in this method compared to previous methods. However, this work, such as HayesGAN, is not guaranteed to extract the hidden message perfectly.

Tang *et al* [53] proposed an automatic steganographic distortion learning framework called ASDL-GAN. The GAN, which they constructed consists of a generator (G) that produces a feature map from an input image. They use Xu-Net steganalysis as the discriminator of the proposed GAN. Also, they proposed a sub-net called TES to simulate the embedding process. In fact, TES acts as an activation function and should be pre-trained. After training the ASDL-GAN, the generator learned to give the change probability of input image pixels. The greatest advantage of this method is that ASDL-GAN can automatically learn steganography distortion, but the performance is lower than traditional steganography methods like S-Uniward.

Zhu *et al* [54] submitted a steganography model based on HayesGAN called hiding data with deep network (HiDDeN). They used encoder and decoder in their structure and introduced different types of noises between encoding and decoding to help the model be most robust. They got a lower error rate in comparison with HayesGAN and improved hidden data extraction performances.

Yang *et al* proposed UT-6HPF-GAN [55] inspired by ASDL-GAN, the components of UT-6HPF-GAN are a generator network that generates a map (modification probability map) from the cover image, a discriminator network, and an embedding simulator. They proposed an activation function based on TanH to propagate gradient in this work instead of the TES (A subnet for embedding simulator in ASDL-GAN) to decrease the training epoch, so UT-6HPF-GAN is faster than ASDL-GAN. The generator that has been used in this model is based on U-Net [56]. The discriminator takes a cover and the generator output (generated stego-noise) and distinguishes between the cover and the stego image. Like ASDL-GAN, UT-6HPF-GAN used Xu-Net with 30 HPF (high-pass filter) of SRM as the discriminator. They also added SCA (selection channel awareness) to the discriminator to improve the model's resisting performance.

Rahim *et al* [57] proposed a decoder–encoder network for large-capacity steganography to hide a gray image as secret information into an oleograph as a cover of the same size. The stego image has good quality, but the color difference is noticeable between the cover and stego.

Baluja [58] proposed a CNN steganographic model based on encoder–decoder to hide an oleograph as secret information in another color cover image. The encoding process is trained to conceal the secret image in the cover image entirely. The first step is to extract features from the secret image. To achieve the stego image, the extracted features and the cover image are encoded through the hiding network. Simultaneously, the trained decoder is used for educating the secret image. Experimental results showed that the security of this method has some critical problems. Figure 5.14 shows the architecture of this method.

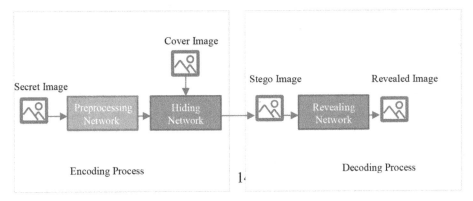

Figure 5.14. Architecture of Baluja encoder–decoder model.

Another way to use an encoding-decoding strategy for image steganography is called STEGANOGAN, proposed by Zhang *et al* [59]. The architecture of this method consists of three parts: encoding, decoding, and critic. The encoder part of the network used secret message and cover image to generate a stego image. The decoding network is used to reveal the secret message from the stego image. The critic network is also used for evaluation and to improve the quality of the generated stego image.

Shang [60] proposed a model for steganography that has two main modules. The first module is a GAN-based model containing encoder, decoder, and a steganalyzer (discriminator). The encoder–decoder part is tructured like the Baluja [58] method. The discriminator part job is to detect stego from cover media and make the encoder stronger. The second module is the security enhancement module. The encoder tries to fool the discriminator, so the encoder's power completely depends on the discriminator. After training the first module, an independent steganalyzer is used to make the encoder much more powerful to overcome this problem.

One of the main problems in the previously mentioned models is that the secrete image size must be much smaller than the cover image. Duan [61] proposed a model to face this problem. The method is based on a quantized variational auto-encoder for secret image compression. Also, the SegNet, which is based on encoder and decoder, is used for hiding and extracting the secret image (message).

5.3 Conclusion

In this chapter, the applications of deep learning in image steganography and steganalysis is elucidated. In steganalysis, CNNs could achieve considerable results against traditional state-of-the-art steganography methods. Also, steganography by using GANs and other deep-learning-based methods like encoder–decoder and VAE could become more secure against deep-learning-based steganalysis. GANs are used in steganography in different ways. They usually have steganalysis inside their architecture to build a robust model. They are learned to be used in a steganography scheme for generating cover images, stego images, and image modification maps in an adversarial domain. Steganalysis tends to use some machine learning methods like ensemble methods alongside the CNNs. Also, using deeper and wider networks to increase detection accuracy is another trend of new steganalysis.

References

[1] Lee Y-K and Chen L-H 1999 An adaptive image steganographic model based on minimum-error LSB replacement *Ninth National Conf. on Information Security: Citeseer* pp 8–15

[2] Crandall R 1998 Some notes on steganography *Posted on Steganography Mailing List* 1–6

[3] Fridrich J and Soukal D 2006 Matrix embedding for large payloads *IEEE Trans. on Information Forensics and Security* **1** 390–5

[4] Liu G, Liu W, Dai Y and Lian S 2011 An adaptive matrix embedding for image steganography *2011 Third Int. Conf. on Multimedia Information Networking and Security* (Piscataway, NJ: IEEE) pp 642–6

[5] Sarkar A, Madhow U and Manjunath B 2010 Matrix embedding with pseudorandom coefficient selection and error correction for robust and secure steganography *IEEE Trans. Inf. Forensics Secur.* **5** 225–39

[6] Mao Q 2014 A fast algorithm for matrix embedding steganography *Digit. Signal Process.* **25** 248–54

[7] Pevny T, Bas P and Fridrich J 2010 Steganalysis by subtractive pixel adjacency matrix *IEEE Trans. Inf. Forensics Secur.* **5** 215–24

[8] Masjedi P and Taheri M 2020 A local optimum matrix construction for matrix embedding steganography *2020 6th Int. Conf. on Web Research (ICWR)* (Piscataway, NJ: IEEE) pp 15–20

[9] Tian H, Qin J, Huang Y, Chen Y, Wang T, Liu J and Cai Y 2015 Optimal matrix embedding for voice-over-IP steganography *Signal Process.* **117** 33–43

[10] Filler T, Judas J and Fridrich J 2011 Minimizing additive distortion in steganography using syndrome-trellis codes *IEEE Trans. Inf. Forensics Secur.* **6** 920–35

[11] Holub V and Fridrich J 2012 Designing steganographic distortion using directional filters *2012 IEEE Int. Workshop on Information Fforensics and Security (WIFS)* (Piscataway, NJ: IEEE) pp 234–9

[12] Holub V, Fridrich J and Denemark T 2014 Universal distortion function for steganography in an arbitrary domain *EURASIP J. Inform. Secur.* **2014** 1

[13] Fridrich J and Kodovsky J 2012 Rich models for steganalysis of digital images *IEEE Trans Inf. Forensics Secur.* **7** 868–82

[14] Denemark T, Sedighi V, Holub V, Cogranne R and Fridrich J 2014 Selection-channel-aware rich model for steganalysis of digital images *2014 IEEE International Workshop on Information Forensics and Security (WIFS)* (Piscataway, NJ: IEEE) pp 48–53

[15] Kodovsky J, Fridrich J and Holub V 2011 Ensemble classifiers for steganalysis of digital media *IEEE Trans. Inf. Forensics Secur.* **7** 432–44

[16] Reinel T-S, Raul R-P and Gustavo I 2019 Deep learning applied to steganalysis of digital images: a systematic review *IEEE Access* **7** 68970–90

[17] Hinton G E and Salakhutdinov R R 2006 Reducing the dimensionality of data with neural networks *Science* **313** 504–7

[18] Gu J, Wang Z, Kuen J, Ma L, Shahroudy A, Shuai B, Liu T, Wang X, Wang G and Cai J 2018 Recent advances in convolutional neural networks *Pattern Recognit.* **77** 354–77

[19] Hinton G E 2009 Deep belief networks *Scholarpedia* **4** 5947

[20] Boroumand M, Chen M and Fridrich J 2018 Deep residual network for steganalysis of digital images *IEEE Trans. Inf. Forensics Secur.* **14** 1181–93

[21] Nair V and Hinton G E 2010 Rectified linear units improve restricted Boltzmann machines *Proc. 27th Int. Conf. on Machine Learning (ICML)*

[22] Karlik B and Olgac A V 2011 Performance analysis of various activation functions in generalized MLP architectures of neural networks *Int. J. Artif. Intell. Expert Syst.* **1** 111–22

[23] Goodfellow I, Pouget-Abadie J, Mirza M, Xu B, Warde-Farley D, Ozair S, Courville A and Bengio Y 2014 Generative adversarial nets *Adv. Neural Inf. Process. Syst.* **27** 2672–80

[24] Tan S and Li B 2014 Stacked convolutional auto-encoders for steganalysis of digital images *Signal and Information Processing Association Annual Summit and Conf. (APSIPA), 2014 Asia-Pacific* (Piscataway, NJ: IEEE) pp 1–4

[25] Holub V and Fridrich J 2013 Random projections of residuals for digital image steganalysis *IEEE Trans. Inf. Forensics Secur.* **8** 1996–2006

[26] Qian Y, Dong J, Wang W and Tan T 2016 Learning and transferring representations for image steganalysis using convolutional neural network *2016 IEEE International Conference on Image Processing (ICIP)* (Piscataway, NJ: IEEE) pp 2752–6

[27] Qian Y, Dong J, Wang W and Tan T 2015 Deep learning for steganalysis via convolutional neural networks *Media Watermarking, Security, and Forensics 2015: International Society for Optics and Photonics* 94090J

[28] Pibre L, Pasquet J, Ienco D and Chaumont M 2016 Deep learning is a good steganalysis tool when embedding key is reused for different images, even if there is a cover source mismatch *Electron. Imag.* **2016** 1–11

[29] Salomon M, Couturier R, Guyeux C, Couchot J-F and Bahi J M 2017 Steganalysis via a convolutional neural network using large convolution filters for embedding process with same stego key: a deep learning approach for telemedicine *European Research in Telemedicine/La Recherche Européenne en Télémédecine* **6** 79–92

[30] Xu G, Wu H-Z and Shi Y-Q 2016 Structural design of convolutional neural networks for steganalysis *IEEE Signal Process. Lett.* **23** 708–12

[31] Xu G, Wu H-Z and Shi Y Q 2016 Ensemble of CNNs for steganalysis: an empirical study *Proc. of the 4th ACM Workshop on Information Hiding and Multimedia Security* pp 103–7

[32] Wu S, Zhong S-h and Liu Y 2019 A novel convolutional neural network for image steganalysis with shared normalization *IEEE Trans. Multimedia* **22** 256–70

[33] Ye J, Ni J and Yi Y 2017 Deep learning hierarchical representations for image steganalysis *IEEE Trans. Inf. Forensics Secur.* **12** 2545–57

[34] Li B, Wei W, Ferreira A and Tan S 2018 ReST-Net: diverse activation modules and parallel subnets-based CNN for spatial image steganalysis *IEEE Signal Process. Lett.* **25** 650–4

[35] Song X, Liu F, Yang C, Luo X and Zhang Y 2015 Steganalysis of adaptive JPEG steganography using 2D Gabor filters *Proc. of the 3rd ACM Workshop on Information Hiding and Multimedia Security* pp 15–23

[36] Li B, Wang M, Huang J and Li X 2014 A new cost function for spatial image steganography *2014 IEEE Int. Conf. on Image Processing (ICIP)* (Piscataway, NJ: IEEE) pp 4206–10

[37] Li B, Wang M, Li X, Tan S and Huang J 2015 A strategy of clustering modification directions in spatial image steganography *IEEE Trans. Inf. Forensics Secur.* **10** 1905–17

[38] Yedroudj M, Comby F and Chaumont M 2018 Yedroudj-net: an efficient CNN for spatial steganalysis *2018 IEEE Int. Conf. on Acoustics, Speech and Signal Processing (ICASSP)* (Piscataway, NJ: IEEE) pp 2092–6

[39] Bas P, Filler T and Pevný T 2011 Break our steganographic system: the ins and outs of organizing BOSS *International Workshop on Information Hiding* (Berlin: Springer) pp 59–70

[40] Bas P and Furon T 2008 BOWS-2 contest (break our watermarking system) *Organised within the Activity of the Watermarking Virtual Laboratory (Wavila) of the European Network of Excellence ECRYPT*

[41] Zhang R, Zhu F, Liu J and Liu G 2019 Depth-wise separable convolutions and multi-level pooling for an efficient spatial CNN-based steganalysis *IEEE Trans. Inf. Forensics Secur.* **15** 1138–50

[42] Guo L, Ni J, Su W, Tang C and Shi Y-Q 2015 Using statistical image model for JPEG steganography: uniform embedding revisited *IEEE Trans. Inf. Forensics Secur.* **10** 2669–80

[43] He K, Zhang X, Ren S and Sun J 2015 Spatial pyramid pooling in deep convolutional networks for visual recognition *IEEE Trans. Pattern Anal. Mach. Intell.* **37** 1904–16

[44] Lu J, Zhou G, Yang C, Li Z and Lan M 2019 Steganalysis of content-adaptive steganography based on massive datasets pre-classification and feature selection *IEEE Access* **7** 21702–11

[45] Hussain I, Zeng J and Tan S 2020 A survey on deep convolutional neural networks for image steganography and steganalysis *KSII Trans. Internet Inform. Syst.* **14** 1228–48

[46] Abazar T, Masjedi P and Taheri M 2020 An efficient ensemble of convolutional deep steganalysis based on clustering *2020 6th Int. Conf. on Web Research (ICWR)* (Piscataway, NJ: IEEE) pp 260–4

[47] Abazar T, Masjedi P and Taheri M 2020 A binary relevance adaptive model-selection for ensemble steganalysis *2020 17th Int. ISC Conf. on Information Security and Cryptology (ISCISC)* (Piscataway, NJ: IEEE) pp 77–81

[48] Hayes J and Danezis G 2017 Generating steganographic images via adversarial training *Adv. Neural Inf. Process. Syst.* pp 1954–63

[49] Volkhonskiy D, Nazarov I and Burnaev E 2020 Steganographic generative adversarial networks *Twelfth Int. Conf. on Machine Vision (ICMV 2019): Int. Society for Optics and Photonics* p 114333M

[50] Shi H, Dong J, Wang W, Qian Y and Zhang X 2017 SSGAN: secure steganography based on generative adversarial networks *Pacific Rim Conf. on Multimedia* (Berlin: Springer) pp 534–44

[51] Arjovsky M, Chintala S and Bottou L 2017 Wasserstein gan *arXiv preprint arXiv:*1701.07875

[52] Hu D, Wang L, Jiang W, Zheng S and Li B 2018 A novel image steganography method via deep convolutional generative adversarial networks *IEEE Access* **6** 38303–14

[53] Tang W, Tan S, Li B and Huang J 2017 Automatic steganographic distortion learning using a generative adversarial network *IEEE Signal Process Lett.* **24** 1547–51

[54] Zhu J, Kaplan R, Johnson J and Fei-Fei L 2018 Hidden: hiding data with deep networks *Proc. of the European Conference on Computer Vision (ECCV)* pp 657–72

[55] Yang J, Ruan D, Huang J, Kang X and Shi Y-Q 2019 An embedding cost learning framework using GAN *IEEE Trans. Inf. Forensics Secur.* **15** 839–51

[56] Ronneberger O, Fischer P and Brox T 2015 U-net: convolutional networks for biomedical image segmentation *Int. Conf. on Medical Image Computing and Computer-Assisted Intervention* (Berlin: Springer) pp 234–41

[57] Rahim R and Nadeem M S 2017 End-to-end trained CNN encode-decoder networks for image steganography *arXiv preprint arXiv:*1711.07201

[58] Baluja S 2017 Hiding images in plain sight: deep steganography *Adv. Neural Inf. Process. Syst.* pp 2069–79

[59] Zhang K A, Cuesta-Infante A, Xu L and Veeramachaneni K 2019 SteganoGAN: high capacity image steganography with GANs *arXiv preprint* arXiv:1901.03892

[60] Shang Y, Jiang S, Ye D and Huang J 2020 Enhancing the security of deep learning steganography via adversarial examples *Mathematics* **8** 1446

[61] Duan X, Guo D and Qin C 2020 Image information hiding method based on image compression and deep neural network *Comput. Model. Eng. Sci.* **124** 721–45

Chapter 6

Recent trends in reversible data hiding techniques

V M Manikandan

Data hiding or information hiding is a well-explored way of securing some secret data by concealing it using a digital cover medium. A variety of digital cover media are used in practice, such as text files, images, audio, videos, etc. Data hiding techniques are useful for secret message communication, authentication of data, and protection of ownership. The secret data transmission popularly in use is known as steganography and the data hiding methods for data authentication or ownership protection are called digital watermarking. Reversible data hiding (RDH) is a newly emerged area in which the cover medium can be restored during the extraction of hidden messages. RDH in images is a widely explored topic. In this chapter, we give an overview of the RDH schemes for images, their applications, and recent advancements in this domain. A few research challenges in the field of reversible data hiding also will be discussed in this chapter on which researchers can work in the future.

6.1 Introduction

Data hiding is a way to protect some secret data by concealing it using a digital cover medium. Various kinds of digital media are used as a cover medium in which the digital image is the most commonly used one. Data hiding is used for different applications of which the most important are described briefly below:

1. **Secret message communication**: Use of algorithms to transmit the messages securely by embedding in an image is a well-known approach and it is termed steganography [1]. In this scheme, the private message will be inserted in a cover image. The image which contains the secret message is called a stego image. The disparity between the cover image and the stego image will not be observed by the naked eye. If an unauthorized third party gets the stego image they would not able to get any information about the hidden message.

doi:10.1088/978-0-7503-3735-9ch6

The steganography approaches can be used with some good objectives but also for some illegal communications. It might be noted that the steganography scheme has been used by terrorists for their communication and intelligence security agencies may completely fail to get any clue about terrorist attacks.

2. **Data authentication or copyright protection**: Copyright protection of digital images and image authentication can be achieved through the data hiding process. The schemes used to meet these two objectives are termed digital watermarking [2, 3]. The information that we use to embed in the image is termed the watermark. The data integrity will be verified by extracting the watermark. The closeness measure between the watermark taken out from the image and the original watermark will decide the integrity of the mage. The owners' unique identification details are generally used as the watermark. The copyright of the digital content can be claimed by extracting the hidden watermark.

The outline of a steganography scheme is given in figure 6.1. The data hiding key in a steganography scheme ensures that the authorized person (who has the data hiding key) only will be able to extract the hidden message.

Outline of the digital image watermarking scheme is given in figure 6.2. In figure 6.2, the watermark can be a sequence of bits or some image itself.

The traditional data hiding approach permanently modifies the pixels of the image that we are using for the concealing purpose. The use of the modified images leads to several concerns in crucial applications like the medical image transmission environment. The use of the conventional watermarking scheme to authenticate medical images is not appreciated since the pixel change in the image may end up with the wrong diagnosis. The tools to analyze the medical images are very sensitive and some small alterations will lead to wrong conclusions.

The current research in this field is focused on a topic called RDH. The original image can be restored at the time of taking out the hidden message in an RDH scheme. The outline of the RDH scheme is given in figure 6.3.

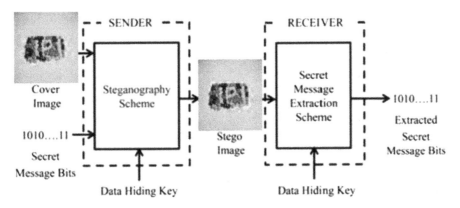

Figure 6.1. Overview of steganography scheme.

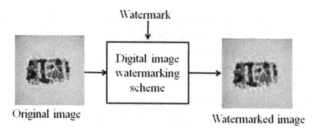

Figure 6.2. Overview of digital image watermarking (invisible watermarking).

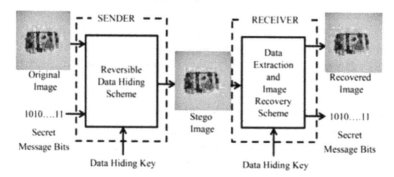

Figure 6.3. Overview of RDH scheme.

RDH schemes will be helpful in the communication of patient details or diagnosis reports by hiding them in the image. Otherwise, the medical images and report should be transmitted separately. The receiver of medical images can take out the report using a predefined scheme and the actual image can be restored. While using RDH schemes there is no need to worry about the wrong diagnosis which may arise due to the modification in the image [4, 5].

The RDH schemes can be used to transmit biometric data in a cloud-based authentication system. In addition to all these applications, the cloud service provider (CSP) can utilize the RDH to insert metadata in the data stored by the users. The CSP does not have the right to make permanent alterations in the data which is owned by the user [6].

6.2 Types of RDH schemes

The existing RDH schemes can be classified into three categories:
1. RDH in natural images;
2. RDH in encrypted images;
3. RDH through encryption.

RDH in natural images: In this type of RDH process, the data hider (those who want to hide the data) can see the actual contents of the image. The basic assumption is that the data hider is a trusted person. The pixels of the cover image will be updated in a predefined way during the data hiding process. The overview of the RDH in a natural image is given in figure 6.4.

RDH in encrypted images: This framework assumes that the content owner does not want to share the actual data with the data hider due to various security reasons. So the content owner will encrypt the image before handover to the data hider. Since the data hider is getting an encrypted image the secrecy of the content is protected. Further, the data hider will keep the additional data in the image which is in encrypted form with the assistance of an RDH method. The outline of the RDH in the encrypted image is given in figure 6.5.

RDH through encryption: In this type of RDH scheme, the embedding process and the encryption of image are merged into a single algorithm. The receiver can take

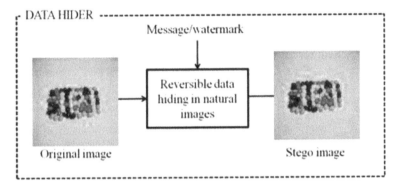

Figure 6.4. Overview of RDH in natural image.

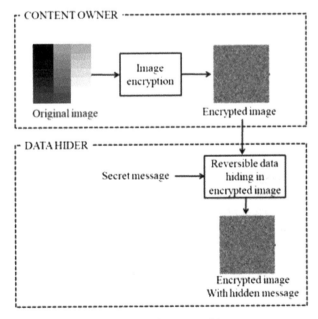

Figure 6.5. RDH in encrypted image.

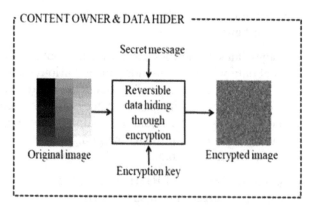

Figure 6.6. RDH through encryption.

out the embedded message during image decryption. The outline of RDH through the encryption scheme is given in figure 6.6.

In the remaining subsections all the three types of RDH schemes are briefly reviewed.

6.2.1 RDH in natural images

As mentioned earlier, RDH in natural images considers the original image in its original form during the data hiding process. The actual pixels of the image will be updated to get the stego image. The stego image and the actual image that we have taken during the hiding process will be almost the same when we are seeing them with the naked eye. There are several RDH schemes introduced for RDH in natural images and they can be mainly classified into two categories (note that many other schemes that are not in this category are also available):

1. Histogram shifting based RDH;
2. Difference expansion based RDH.

Histogram shifting based RDH scheme

The histogram shifting based RDH scheme was introduced in 2006 and widely studied and improved in later years [7]. The basic histogram-based shifting RDH scheme process is given below:

Input	: The message D that the sender wants and the cover image I
Output	: The image I' treated as stego image without much deviation from I
1.	: Compute the number of times each pixel is present and generate a histogram H corresponding to image I
2.	: Find the pixel value P that is present a greater number of times in I
3.	: Increment all the pixels in I which is greater than P to get a temporary image I'. Note that after this process in T the pixel value $(P + 1)$ will not be present due to this shifting process
4.	: The pixels in I' will be considered one by one and a single bit B from the D at a time, and B can be embedded in the pixel if its value is P

(*Continued*)

Case 1: If we need to embed 0 on a pixel with pixel value P we do not want to do any changes.

Case 2: If we need to embed 1 on a pixel value P, increment the value by one.

5. : Return the stego image I'

The process for taking out the hidden message and to restore the original image in an RDH scheme using histogram shifting approach is given below:

Input : The image I' (stego), the pixel intensity value P used during data hiding

Output : The image I which is recovered from stego image and the retrieved message D

1. : The pixels X in image I' will be accessed one by one and one and the following steps will be carried out to extract and recover the image:

$X = P$: Extract bit value 0 from X

$X = (P + 1)$: Extract the bit value 1 from X and the recovered pixel value $(X - 1)$

$X < P$: The pixel X we can keep as it is in the final recovered image I

$X > (P + 1)$: Recover the pixel value by decrementing X by one.

2. : Return the recovered image I and the extracted message D

A few key points/challenges in the histogram shifting based RDH scheme are listed below:

- The bits in the lengthiest message that we can embed in the image will be dependent on the peak in the histogram obtained from the image that we are using for concealing purpose (occurrences of the pixel value X).
- The overflow is another issue in the RDH schemes that uses histogram shifting, which will happen when the original image itself consists of the pixel values 255 and during the histogram shifting process it supposes to be incremented by one. But it may be noted that the pixel value 256 cannot be represented using 8 bits. So in the final image 255 will stay as it is and the pixels with the grayscale value 254 will be incremented by one and will become 255. So on the receiver side, we need to distinguish pixels that are originally 255 and the pixels with intensity value 254. Additional location map details need to be used to handle the overflow pixels but it will lead to reducing the effective embedding rate.

Recently, a scheme to handle overflow was introduced in [8] in which the overhead of overflow handling bits is reduced efficiently. To improve the embedding rate without compromising the perceptual quality of the stego image, an efficient histogram shifting which processes block-wise is discussed in [9]. In this block-wise histogram shifting approach, the image is divided into blocks and the histogram computed from each of those blocks is separately considered during the data hiding process. The peak in a histogram should be sufficiently high to select a block for data hiding. The scheme also ensures that the data hider does not want to share the peak intensity value with the receiver. The peak information will be extracted from the block itself. The overflow issues are also handled in this scheme efficiently with the similar approach discussed in [8].

Since the peak of the histogram decides the message length that is possible to insert using an RDH scheme based on shifting of the histogram, an improved scheme is discussed in [10] in which the prediction error histogram is considered during data hiding. The quality of the pixel prediction will determine the shape of the prediction error histogram and the experimental study shows that the prediction error histogram will have a bell shape in which the prediction errors with 0 will be the maximum. The prediction error E is defined below:

$$E = X - X' \tag{6.1}$$

Where X is the actual pixel value present in an image and X' is the predicted value. There is a high probability that X is very close to X' when we are using a good prediction technique. In most cases, the actual value and the predicted value will be the same results in a prediction error of 0. This will lead to a bell-shaped prediction error histogram in which the peak will be at 0. The same process which is used in the conventional histogram shifting technique will be used here also for data hiding. But the prediction errors ensure superior embedding rate while comparing the same from the conventional histogram shifting based RDH. A set of pixels are considered as reference pixels and those pixels will be used for the prediction. Various prediction techniques have been tried by the researchers to get a greater number of 0's as the prediction errors. A two-dimensional prediction error histogram was also explored for RDH purposes [11].

Several approaches are reported in the literature that use the concept of histogram [12–15].

Difference expansion based RDH

In this approach, the difference of two pixels will be expanded to hide single bit information [16]. Let x and y be two pixels where $0 \leqslant x, y \leqslant 255$. The first step in the difference expansion based RDH is to find l and the h in the following way:

$$l = \left\lfloor \frac{(x + y)}{2} \right\rfloor \tag{6.2}$$

$$h = x - y \tag{6.3}$$

During difference expansion based RDH, to insert a single bit b, following sequence of operations we will follow:

$$h' = 2 \times h + b \tag{6.4}$$

The new values for the pixels in the stego image x' and y' will be computed in the following way and will be placed in the stego image instead of x and y.

$$x' = l + \left\lfloor \frac{(h' + 1)}{2} \right\rfloor \tag{6.5}$$

$$y' = l - \left\lfloor \frac{h'}{2} \right\rfloor \tag{6.6}$$

For data extraction and image recovery, the same pair of pixels from the stego image will be accessed and we have to follow the following steps to extract the hidden bit b and the recovered pixel values x and y.

$$l' = \left\lfloor \frac{(x' + y')}{2} \right\rfloor \tag{6.7}$$

$$h' = x' - y' \tag{6.8}$$

From h', we can find the hidden bit b by extracting the last bit of h', then find the h value by the following way:

$$h = \left\lfloor \frac{h'}{2} \right\rfloor \tag{6.9}$$

From l' and the h, we can recover the original pixel values x and y.

The difference expansion scheme is further extended to design RDH schemes with better embedding rate. A scheme for data hiding based on difference expansion concept with a modulus function is introduced in [17]. This scheme uses both positives and negative values which we may obtain while finding the difference to conceal bits from the message.

Other RDH schemes in natural images

An efficient sudoku based RDH scheme is introduced in [18] to improve the embedding rate. A sudoku matrix is used as a reference matrix and it decides the modification required to be done in the original pixel values to embed a specific bit sequence. A bit-plane compression based RDH is discussed in [19]. In this scheme, a bit-plane of the grayscale image is compressed using the run-length encoding scheme. The run-length sequence is encoded with the variable-length encoding scheme called Elias gamma encoding. The space created using bit-plane compression is used for placing the message. The lower bit-planes may not give enough compression while applying run-length and this motivates the use of higher bit-planes. But the modification of higher bit-planes may drastically reduce the visual quality. To overcome this issue, the Arnold transform technique is efficiently used to find a modified version of the bit-plane which is very close to the original bit-plane. Another image scaling based RDH scheme is discussed in [20]. In this scheme, the image of size $N \times N$ pixels and the stego image will have a size of $2N \times 2N$ pixels. This is scheme is further studied and improved in [21] to better obtain stego images with better visual quality. A few other well-known RDH schemes are discussed in [22–26].

6.2.2 RDH in encrypted images

The RDH scheme capable of embedding messages in encrypted images is introduced in [27]. The algorithm discussed in [27] allows the data hider to insert one-bit data in a block from the image. During data hiding, the pixels of a block will be categorized into two sets called S^0 and S^1. Based on the pixel value that we need to hide on a block, the last three least significant bits (LSBs) of values in S^0 or S^1 will be flipped. The three LSBs of S^0 pixels will be inverted to embed bit 0 and the three LSBs of S^1 should be inverted to hide a secret bit 1. During the message extraction and image restoration process, from each block of the image, two different versions V^0 and V^1 will be generated by flipping the three LSBs S^0 and S^1 pixels. For the correctly decrypted form of the image blocks the smoothness measure will be less. The measure M for an image block having size $S \times S$ pixels is:

$$M = \sum_{x=2}^{S-1} \sum_{y=2}^{S-1} \left| P_{x,y} - \frac{P_{x-1,y} + P_{x,y+1} + P_{x+1,y} + P_{x,y-1}}{4} \right| \qquad (6.10)$$

where $P_{x,y}$ is a pixel at location (x, y) of the given block. The approach discussed in [27] faced a large number of errors during image recovery while using a small block size. The amount of information that the data hider can hide will be much less due to the selection of a large block size for reducing the errors during image recovery.

The algorithm discussed in [27] is improved by using a side-match technique in [28]. Recently, the scheme has been improved in [29]. In this scheme, the pixels in each block are split into two groups: black pixels and white pixels. The classification is done by considering a checkerboard pattern. In the scheme, one category of pixels (all the bits in the pixels) is flipped to embed a single bit. An efficient measure is also introduced in this scheme to ensure better image recovery.

An RDH scheme that uses the prediction of the most significant bits (MSBs) is discussed in [30]. In this work, the authors presented two approaches, one with a high capacity RDH scheme that uses prediction error correction and the second one with the high capacity RDH approach which embeds the prediction errors. The authors experimentally analyzed and reported a good embedding rate with better image recovery capability. An RDH scheme that considers integer wavelet transform (IWT), along with the shifting of the histogram is introduced in [31]. This approach utilized the benefits of the Laplacian-like arrangement of high-frequency coefficients in IWT. A block-level predictor (BLP) based RDH scheme is introduced in [32]. An RDH scheme for encrypted images obtained from homomorphic encryption is proposed in [33]. In this scheme, the preprocessed image will be encrypted, after that two different embedding methods are applied to the encrypted image.

6.2.3 RDH through encryption (RDHTE)

The RDHTE schemes will insert the message in an image at the time of the encryption process. Both image encryption and hiding tasks are combined into one. The RDHTE scheme was first reported in [34] 2018 in which the data hiding process and the image encryption process are combined into a single task. In this scheme, the content owner who wants to encrypt the image and also wants to hide the secret message will pick three different encryption keys. The scheme uses a symmetric encryption scheme so the content owner will share the same keys as the receiver also.

The original image is partitioned into non-overlapping blocks, and one-bit message is possible to insert in a single block through the process. The bit value that the data hider wants to hide in a selected block will determine the key used for encrypting that block. In each block, there are three possibilities: embed bit value 0, embed bit value 1, and do not want to embed anything. The image restoration and extraction of the hidden message is carried by attempting the decryption of every block using three different keys and the blocks that are correctly decrypted will be more smooth (pixels will be highly correlated). An entropy-based measure is discussed in this paper for analyzing the randomness of the image blocks.

The scheme discussed [34] is further studied and improved in [35] by using a machine learning technique. A support vector machine model is trained to categorize a block into either a normal block or an encrypted block. The scheme reduced the bit error rate during the recovery. The embedding rate observed from the schemes reported in [34] and [35] remains unchanged. To improve the embedding rate, a new scheme is introduced in [36] in which in every block the data hider can insert 3 bits from the message. In this scheme, by using three different encryption keys eight different versions of stream ciphers are generated using predefined bit-wise operations. The bit combinations that the data hider wants to hide in a block will decide the stream cipher for encryption. Another RDHTE scheme is discussed in [37] in which the error-free image recovery is ensured with the help of a block prechecking. If some of the blocks lead to the wrong recovery at the receiver side, it will be handled as a special case in this scheme.

6.3 Analysis of RDH schemes

The analysis of RDH schemes can be carried out using the following measures:
1. **Embedding rate (ER):** Embedding rate is defined as follows:

$$ER = \frac{L}{N} \qquad (6.11)$$

Where L is maximum number of bits that we can insert in an image that contains N pixels. If the image is a grayscale image having $R \times C$ pixels then $N = R \times C$. An RDH scheme capable of providing high embedding rate is preferred since we want to hide more information in an image in practical applications.
2. **Bit error rate (BER):** The BER is a parameter which helps to know the status of message extraction. The BER ratio is between the W_L and M_L where W_L indicates the number of wrongly extracted bits and M_L is the length of the message (in bits). From an RDH scheme we expected to get a BER of 0, but due to various reasons it need not be 0 always. So to make sure that an RDH scheme is efficient we have to evaluate the BER from the scheme, and a scheme with a low bit error rate is preferred over a scheme with a high bit error rate.
3. **Peak signal to noise ratio (PSNR):** The PSNR is one of the parameters that can be used to compare an image with another reference image [38]. The

PSNR between the image P and Q having size R × C pixels is defined as follows:

$$MSE = \frac{1}{(R \times C)} \sum_{i=1}^{R} \sum_{j=1}^{C} [P_{i,j} - Q_{i,j}]^2 \tag{6.12}$$

$$PSNR = 10.\log_{10}\left(\frac{M^2}{MSE}\right) \tag{6.13}$$

In equation (6.12), the M is the maximum possible pixel value in an image possible. The M value will be $2^8 - 1 = 255$ while finding the PSNR for a grayscale image which uses 8 bits to store each of the pixels in the image.

The PSNR measure can be used to compare the recovered image with the original image. If the mage which is recovered is the same as the original image then we will get a PSNR of ∞ since the MSE will be 0. In some cases, the recovered image may be slightly different from the original image due to the wrong recovery of some of the pixels. The unit of the PSNR is the decibel (dB).

4. **Structural similarity index (SSIM):** The SSIM is another measure to compare the structural similarity between two images. The SSIM value while comparing two images will vary between 0 and 1. The SSIM measure 1 between two images claims that both are the same.

6.4 Image dataset for experimental study

One of the well-known image datasets that is widely used by researchers working in the domain of RDH is the USC-SIPI dataset. The USC-SIPI was published on the website of University of Southern California [39]. This image dataset consists of four categories of images: *miscellaneous, textures, sequences*, and *aerials*. The image dataset is a combination of grayscale images and color images. The details about the image dataset are given in table 6.1.

The miscellaneous category consists of the well-known images such as *peppers, boat, baboon, airplane*, etc. In most of the research works, the grayscale versions of the images from USC-SIPI datasets are considered. Note that any algorithms designed for a grayscale image can be easily extended to the color images with some minor modifications.

Table 6.1. Details USC-SIPI image dataset.

Serial No.	Image category	Number of images
1	Miscellaneous (Misc)	39
2	Sequences	69
3	Textures	64
4	Aerials	38

6.5 Future scope of the research in RDH

The RDH schemes have wide application in the secure transmission of data, especially medical image transmission and cloud computing. A few challenges in some of the existing RDH schemes are discussed in this section so that researchers working on these problems might come up with some solutions.

The histogram-based RDH schemes and difference expansion based RDH schemes focus on the overflow or underflow during the data hiding phase. An additional location map is required to be handled. The recent overflow handling approach limited the additional number of overflow bits to the total count of 254's and 255's in the cover image. While considering underflow, the same scheme can be used and the overhead bits will be equivalent to the number of 0's and 1's in the image. Alternative approaches can be studied to reduce the overhead bits.

In an RDH scheme that uses histogram shifting, the embedding rate is purely decided by the pixel distribution in the image. Or in other words, the peak in the histogram of the image will decide the rate of embedding. Intensive research has happened in this domain to improve the embedding rate in recent years and one solution that came out of the research is to use a histogram of prediction errors rather than using the histogram of the original image. The prediction error histogram may have a bell-shaped property where the number of prediction errors with 0 will be high. The embedding rate in a prediction error based histogram shifting approach relies on the quality of the prediction techniques that we are using. This domain can be further explored to come up with new prediction techniques to increase the embedding rate. The overflow and underflow concerns are also here and the same should be handled efficiently.

The block-wise histogram shifting based approach is explored in the literature to increase the embedding rate. Instead of using predefined block sizes, the histogram of the objects can be taken into consideration. It might be noted that if we create a histogram that corresponds to an object's pixels there is a high chance to get large peak in the histogram. But the major issue is that the segmentation process in the stego image also should select the same set of pixels as part of the objects. The point that we have mentioned here needs to be studied in detail to explore further. The use of histograms after image quantization can also be studied for bringing new solutions in histogram shifting based RDH.

The histogram shifting based approaches are not good for performing the RDH in encrypted images. The histogram computed from the encrypted images is expected to be flat in nature. If we do some histogram shifting based RDH in the encrypted images it may generate a new encrypted image with a histogram of different shapes that may not meet the histogram that we are expecting from an encrypted image. The cyber attackers can analyze the histograms and they can easily identify the presence of some hidden information. They may try some steganalysis in such images to extract the hidden message. The use of a histogram shifting based approach in the encrypted image may not be capable of providing a sufficient ER since the peak need not be high in the histogram.

The difference expansion based RDH schemes take two pixels and embed the secret bit by expanding the difference. It is observed that the difference between the pixel value X and the modified pixel value X' after data hiding will be directly proportional to the difference D between the pair of pixels X and Y. To our knowledge the pair of pixels are selected in the existing schemes based on a data hiding key or in a predefined order. The actual difference between the pair of pixels is not taken into consideration. This can be explored in the future, and researchers can come up with an efficient pixel pair selection technique which will select the pixels X and Y in such a way that the difference between original pixel X or Y and the corresponding pixels in the stego image X' and Y' will be very close.

There is a lot of scope to work in the design and implementation of algorithms for RDH in encrypted images. One of the major concerns while hiding data in an encrypted image is that it will affect the security of the image. In general, from an encrypted grayscale image, we are expecting an entropy value of 8 and a flat histogram. But if we do data hiding in encrypted images it will surely change the pixel distribution and may affect the randomness. Readers may note that entropy helps to check the randomness in the distribution of an image. The entropy measure from a natural image will be comparatively low since the repetition of some of the pixel values will be there. Researchers can focus work on RDH schemes in encrypted images that will not change the entropy or histogram of the encrypted image. This problem will get much attention in the upcoming years.

RDH through encryption schemes was recently introduced for symmetric encryption techniques and it uses stream ciphers. There is wide scope to explore the fine-tuning of other well-known image encryption processes to support data hiding during encryption. The existing RDH schemes are not efficient against the texture images due to their random texture property. RDH through the encryption process uses a smoothness measure (closeness between the pixels in a block) as the major criteria and the texture images do not have a good correlation between adjacent pixels. Future works can be focused to consider the pattern of pixel distribution also rather than just considering the closeness between adjacent pixels. In the texture images, the same patterns are repeating in different regions and the incorporation of pattern extraction techniques such as local binary patterns in a clever way may help to improve the image recovery capability.

In real life, we use images in compressed form to minimize the storage requirement and to reduce the bandwidth requirement during transmission. A very limited number of RDH algorithms have been reported up to this point that will facilitate the data hiding in an encrypted image. This domain can be taken in future research to design efficient RDH schemes in encrypted images.

6.6 Conclusion

This chapter discussed the basics of RDH and its various applications. The motivation for RDH and the major categories of RDH schemes are detailed in this book chapter. A few well-known algorithms are also briefly described with various challenges in the existing schemes. The well-known dataset used in the study of reversible data hiding is also detailed in this chapter. The major challenges in the area of RDH schemes are briefly described along with a detailed description of the common efficiency parameters that we need to consider. This chapter gives an overview of the basic concepts of RDH in images for beginners who wish to work in this domain and an insight into some research problems where there is wide scope to explore further.

References

[1] Bender W *et al* 1996 Techniques for data hiding *IBM Syst. J.* **35** 313–36

[2] Lawandy N and Tillotson S Authentication using a digital watermark *U.S. Patent Application* No. 09/801,445

[3] O'Ruanaidh J J K, Dowling W J and Bowland F M 1996 Watermarking digital images for copyright protection *IEE Proc. Vision, Image Sign. Proc.* **143** 250–6

[4] Loan N A *et al* 2017 Hiding electronic patient record (EPR) in medical images: a high capacity and computationally efficient technique for e-healthcare applications *J. Biomed. Inform.* **73** 125–36

[5] Geetha R and Geetha S 2020 Efficient high capacity technique to embed EPR information and to detect tampering in medical images *J. Med. Eng. Technol.* **44** 55–68

[6] Singh P and Raman B 2017 Reversible data hiding for rightful ownership assertion of images in encrypted domain over cloud *AEU-Int. J. Electron. Commun.* **76** 18–35

[7] Ni Z *et al* 2006 Reversible data hiding *IEEE Trans. Circuits Syst. Video Technol.* **16** 354–62

[8] Manikandan V M and Renjith P 2020 An efficient overflow handling technique for histogram shifting based reversible data hiding *2020 Int. Conf. on Innovative Trends in Information Technology (ICITIIT)* (Piscataway, NJ: IEEE)

[9] Murthy K S R and Manikandan V M 2020 A block-wise histogram shifting based reversible data hiding scheme with overflow handling *2020 11th Int. Conf. on Computing, Communication and Networking Technologies (ICCCNT)* (Piscataway, NJ: IEEE)

[10] Hong W, Chen T-S and Shiu C-W 2009 Reversible data hiding for high quality images using modification of prediction errors *J. Syst. Softw.* **82** 1833–42

[11] He W *et al* 2018 Reversible data hiding using multi-pass pixel-value-ordering and pairwise prediction-error expansion *Inf. Sci.* **467** 784–99

[12] Chen X *et al* 2015 Histogram shifting based reversible data hiding method using directed-prediction scheme *Multimedia Tools Appl.* **74** 5747–65

[13] Kim S *et al* 2018 Skewed histogram shifting for reversible data hiding using a pair of extreme predictions *IEEE Trans. Circuits Syst. Video Technol.* **29** 3236–46

[14] Jia Y *et al* 2019 Reversible data hiding based on reducing invalid shifting of pixels in histogram shifting *Signal Process.* **163** 238–46

[15] Li Y *et al* 2019 A high-imperceptibility and histogram-shifting data hiding scheme for JPEG images *IEEE Access* **7** 73573–82

[16] Tian J 2003 Reversible data embedding using a difference expansion *IEEE Trans. Circuits Syst. Video Technol.* **13** 890–6

[17] Maniriho P and Ahmad T 2019 Information hiding scheme for digital images using difference expansion and modulus function *J. King Saud Univ., Comp. Info. Sci.* **31** 335–47

[18] Nguyen T-S and Chang C-C 2015 A reversible data hiding scheme based on the Sudoku technique *Displays* **39** 109–16

[19] Manikandan V M and Masilamani V 2020 A novel bit-plane compression based reversible data hiding scheme with Arnold transform *Int. J. Eng. Adv. Technol.* **9** 417–23

[20] Parah S A *et al* 2017 Hiding clinical information in medical images: a new high capacity and reversible data hiding technique *J. Biomed. Inform.* **66** 214–30

[21] Manikandan M V and Vedhanayagam M 2021 A novel image scaling based reversible watermarking scheme for secure medical image transmission *ISA Trans.* **108** 269–81

[22] Yi S and Zhou Y 2018 Separable and reversible data hiding in encrypted images using parametric binary tree labeling *IEEE Trans. Multimedia* **21** 51–64

[23] Mandal P, Chandra I, Mukherjee and Chatterji B N 2020 High capacity reversible and secured data hiding in images using interpolation and difference expansion technique *Multimedia Tools Appl.* **80** 3623–44

[24] Liu Z-L and Pun C-M 2018 Reversible data-hiding in encrypted images by redundant space transfer *Inf. Sci.* **433** 188–203

[25] Wu H-T *et al* 2018 A novel reversible data hiding method with image contrast enhancement *Signal Process. Image Commun.* **62** 64–73

[26] Hassan F S and Gutub A 2020 Novel embedding secrecy within images utilizing an improved interpolation-based reversible data hiding scheme *J. King Saud Univ., Comp. & Info. Sci. at press* https://doi.org/10.1016/j.jksuci.2020.07.008

[27] Zhang X 2011 Reversible data hiding in encrypted image *IEEE Signal Process Lett.* **18** 255–8

[28] Hong W, Chen T-S and Wu H-Y 2012 An improved reversible data hiding in encrypted images using side match *IEEE Signal Process Lett.* **19** 199–202

[29] Korivi K N and Manikandan V M 2020 Reversible data hiding in encrypted image using checkerboard pattern based pixel inversion *2020 5th Int. Conf. on Computing, Communication and Security (ICCCS)* (Piscataway, NJ: IEEE)

[30] Puteaux P and Puech W 2018 An efficient MSB prediction-based method for high-capacity reversible data hiding in encrypted images *IEEE Trans. Inf. Forensics Secur.* **13** 1670–81

[31] Xiong L, Xu Z and Shi Y-Q 2018 An integer wavelet transform based scheme for reversible data hiding in encrypted images *Multidimension. Syst. Signal Process.* **29** 1191–202

[32] Yi S, Zhou Y and Hua Z 2018 Reversible data hiding in encrypted images using adaptive block-level prediction-error expansion *Signal Process. Image Commun.* **64** 78–88

[33] Wu H-T *et al* 2019 A high-capacity reversible data hiding method for homomorphic encrypted images *J. Visual Commun. Image Represent.* **62** 87–96

[34] Manikandan V M and Masilamani V 2019 A novel entropy-based reversible data hiding during encryption *2019 IEEE 1st Int. Conf. on Energy, Systems and Information Processing (ICESIP)* (Piscataway, NJ: IEEE)

[35] Manikandan V M and Masilamani V 2018 Reversible data hiding scheme during encryption using machine learning *Procedia Comput. Sci.* **133** 348–56

[36] Manikandan V M and Masilamani V 2019 An improved reversible data hiding scheme through novel encryption *2019 Conf. on Next Generation Computing Applications (NextComp)* (Piscataway, NJ: IEEE)

[37] Manikandan V M and Bini A A 2020 An improved reversible data hiding through encryption scheme with block prechecking *Procedia Comput. Sci.* **171** 951–8

[38] Sara U, Akter M and Uddin M S 2019 Image quality assessment through FSIM, SSIM, MSE and PSNR—a comparative study *J. Comput.-Mediat. Commun.* **7** 8–18

[39] USC-SIPI image dataset: http://sipi.usc.edu/database/

Chapter 7

Anatomized study of security solutions for multimedia: deep learning-enabled authentication, cryptography and information hiding

Ameya Kshirsagar and Manan Shah

The continuous growth and usage of multimedia-based applications and services have put up a lot of multimedia traffic due to which security and authentication are critical for wireless multimedia networks, especially in this information era of the internet of everything. Hence, security provisioning has become a major issue in the current multimedia network due to the vital roles they play in conveying thought and supporting various causes. Multimedia data and its path of transmission face several threats ranging from eavesdropping, content manipulation, content theft, piracy. Further, issues like unbalanced growth in low computational costs and high security can be overcome by concepts based on multimedia security like, cryptography, information hiding which further includes steganography and watermarking followed by hybrid deep learning or artificial intelligence-assisted lightweight authentication. New deep learning, blind feature learning and lightweight physical layer authentication can be implemented to increase the overall security of the multimedia over the wireless network.

7.1 Introduction

Multimedia security is rapidly becoming a topic of concern for content creators, artists, companies, the entertainment industry, healthcare etc [1]. In recent times people have witnessed a lot of help for the need of a robust mechanism to safeguard the multimedia content and protect it from any kind of leaks [2], tampering [3] or tweaking of the media to convey the wrong information. These security issues arise as a result of a user wanting to share the content or the information via a cheaper source, henceforth possibly violating the terms of content copyrights. As new technology like digital newspapers and content sharing platforms are skyrocketing in the recent times, the traditional methodologies like magazines, cassettes, DVDs etc are being cast-off totally. Now it is more manageable for the multimedia content to be stored, edited, shared, and viewed by many on a single click. Since there is an advancement in the multimedia related technological world it also gives rise to the problems related to it, ranging from piracy [4] to unlawful morphing [5] of the content. The content is created and shared among users and each user acts as a node; at any point in the sharing the multimedia content can be tampered with and end up giving a false message in the system [6, 7].

The reason for not having many cases of piracy and content violation in the past was due to the default or maybe faulty build of cassettes or tapes (VHS tapes) and the minimality of the technology. Traditionally, for tapes and cassettes that were used, when copied to another piece, the quality used to degrade to a greater extent, making it unsuitable for use and thereby avoiding the high scale piracy existing now [8]. In fact, now one can copy the content or share it via online storage drives, pen drives, SSDs, HDDs etc and the copy is so near to perfect that it makes it difficult to distinguish between the authentic and the fake multimedia content let it be videos, audios, arts, gifs, songs, texts etc.

The significant multimedia threats [9], security risks and attacks can lead to drastic irreversible damage in this sector [10]. Additionally, the use of multimedia is very prone to these kinds of threats and attacks causing a disruption in the system via morphing, data injection [11], piracy, eavesdropping [12] and more. Hence there is a necessity for a robust system to avert these mishaps and ensure security and privacy is maintained. Authentication [13], watermarking [14] and access control [15] are considered as the vital contributors towards the identity confirmation and access to multimedia resources.

In order to prevent attacks in the multimedia world, this chapter focuses on the threats faced by multimedia data and thereby states the state-of-the-art methodologies to overcome the same. In the following section, we will look into the hurdles faced in the security approaches followed by threats to multimedia content. Later we meticulously analyse the security solutions, namely cryptography, bio-cryptography, data hiding strategies like steganography and watermarking. We also anatomize several studies in concise form in a tabular format for easy understanding of the application of robustness in watermarking techniques. And followed by discussing the novel deep learning-based security and authentication solutions. Finally, we propose some of the possible future work and conclude the chapter.

7.2 Hurdles in conventional approaches for security

Traditionally due to less availability of the technology, the sharing of media content was based on a one-to-many perspective, whose main aim was to focus on the information, and this followed a strict pattern or format and it lacked interactivity, whereas the case today is totally contrasting making the multimedia content versatile in nature (audio, video, excerpts etc), and making it possible for many people to communicate en masse in an instant in an interactive form [16–18].

Even though differences exist between the conventional and latest media, the one thing that remains constant is the security and the authenticity of the content [19]. Some of the threats to the security approaches, as shown in figure 7.1, are addressed below.

7.2.1 Vulnerability due to expansion

Traditional security solutions may not be capable enough to cope up with the rising needs of multimedia and its applications (like communication, healthcare etc). As there is a rise in the need to share multimedia the number of nodes (multimedia sensors) in the system rises making it more prone to threats and attacks. Although in a communication mechanism the higher layers are thoroughly protected, they can be undermined by attack or injection of malicious content on the lower levels, which in turn result in forged keys thereby damaging the authentication mechanism [20, 21].

7.2.2 Authentication and computational latency

The conventional mechanism requires more time and effort to decipher the authentication key and with a rising number of multimedia sensors, the complexity of these key rises significantly giving rise to slower computation [22], which in turn increases the overhead time and results in latency [23] in the system and increases traffic. Additionally, due to the non-adaptive nature of the customary method-ologies, the overall time also increases due to the involvement of the manual selection of the statistical characteristics.

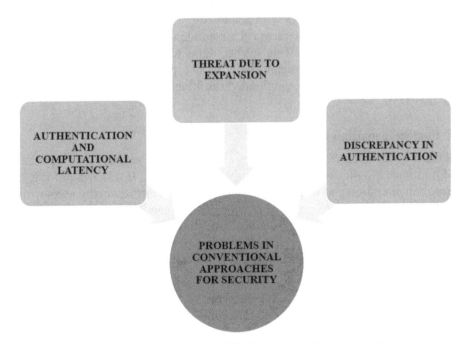

Figure 7.1. Multimedia security difficulties in conventional approaches.

7.2.3 Discrepancy in authentication

The traditional mechanism is very specific to the model and non-adaptive in nature, hence implementing one verification model with another set results in false outcomes. These techniques face difficulties in setting up the most suitable model in an unknown environment. These drawbacks of the conventional model pose a significant threat to the system, leaving it vulnerable to attacks [24]. Hence there is a need for a more intelligent authentication system that is versatile in nature with no explicit programming.

7.3 Vulnerability to multimedia content

In a network of users, multimedia content sharing is a major chunk of the data that is been shared amongst them. The user can share photos, videos, gifs, songs, documents and so on. Multimedia sharing is not only limited to individuals but also extends to vast organizations and businesses, such as hospitals, courts, restaurants etc; as there is a rise in the use of multimedia, similarly there will be a rise in the threats targeted towards it. Features like location sharing, face recognition, web searches increases the possibility of them being utilized for illegal deeds. Here in this section, we will discuss some of the threats to the content shared by the user, as shown in figure 7.2.

7.3.1 Data disclosure

In most of the cases, the user has to share their data to gain the benefits of the service. The data that has been shared is subjected to confidentiality issues or leaks. For instance, the user who shares with healthcare providers their personal information are subject to having it extracted for some kinds of studies, which might be against the will of the user sharing his/her data. Moreover, a user sharing their location, videos, photos over social media is also prone to illegal use. It can be downloaded, manipulated and re-uploaded resulting in tampering with the privacy of the user [25].

7.3.2 Content manipulation

Facilitated by the internet, people are very closely knit in a network and they share a lot of multimedia data over the vast number of platforms. But sharing of this data can result in alteration and distortion of the content by untrustworthy users without consent. One can take an example of how Photoshop can be used to manipulate the image to such a great extent that it becomes difficult to interpret the difference between the original and the fake [26].

7.3.3 Link sharing

Nowadays, due to the vast variety of the types of multimedia data, it has become difficult for platforms to support all kinds at once. For instance, Instagram does not support meeting invites [27], on the contrary, it is supported by e-mail or networking groups of users. There are scenarios where a user needs to share a file or document

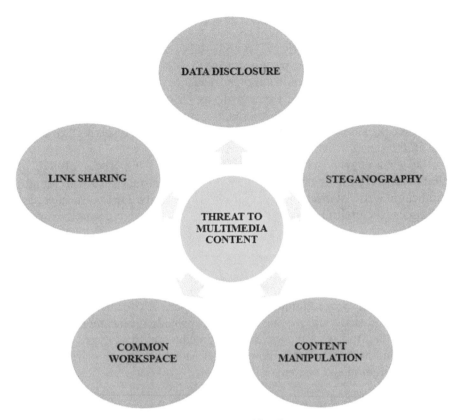

Figure 7.2. Threats to multimedia content.

with a particular number of people, and they make use of a link to do so. Due to the sharing of the link, the link's data is now in the hands of multiple users, making it vulnerable to attacks or manipulation of the content. Similar is the case of meeting invites that are sent for an online meeting being prone to intrusion, despite a layer of protection in the application. Moreover, when a picture is tagged and uploaded to a group by an individual, then the sharing can affect the privacy of the users in the image. These links and tagging [28–30] might result in malicious content being uploaded to the system to spy on the user [31].

7.3.4 Steganography

Though steganography has legal use, it can be used as a medium to convey an illegitimate message hidden under or shared as another medium of data. Stenograpy has a very crucial role in the courtroom as it is used for noting down the statements of both the sides involved in the debate and later that transcript is used for investigation purposes. But when steganography is used for illegal purposes it is quite difficult to get hold of it as the message is hidden under the images and conveyed. Due to this, an innocent individual can get entangled in an illicit act [32].

7.3.5 Common workspace

Due to the rise in technology, there is no possibility to mend the software problems remotely with the help of third-party software [33]. The person takes control of the individual device and operates it remotely, which can cause a huge extent of the threat to the private content of the user device. Moreover, the concept of shared drives [34] allows multiple people to share a single storage device among many people. This can cause a breach of personal space and might result in illicit use of the content in the shared drive [29].

As the technology is increasing rapidly to serve the purpose of individuals simultaneously, the threat to the content is also increasing, which necessitates the requirement of a robust mechanism of multimedia security. Hence, the later sections aim to discuss the multiple aspects and the solutions to overcome such a scenario.

7.4 Analysis of security solutions for multimedia content

In the recent past, multimedia security has been an intriguing field of study for researchers and enthusiasts in the industry sector as well as in academia. We have analysed a vast variety of solutions, as shown in figure 7.3, for the above-mentioned threats. Here in this section, we anatomize and provide several methodologies and approaches in the studies on the topic of multimedia security to yield beneficial and secure solutions and to achieve more user trust and a better privacy conscious ecosystem for multimedia content.

7.4.1 Cryptography

In digital communication where multimedia data sending and information sharing are playing a major role, it also brings forth the necessity of security for the data. Encryption is a manner in which this can be achieved. Here the data is protected with a key which is only known to the sender and receiver of the content. This technique allows only the selected mass of people, with the key, to view the content. Cryptography is employed to prevent any kind of illicit operations towards the

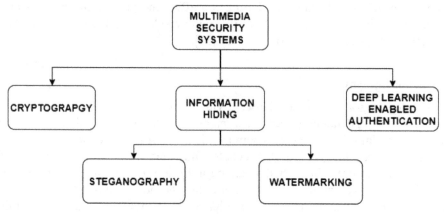

Figure 7.3. Multimedia security solutions.

multimedia files. The data is encrypted and sent to the receiver [35, 36]. The receiver then decrypts the message to extract the original meaningful data. Cryptography predominantly consists of three types: symmetric cryptography [37], asymmetric cryptography [38] and hash function [39]; but there is a more novel type of cryptography which overcomes the limitations of the mentioned three, i.e., biometric cryptography, as shown in figure 7.4.

Basic terminologies of cryptography [40] are as follows:
- Plain text: original data which is meant to be communicated to the receiver's end is known as plain text or original data.
- Encryption: the method of transforming plain text into meaningless and imperceptible text at the sender's end is known as encryption. This procedure requires two parts, i.e. encryption algorithm and a key.
- Cipher text: the meaningless text which is inconceivable by any means is known as cipher text. The cipher text is the output received when the plain text is encrypted.
- Key: the key is a script or specific dictionary-type collection of signs. This is used at the time of converting plain text to ciphered text and vice versa. The key is a requirement at the time of encryption and decryption.
- Decryption: this method is the converse of encryption. Where the ciphered text is converted to plain or meaningful text. This step takes place at the receiver's end.

Now we will look into the types of cryptography.

7.4.1.1 Symmetric cryptography
Figure 7.5 shows the working of secret key cryptography or symmetric key algorithm; here the same key is used for encrypting and decrypting the data or the media file. The sender applies the key to encrypt the data, the same key has to be used by the receiver to decrypt the data. Since there is only one key to encrypt and decrypt the data, there is a need to share the key with every receiver prior to the sending of data. This provides a significant scale of protection to the contents but prior key sharing is a drawback to this procedure. Some of the implemented tools of symmetric key algorithms are DES, 3DES, AES [41] and Blowfish [42].

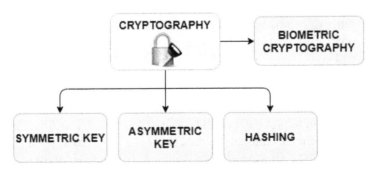

Figure 7.4. Types of cryptography.

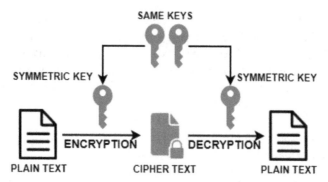

Figure 7.5. Working of symmetric cryptography.

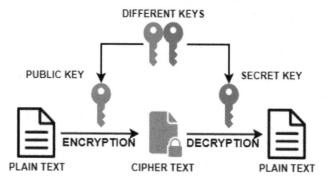

Figure 7.6. Working of asymmetric cryptography.

7.4.1.2 Asymmetric cryptography

Figure 7.6 shows the working of public key cryptography or asymmetric key algorithm [43]; here different keys are used for encrypting and decrypting the data or the media file. For this crypto methodology, there is a necessity of both keys having access to the data. Here the public key is used for the encryption of the data and the private key is used for decryption of the data. Here, since the public key is not private it is shared among the group with whom one wishes to communicate, whereas the private key is private to the individual and not revealed to anyone. Moreover, there is no possible way in which private key can be derived from the public key. Hence due to these two keys the protection of the overall model increases manyfold. Some of the implemented tools of symmetric key algorithms are RSA, XTR, EES etc [44].

7.4.1.3 Hash function

Figure 7.7 shows the working of the hash function [45]. The hash function is a one-way function with no requirement of a key, but rather a hash function. On the other hand, it takes a variable amount of data as input and generates a fixed-length ciphered or hashed text also called hash values. It is practical, and not possible to revert. Hence they are used for checking the integrity of the process and determining

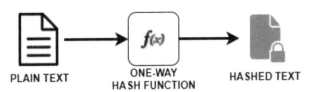

PLAIN TEXT   ONE-WAY   HASHED TEXT
HASH FUNCTION

Figure 7.7. Working of hash function.

whether there is the presence of altered data [46] or virus attack, thereby ensuring the veracity of the records. Some of the implemented tools of symmetric key algorithms are MD5, Whirpool, SHA-1 etc [47].

7.4.1.4 Bio-metric cryptography

Biometric cryptography is one of the emerging forms of cryptography which overcomes the limitations of the above-mentioned methodologies [48]. Since there is no use of a key, the overheads and time consumption for key sharing and creation is avoided. Since there is no key, there is no necessity for storage and hence it can be used for other purposes. The key cannot be copied, such as when a fingerprint is used, as the key is unique to each individual. Hence biometric cryptography is a highly secure mechanism for sharing content with high security as it is an amalgamation of both biometrics and cryptography. The authors of [49, 50] worked towards biometric-based cryptography for multimedia content protection. In their process, they extracted the user's fingerprint information via sensors and extracted features by making use of the convolution coding principle. This recently generated code is used in making of the cryptographic key for encryption and decryption of the multimedia content. With this procedure, they were able to achieve 95.12% true positive and 0% as false-negative values. Next, we will look into another approach, data hiding, mainly discussing steganography and watermarking.

7.4.2 Data hiding

The main purpose behind data hiding is to embed data into another type, i.e. hiding one form of the data file in another file [51]. This is crucial for many of the multimedia files that need to be protected from any kind of attacks or posed theft of the content or the ownership. The data are hidden initially and the final hidden data (i.e. maybe after theft or tampering) is compared to judge whether there was any kind of illicit activity that took place.

Data hiding in general is a simple stepped process. Here, as shown in figure 7.8, the multimedia content and secret message (the data to be hidden) are taken into consideration and passed via the embedding algorithm. The embedding algorithm is the step where the secret message is made to be hidden inside the multimedia host file [52]. Further, this step is protected with a 'secret key' to increase the security of the content which is owned by the owner of the content. Then the multimedia content is published for viewers to view and gain knowledge. If any kind of attack is performed then the same embedding algorithm (as decoding algorithm) is used to

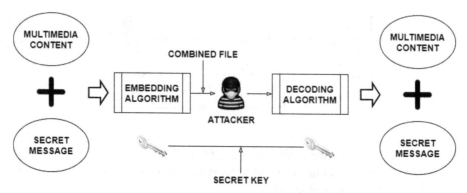

Figure 7.8. Generic working of data hiding technique.

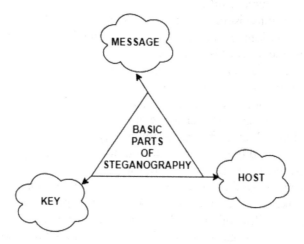

Figure 7.9. Basic terms of steganography.

separate the host multimedia file and the secret message. Later this secret message is compared with the original secret message to compare and analyse if there was any attack. Further, data hiding is predominantly divided into two types, stenography [53] and watermarking, which is further elaborated in the next section.

7.4.2.1 Steganography

Steganography is a method to convey a message in a hidden manner. The information shared is only meaningful to the sender and the receiver of the message, file or the multimedia content. Steganography is terminology derived from the Latin word 'steganographia'. The main goal of this method is to hide data inside the host data. Steganography dates back to the ancient past where symbols were engraved in cave walls to convey the message, and at the present time audio, video etc is used as a carrier for steganography [54]. In the end, the prime purpose of this methodology is to hide the data so that it can only be discerned by the targeted mass of people [55].

There are three major parts of the basic model of steganography, as shown in the figure 7.9, i.e. the host, the message and the key [56]:

1. The host: This is also known as the carrier image or cover object. The hidden message or the content is camouflaged under this file. And this file is shared among the targeted sources.
2. The message: This is the content (audio, video, text etc) that is being hidden or concealed in the host. This is the main file which is hidden to make it indiscernible.
3. The key: this key is used by the sender and the receiver to encrypt and decrypt the data (the message) that is hidden with the use of the host file.

Further, we will discuss the four major types of steganography, as shown in figure 7.10, to be able to hide the desired content and increase the security of the multimedia data transfer

7.4.2.1.1 *Image steganography*

In this process, the data is concealed under an image format host. After the data is concealed within the image the result is known as a stego-image [57]. The addition of the secret message is done by altering some of the pixels of the image which is performed by the embedding algorithm. The sender and receiver should be familiar with the same algorithm to embed and extract the information with the aid of a key, which is necessary for the algorithm to work. Newer and sturdy steganalysis models [58–60] are built to enhance the security of the transmission of the message by the inclusion of a deep neural network, as done by You *et al* [61] where they compared the noise of other subparts of the different region of the image, thereby giving resulting comparative output. Also, analysis is being done to catch terrorists who are making use of this methodology for illicit purposes [62].

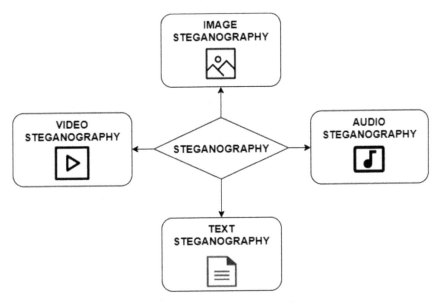

Figure 7.10. Types of steganography.

7.4.2.1.2 Audio steganography

Audio steganography makes use of the audio file as the host and other formats as the hidden content. Compared to image steganography audio steganography is quite a difficult task to achieve. Altering or tweaking the audio file is a challenging task as the tendency of human auditory system has a wide range of different recognition in the file if any changes are made and the same goes for the case for frequency [63]. On the other hand, due to the high level of redundancy in the audio host, the capacity of the host file is much larger as compared to others [64].

Agarwal and Venkatraman [65] suggested a novel methodology where deep learning mechanism is taken into consideration to embed RGB images without any perpetual loss. They achieved this by following a three-step process. Initially, they encrypted the message at the sender's end, followed by decrypting at the receiver's end and finally by enhancing the reconstructed image at the receiver's end. Moreover, Chaharlang et al [66] suggested another method making use of frame-based least significant fractional qubit (LSFQ) and quantum K-nearest neighbour (QKNN) algorithm. They made use of LSQF at the user's end to embed the information onto the audio file followed by, at the receiver's end utilising the QKNN for the recognition purpose. With this novel methodology, they were able to achieve a high accuracy of 90%.

7.4.2.1.3 Text steganography

Text steganography is more difficult compared to the above-mentioned method-ologies (image and audio steganography) as there is very much an absence of redundant data which can be altered to store the hidden data. Due to the vast variety in the other cover types (host multimedia file), it is easier to conceal the secret in them as compared to text, as text files are showing text which is visually detectable by humans. However, despite this limitation, text steganography provides high capacity for cost expenditure as it takes much less memory compared to other host media files [67]. It has a vast variety due to the enormity of linguistic extensiveness and hence many researchers are extensively researching it [68].

Xiang et al [69] made use of the convolutional neural network (CNN) for steganalysis. They divide the task into two parts, where in the first step they collected and made a pool of the required sentences and in the second one with the modified sentences. These are then fed to the model to compare whether the sentences were changed or not, whether there was any kind of replacement with synonyms. Their model was 82.245% accurately able to detect the stego-texts from cover texts.

7.4.2.1.4 Video steganography

A video is a compilation of fast-moving image with audio. Video steganography tends to overcome almost all the problems faced by other formats (text, audio, and image). Video steganography is more invisible, making it more undetectable to the naked eye, has a higher capacity per bit and is more robust compared to other host formats. Due to the composite nature of audio and images, there is a lot of redundancy making it easy to hide the data. Image and video differ highly when compared with respect to the increased or decreased frame rate, addition or deletion of frames, compression etc, moreover, due to this nature an attacker or malpractitioner will be forced to analyse each frame to spot and attack the hidden content [70].

Abdolmohammadi *et al* [71] focused on the least significant bits (LSBs) of video. The process of discerning these LSBs and assigning the secret value or content is still a challenging task but they made use of a proposed model. They employed a 3D convolutional neural network by exploiting the spatial and temporal features at once. They made use of a UCF101 dataset to implement their model and to test it. They observed an overall improvement of 22.75 bits per pixel.

Here we looked into how steganography can aid in hiding the data in text, audio, video and images. Next, we will look into another technique known as water-marking whose main purpose is also the same, i.e. hiding of data.

7.4.2.2 Watermarking

Digital watermarking is a methodology that is being used to prove the ownership of the product. Here typical data is embedded into the multimedia file that can aid in proving the proprietorship of the content. As we can see from figure 7.11, audio and video both incorporate the use of a watermarking type security function for showing ownership. The watermarking is predominantly divided into two parts, visible and invisible. Visible watermarking [72] as the name suggests, is visible over the image, video or audio file, i.e. it can be viewed by human eyes and clearly identifies the owner, whereas invisible watermarking [73] is not decipherable by the human eye and it is mainly segregated in three parts: robust, semi-fragile and fragile.

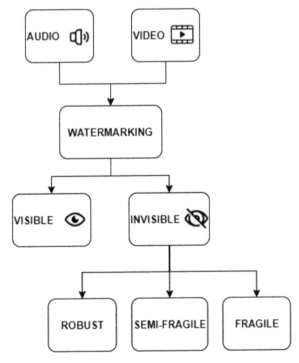

Figure 7.11. Types of watermarking.

In robust watermarking [74], the data or the content that was being can be recovered after the attack, whereas in fragile watermarking [75] the recovery or the authentication after the signal procession is not possible. Lastly, semi-fragile [76, 77] watermarking is a hybrid of robust and fragile watermarking. In this, Zigomitros *et al* [77] suggested a process where there is a use of dual watermarking, that is, the usage of both robust and fragile watermarking, thereby giving one more layer of protection to the user media content. With the aide of semi-fragile watermarking it enables the owner to keep track of his/her media content by tracking its status, such as whether some user is creating a copy or if there is a re-upload, editing etc [78]. This aids in addressing the issue of data disclosure on various multimedia platforms by using public watermarking techniques for unified privacy regulations over the various platforms.

In this section, we mainly discuss and focus on the necessary and vital property requirements for digital watermarking. Security, robustness, imperceptibility and capacity are the major requirements for watermarking, as shown in figure 7.12. These requirements are tweaked according to the application. One major issue that persists is that these requirements go hand-in-hand and compete with each other, thereby making it a challenge for researchers [79–85].

7.4.2.2.1 Robustness

Robustness can be defined as the capability of the methodology to withstand against the malicious act of modifying or morphing [86] the data [87]. It plays a major role in proving ownership, copy control, and authenticity of the content. The watermarks are intricately implanted into the video or audio or multimedia file and are designed in such a manner to withstand any kind of changes or attack. Further, these watermarks can be retrieved from the multimedia data or content. Later the watermark is tested and compared to look out for any kind of changes, distortion or removal, if they exist. Figure 7.13 shows the removal of the watermark. The blue circle indicates the watermark that is being used. The black circle in the later image shows the removed watermark area which is been filled by the approximation of the

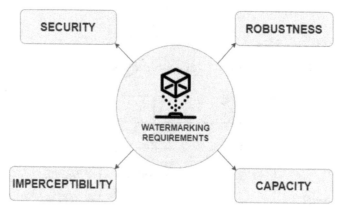

Figure 7.12. Watermarking property requirements.

BEFORE WATERMARK REMOVAL   AFTER WATERMARK REMOVAL

Figure 7.13. Distortion due to watermark removal.

surrounding bits to make it look natural, on the other hand, it is quite visible that the watermark has been removed due to the image distortion present in the black circle.

There isn't an exact measure to gauge the strength of the robust system [88–91], but if the system is able to withstand the formatting, content and other mentioned robustness impairing attacks mentioned in figure 7.14 then it is considered a robust watermarking system. In content-based manipulation the content's voice, tense, syntactic formation is done to change the content but the resultant data or the multimedia file has the same meaning. In format base attack the format of the data is changed like degrading the quality, performing optical character recognition, font changing etc. Watermark accuracy rate (WAR) and watermark distortion rate (WDR) are calculated for the image with the mentioned equations (equation (7.1), equation (7.2)), and the smaller the value of WDR the less is the distortion in the content. N_c is the number of matching and correctly detected bits or pattern and N_w defines the number of bits or pattern in the watermark [92]. Hence one can take these parameters into consideration when one needs to build a robust watermarking system.

$$WAR = \frac{N_c}{N_w} \tag{7.1}$$

$$WDR = 1 - \frac{N_c}{N_w} \tag{7.2}$$

Further, in table 7.1 we scrutinize several studies in concise tabular format for better understanding of the application of robustness in watermarking techniques. The studies were selected whose main aim was to test the robustness of their suggested techniques. Most of the techniques implemented were able to detect the insertion, deletion and syntactic transformation, whereas that is not the case for synonym substitution.

7.4.2.2.2 Imperceptibility
Imperceptibility is the tendency of the watermark to what range it can (watermark) be hidden or invisible to the naked human eye. This can be achieved via high scale combination of the original video or image or audio or any other form of

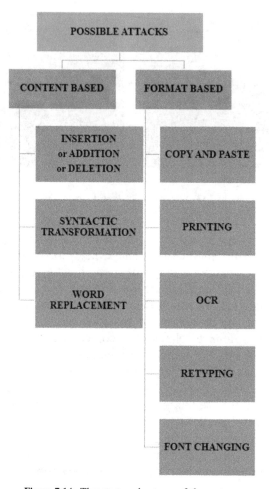

Figure 7.14. Threats to robustness of the system.

multimedia data and the watermark data. After the step to embed the watermark onto the original content or file the quality and the originality of the data should not be reduced or degraded in any manner. The purpose of this step is to add hidden data to the main data (i.e. multimedia data) to assign copyright, mark ownership and preserve the integrity of the same. Although the main purpose of impercept-ibility is to be concealed, sometimes the owner wishes to clearly show the watermark to aver the ownership. Hence imperceptibility is divided into two parts, as shown in figure 7.15, invisible and visible [108]. Visible watermarking is to show that any kind of theft or tampering to the data is not lawful, whereas invisible watermark is embedded in such a way that it is only detectable by a specific algorithm.

7.4.2.2.3 Capacity
Capacity [109], payload or bit rate in watermarking all points toward one thing, that is, how many numbers of bits of the watermark are to be made hidden in the original audio [110], video, image [111] or any multimedia content. Its metric is bits per

Table 7.1. Robustness analysis of various studies.

Serial no.	Reference	Insertion	Deletion	Reordering	Syntactic transformation	Copy and past	Synonym substitution
1	[93]	✔	✔		✔	✔	
2	[94]				✔		✔
3	[95]			✔	✔	✔	
4	[96]	✔	✔				✔
5	[97]	✔			✔	✔	
6	[98]	✔	✔				
7	[99]	✔		✔	✔	✔	
8	[100]	✔	✔		✔		
9	[101]		✔				
10	[102]	✔	✔	✔			
11	[103]	✔	✔		✔	✔	
12	[104]		✔	✔	✔	✔	
13	[105]	✔	✔	✔			
14	[106]	✔			✔	✔	
15	[107]	✔	✔	✔	✔		

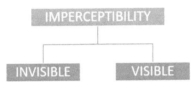

Figure 7.15. Types of imperceptibility.

second, therefore it can be depicted as in equation (7.3) [112]. The more the number of the bits are embedded and hidden the more is the capacity. Higher capacity means higher utilization of the watermark but crossing a certain limit may tamper with the watermark's invisibility. Hence the capacity of the watermark should be high but shouldn't affect the invisibility. Moreover, the capacity varies from type to type of multimedia content. For instance, healthcare related multimedia files have higher capacity as they should be least prone to any kinds of attack [113].

$$\text{Capacity} = \frac{\text{Total number of watermarked data bits}}{\text{Total number of content data (kb)}} \times 100 \qquad (7.3)$$

7.4.2.2.4 Security
Security should ensure prevention of the content being manipulated by unauthorized tampering or removal of the hidden data [114] and should only be alterable by the owner of the content [115]. The fact cannot be ignored that the attackers or the malpractitioners are aware of the embedding process that the watermark went

through [116]. Much of the robustness of the watermark relies on this factor, i.e. the process is kept confidential or hidden. But once the process is out it is very easy for the attacker to remove the watermark with very little computational complexity and power. The embedding processes are protected with the security key which is kept safe to prevent any kind of theft or leak of the authenticated data. For further protection, the key is made to be well hidden from malpractice with the use of cryptographic security and a digital signature. Since the attacker will be short of the key they will need to analyse and destroy the watermark, which will also lead to tampering with the multimedia data. Hence, in this scenario the watermark is considered as secured. Hence it is a necessity to take into consideration the cryptographic security and digital signature to scale up the effectivity of the watermarking system [117]. Security can also be considered as the sum of robustness, capacity and imperceptibility. Li *et al* [118] suggested a novel CNN based security system for image watermarking. They made use of synergetic neural networks. They processed over the gray-watermark image followed by inculcating it as a watermark over the block discrete cosine transform (DCT) component. This in turn aids in simultaneous detection and extraction of the watermark attribution on further comparison to other state-of-the-art models that had significant peak signal-to-noise ratio (PSNR) with an average value around 50.

Further, we aim to look into some of the novel state-of-the-art techniques for multimedia data and its transmission security which make use of deep learning methodologies to enhance the working, effectiveness and impregnability of the overall security system.

7.4.3 Deep learning enabled authentication

Due to the dynamic age of our society, where data is transferred and shared amongst people for enjoyment, study and work purposes, the rate of data transfer has increased manyfold. Due to this high capacity of multimedia data transfer, there is a necessity of an advanced system which can keep up with the speed. The security system should be easy to implement, robust and should not be prone to any kinds of attack. If a breach or attack or illicit act has been made one should be able to detect and rectify it. Hence due to the rise in multimedia data, to secure, verify and authenticate the data novel technologies are employed which involve deep learning to authenticate the user and the data [119].

Centeno *et al* [120] suggests that due to continuous online services there was a need for an online authentication service. A service that can protect the data and authenticate it in a real-time and real-world scenario. They proposed a deep learning-enabled autoencoder. They considered the real-world scenarios where the profundity of the architecture is considered, time taken prior to re-building the model and length of the training dataset. They also considered the balance between the re-authentication time and the number of dimensional features considered for the analysis. Due to these steps and the model's reliability on the accelerometer data the models do not require a high number of features, thereby reducing the computational load on the system and yielding a low error rate equivalent to 2.2%.

Moreover, Ferdowsi and Saad [121] stated that to make sure that a proper sharing of multimedia is carried out, a communication path should be taken care of that should prevent any kind of data injection, eavesdropping, altering, and tampering with the data and man-in-the-middle threats. For this purpose they suggested a method making use of deep learning methods to detect the attacks via dynamic watermarking of IoT signals. They used the LSTM (long short-term memory) framework to extract the basic features and watermarked them dynamically into the signal. With the aid of this method, the receiver of the signal can analyse the signal and validate whether there was a presence of any malpractice or tampering with the signal and the data. This method assists in preventing the issue of eavesdropping and data tampering. Their model was capable of detecting the attack in under one second, thereby providing an almost 100% reliable source of communication and data sharing.

However, Ferdowsi and Saad [121] covered the security aspects related to the transmission of the data but only of the upper-layer authentication, whereas Qiu et al [122] focused on the physical layer authentication with the assistance of artificial intelligence-based security authentication with blind feature learning (BFL) and lightweight physical layer authentication (LPLA). The main aim of the study was to identify any malicious multimedia devices. For the model, they estimated the physical attributes of a legitimate multimedia sharing device with which the recognition model (LPLA model) was trained, and for a later step the unknown devices were used to test the efficiency of the model. Their analysis verified the superiority of the suggested model to increase and achieve an AI-enabled lightweight authentication for the safety of the wireless multimedia device and the data transferred.

7.5 Future scope

The possible challenges the current multimedia data security can face or the issues that can be looked into to enhance the overall content sharing system are:
- The suggested methods in this chapter can extend their scope to more types of multimedia data like zip files, meeting invite links, dithered image, etc.
- Interdependency of the robustness, imperceptibility, and capacity can be further studied to increase them simultaneously without lowering the impact of others.
- Concomitantly reduce computation cost and computational power to provide a more resilient methodology.
- The difficulty of embedding content in the video, because of the varying number of bits, can be further studied.
- Emphasis over adaptive embedding approaches to achieve an optimized algorithm.

More machine learning and deep learning-based applications can be implemented to enhance the verification, tampering detection and theft detection, and better authentication can be achieved.

7.6 Conclusion

The current chapter introduced the different multimedia security systems based on the application under concern, such as data hiding and protection algorithms for images, video, texts etc for data hiding applications in image/video communication. We looked into different hurdles in the security systems due to discrepancy in authentication, threat due to expansion and computational latency. Followed by the threat to multimedia data ranging from data disclosure to content manipulation. Additionally, we looked into different methodologies to aid in increasing the security of the multimedia content and its sharing mechanism by deeply anatomizing the data hiding techniques. In cryptography, biometrics work as the most efficient model to overcome the issues of other suggested cryptography types. We also looked into types of steganography and watermarking techniques. Further, we discussed how deep learning can be inculcated to improve the overall security of the multimedia data and the security of its transmission. More researchers, students and enthusiasts can further work on the suggested challenges and future work to supplementarily enhance the overall working and security of multimedia data and its sharing.

Acknowledgements

The authors are grateful to Symbiosis Institute of Technology and Department of Chemical Engineering, School of Technology, Pandit Deendayal Petroleum University for the permission to publish this research.

References

[1] Zhang P, Kang X, Wu D and Wang R 2019 High-accuracy entity state prediction method based on deep belief network toward IoT search *IEEE Wirel. Commun. Lett.* **8** 492–5

[2] Hauer B 2015 Data and information leakage prevention within the scope of information security *IEEE Access* **3** 2554–65

[3] Bestagini P, Milani S, Tagliasacchi M and Tubaro S 2013 Local tampering detection in video sequences. *2013 IEEE Int. Work. Multimed. Signal Process. MMSP* **2013** 488–93

[4] Van Kranenburg H and Hogenbirk A 2005 Multimedia, entertainment, and business software copyright piracy: a cross-national study *J. Media Econ.* **18** 109–29

[5] Canazza S, De Poli G, Drioli C, Rodà A and Vidolin A 2000 Audio morphing different expressive intentions for multimedia systems *IEEE Multimed.* **7** 79–82

[6] Wu D, Si S, Wu S and Wang R 2018 Dynamic trust relationships aware data privacy protection in mobile crowd-sensing *IEEE Internet Things J.* **5** 2958–70

[7] Wu D, Deng L, Wang H, Liu K and Wang R 2019 Similarity aware safety multimedia data transmission mechanism for internet of vehicles *Futur. Gener. Comput. Syst.* **99** 609–23

[8] Jan M A, Usman M, He X and Rehman A U 2019 SAMS: a seamless and authorized multimedia streaming framework for WMSN-based IoMT *IEEE Internet Things J.* **6** 1576–83

[9] Hu H, Zhang H and Yang Y 2018 Security risk situation quantification method based on threat prediction for multimedia communication network *Multimed. Tools Appl.* **77** 21693–723

[10] Fang H, Qi A and Wang X 2020 Fast authentication and progressive authorization in large-scale IoT: how to leverage AI for security enhancement *IEEE Netw* **34** 24–9

[11] Manandhar K, Cao X, Hu F and Liu Y 2014 Detection of faults and attacks including false data injection attack in smart grid using Kalman filter *IEEE Trans. Control Netw. Syst.* **1** 370–9

[12] Dai H N, Wang Q, Li D and Wong R C W 2013 On eavesdropping attacks in wireless sensor networks with directional antennas *Int. J. Distrib. Sens. Networks* **2013** 760834

[13] Zhu B B, Swanson M D and Tewfik A H 2004 When seeing isn't believing *IEEE Signal Process. Mag.* **21** 40–9

[14] Hurrah N N, Parah S A, Loan N A, Sheikh J A, Elhoseny M and Muhammad K 2019 Dual watermarking framework for privacy protection and content authentication of multimedia *Futur. Gener. Comput. Syst.* **94** 654–73

[15] Akyildiz I F, McNair J, Martorell L C, Puigjaner R and Yesha Y 1999 Medium access control protocols for multimedia traffic in wireless networks *IEEE Netw.* **13** 39–47

[16] Ferrari D 1990 Client requirements for real-time communication services *IEEE Commun. Mag.* **28** 65–72

[17] Vina A, Lerida J L, Molano A and del Val D 1994 Real-time multimedia systems *Proceedings Thirteenth IEEE Symposium on Mass Storage Systems. Toward Distributed Storage and Data Management Systems* (Piscataway, NJ: IEEE) pp 77–83

[18] Bruhn M, Schoenmueller V and Schäfer D B 2012 Are social media replacing traditional media in terms of brand equity creation? *Manag. Res. Rev.* **35** 770–90

[19] Zou Y, Zhu J, Wang X and Hanzo L 2016 A survey on wireless security: technical challenges, recent advances, and future trends *Proc. IEEE* **104** 1727–65

[20] Rittenhouse R and Chaudhry J 2016 A survey of alternative authentication methods *Int. Conf. of Recent Advances in Computer Systems (RACS 2015)* pp 179–82

[21] Joshi J B D, Shyu M L, Chen S C, Aref W and Ghafoor A 2008 A multimedia-based threat management and information security framework *Multimed. Technol. Concepts, Methodol. Tools, Appl.* **1** 509–27

[22] Buschek D, Hartmann F, Von Zezschwitz E, De Luca A and Alt F 2016 SnapApp: reducing authentication overhead with a time-constrained fast unlock option *Conf. on Human Factors in Computing Systems—Proc.* (New York: Association for Computing Machinery) pp 3736–47

[23] Perera P and Patel V M 2018 Efficient and low latency detection of intruders in mobile active authentication *IEEE Trans. Inf. Forensics Secur.* **13** 1392–405

[24] Jain A K, Lin H, Pankanti S and Bolle R 1997 An identity-authentication system using fingerprints *Proc. IEEE* **85** 1365–88

[25] Lee J D and Sin C H 2014 PPS-RTBF: privacy protection system for right to be forgotten *J. Converg.* **5** 37–40

[26] Therezza M 2015 Image distortion tool downloads *Softw. Inf.*

[27] Ramzan N, Park H and Izquierdo E 2012 Video streaming over P2P networks: challenges and opportunities *Signal Process. Image Commun.* **27** 401–11

[28] Squicciarini A C, Shehab M and Wede J 2010 Privacy policies for shared content in social network sites *VLDB J.* **19** 777–96

[29] González-Manzano L, González-Tablas A I, De Fuentes J M and Ribagorda A 2014 CooPeD: co-owned personal data management *Comput. Secur.* **47** 41–65

[30] Ahmed F and Abulaish M 2013 A generic statistical approach for spam detection in online social networks *Comput. Commun.* **36** 1120–9

[31] Sams B 2011 *Facebook Photo Exploit Allows you to View Any Albums of Non-friends* (Plymouth, MI: Neowin)

[32] Viejo A, Castellà-Roca J and Rufián G 2013 Preserving the user's privacy in social networking sites *Lect. Notes Comput. Sci. (including Subser. Lect. Notes Artif. Intell. Lect. Notes Bioinformatics)* **8058 LNCS** 62–73

[33] Daniel B 2020 *Best Remote Desktop Software of 2020: Free, Paid and for Business* (TechRadar)

[34] Nitzberg B and Lo V 1991 Distributed shared memory: a survey of issues and algorithms *Computer* **24** 52–60

[35] Gurunathan K and Rajagopalan S P 2020 A stegano—visual cryptography technique for multimedia security *Multimed. Tools Appl.* **79** 3893–911

[36] Pandey A and Som S 2016 Applications and usage of visual cryptography: a review *2016 5th Int. Conf. Reliab. Infocom Technol. Optim. ICRITO 2016 Trends Futur. Dir.* 375–81

[37] Verma V and Kumar R 2014 A unique approach to multimedia based dynamic symmetric key cryptography *Int. J. Comput. Sci. Mob. Comput.* **3** 1119–28

[38] Barak B 2017 The complexity of public-key cryptography *Information Security and Cryptography* ed Y Lindell (Berlin: Springer) pp 45–77

[39] Wang D, Jiang Y, Song H, He F, Gu M and Sun J 2017 Verification of implementations of cryptographic hash functions *IEEE Access* **5** 7816–25

[40] Djordjevic I B and Djordjevic I B 2019 Conventional cryptography fundamentals *Physical-Layer Security and Quantum Key Distribution* (Berlin: Springer) pp 65–91

[41] Bhat B, Ali A W and Gupta A 2015 DES and AES performance evaluation *Int. Conf. on Computing, Communication and Automation, ICCCA 2015* (Piscataway, NJ: IEEE) pp 887–90

[42] Mandal P C 2012 Evaluation of performance of the symmetric key algorithms: DES, 3DES, AES and Blowfish *J. Glob. Res. Comput. Sci.* **3** 67–70

[43] Pradeep K V, Vijayakumar V and Subramaniyaswamy V 2019 An efficient framework for sharing a file in a secure manner using asymmetric key distribution management in cloud environment *J. Comput. Networks Commun.* **2019** 1–8

[44] Al-Shabi M A 2019 A survey on symmetric and asymmetric cryptography algorithms in information security *Int. J. Sci. Res. Publ.* **9** 8779

[45] Tchórzewski J and Jakóbik A 2019 Theoretical and experimental analysis of cryptographic hash functions *J. Telecommun. Inf. Technol.* **1** 125–33

[46] Almazrooie M, Samsudin A, Gutub A A A, Salleh M S, Omar M A and Hassan S A 2020 Integrity verification for digital Holy Quran verses using cryptographic hash function and compression *J. King Saud Univ.—Comput. Inf. Sci.* **32** 24–34

[47] Pittalia P P 2019 A comparative study of hash algorithms in cryptography *Int. J. Comput. Sci. Mob. Comput.* **8** 147–52

[48] Kuznetsov A, Kiyan A, Uvarova A, Serhiienko R and Smirnov V 2019 New code based fuzzy extractor for biometric cryptography *2018 Int. Sci. Conf. Probl. Infocommunications Sci. Technol. PIC S T 2018—Proc.* (Piscataway, NJ: IEEE) pp 119–24

[49] Dwivedi R, Dey S, Sharma M A and Goel A 2020 A fingerprint based crypto-biometric system for secure communication *J. Ambient Intell. Humaniz. Comput.* **11** 1495–509

[50] Panchal G, Samanta D and Barman S 2019 Biometric-based cryptography for digital content protection without any key storage *Multimed. Tools Appl.* **78** 26979–7000

[51] Singh L, Singh A K and Singh P K 2020 Secure data hiding techniques: a survey *Multimed. Tools Appl.* **79** 15901–21

[52] Swanson M D, Zhu B and Tewfik A H 1996 Robust data hiding for images *IEEE Digital Signal Processing Workshop* pp 37–40

[53] Kumar A and Pooja K 2010 Steganography-a data hiding technique *Int. J. Comput. Appl.* **9** 19–23

[54] Swain G and Lanka K L 2012 A quick review of network security and steganography *Int. J. Electron.* **1** 426–35

[55] Khalid M, Arora K and Pal N 2014 A crypto-steganography: a survey *Int. J. Adv. Comput. Sci. Appl.* **5** 149–55

[56] Odeh A, Alzubi A, Hani Q B and Elleithy K 2012 Steganography by multipoint Arabic letters *2012 IEEE Long Isl. Syst. Appl. Technol. Conf. LISAT 2012*

[57] Yang C N, Hsu S C and Kim C 2017 Improving stego image quality in image interpolation based data hiding *Comput. Stand. Interfaces* **50** 209–15

[58] Fridrich J and Goljan M 2002 Practical steganalysis of digital images: state of the art *Secur. Watermarking Multimed. Contents IV* **4675** 1–13

[59] Fridrich J and Kodovsky J 2012 Rich models for steganalysis of digital images *IEEE Trans. Inf. Forensics Secur.* **7** 868–82

[60] Lyu S and Farid H 2006 Steganalysis using higher-order image statistics *IEEE Trans. Inf. Forensics Secur.* **1** 111–9

[61] You W, Zhang H and Zhao X 2021 A siamese CNN for image steganalysis *IEEE Trans. Inf. Forensics Secur.* **16** 291–306

[62] Ruan F, Zhang X, Zhu D, Xu Z, Wan S and Qi L 2020 Deep learning for real-time image steganalysis: a survey *J. Real-Time Image Process.* **17** 149–60

[63] Lu T C, Chi L P, Wu C H and Chang H P 2017 Reversible data hiding in dual stego-images using frequency-based encoding strategy *Multimed. Tools Appl.* **76** 23903–29

[64] AlSabhany A A, Ali A H, Ridzuan F, Azni A H and Mokhtar M R 2020 Digital audio steganography: systematic review, classification, and analysis of the current state of the art *Comput. Sci. Rev.* **38** 100316

[65] Agarwal S and Venkatraman S 2020 Deep residual neural networks for image in audio steganography *(Workshop Paper)* 430–4

[66] Chaharlang J, Mosleh M and Rasouli Heikalabad S 2020 A novel quantum audio steganography–steganalysis approach using LSFQ-based embedding and QKNN-based classifier *Circuits Syst. Signal Process.* **39** 3925–57

[67] Malik A, Sikka G and Verma H K 2017 A high capacity text steganography scheme based on LZW compression and color coding *Eng. Sci. Technol. an Int. J.* Karabuk University **20** 72–9

[68] Tong Y, Liu Y L, Wang J and Xin G 2019 Text steganography on RNN-generated lyrics *Math. Biosci. Eng.* **16** 5451–63

[69] Xiang L, Guo G, Yu J, Sheng V S and Yang P 2020 A convolutional neural network-based linguistic steganalysis for synonym substitution steganography *Math. Biosci. Eng.* **17** 1041–58

[70] Zhao H, Pang M and Liu Y 2020 Intra-frame adaptive transform size for video steganography in H.265/HEVC bitstreams Intelligent Computing Methodologies. *ICIC* (Lecture Notes in Computer Science including subseries Lecture Notes in Artificial Intelligence and Lecture Notes in Bioinformatics) (Cham: Springer) pp 601–10

[71] Abdolmohammadi M, Toroghi R M and Bastanfard A 2020 Video steganography using 3D convolutional neural networks *Communications in Computer and Information Science* (Berlin: Springer) pp 149–61

[72] Santoyo-Garcia H, Fragoso-Navarro E, Reyes-Reyes R, Cruz-Ramos C and Nakano-Miyatake M 2017 Visible watermarking technique based on human visual system for single sensor digital cameras *Secur. Commun. Networks* **2017**

[73] Agrwal S L, Yadav A, Kumar U and Gupta S K 2016 Improved invisible watermarking technique using IWT-DCT *2016 5th Int. Conf. Reliab. Infocom Technol. Optim. ICRITO 2016 Trends Futur. Dir.* 283–5

[74] Kulkarni P R, Mulani A O and Mane P B 2017 Robust invisible watermarking for image authentication *Lect. Notes Electr. Eng.* **394** 193–200

[75] Renza D, Ballesteros L D M and Lemus C 2018 Authenticity verification of audio signals based on fragile watermarking for audio forensics *Expert Syst. Appl.* **91** 211–22

[76] Yu X, Wang C and Zhou X 2017 Review on semi-fragile watermarking algorithms for content authentication of digital images *Futur. Internet* **9** 1–17

[77] Zigomitros A, Papageorgiou A and Patsakis C 2012 Social network content management through watermarking *Proc. 11th IEEE Int. Conf. Trust. Secur. Priv. Comput. Commun. Trust.—11th IEEE Int. Conf. Ubiquitous Comput. Commun. IUCC-2012* 1381–6

[78] Patsakis C, Zigomitros A, Papageorgiou A and Galván-López E 2014 Distributing privacy policies over multimedia content across multiple online social networks *Comput. Networks* **75** 531–43

[79] Liu J L, Lou D C, Chang M C and Tso H K 2006 A robust watermarking scheme using self-reference image *Comput. Stand. Interfaces* **28** 356–67

[80] Lagzian S, Soryani M and Fathy M 2011 A new robust watermarking scheme based on RDWT-SVD *Int. J. Intell. Inf. Process., AICIT* **2** 22–9

[81] Haitsma J and Kalker T 2001 A watermarking scheme for digital cinema *IEEE Int. Conf. Image Process.* **2** 487–9

[82] Tiwari N 2017 Digital watermarking applications, parameter measures and techniques *IJCSNS Int. J. Comput. Sci. Netw. Secur.* **17** 184

[83] Soltani Panah, A., Van Schyndel, R., Sellis, T. and Bertino, E 2016 On the properties of non-media digital watermarking: a review of state of the art techniques *IEEE Access* **4** 2670–704

[84] Hartung F and Kutter M 1999 Multimedia watermarking techniques *Proc. IEEE, IEEE* **87** 1079–107

[85] Petitcolas F A P, Anderson R J and Kuhn M G 1999 Information hiding—a survey *Proc. IEEE* **87** 1062–78

[86] Autherith S and Pasquini C 2020 Detecting morphing attacks through face geometry features *J. Imaging* **6** 115

[87] Matheson L R, Mitchell S G, Shamoon T G, Tarjan R E and Zane F 1998 *Robustness and security of digital watermarks Financial Cryptography.* (Lecture Notes in Computer Science vol 1465) (Cham: Springer) pp 227–40

[88] Kaur M and Sharma V K 2016 Encryption based LSB Steganography Technique for Digital Images and Text Data *IJCSNS Int. J. Comput. Sci. Netw. Secur.* **16** 90–7

[89] Topkara M, Taskiran C M and Delp E J III 2005 Natural language watermarking *Secur. Steganography, Watermarking Multimed. Contents VII* **5681** 441

[90] AminAli A and Saad A S 2013 New text steganography technique by using mixed-case font *Int. J. Comput. Appl.* **62** 6–9

[91] Alotaibi R A and Elrefaei L A 2016 Utilizing word space with pointed and un-pointed letters for Arabic text watermarking *Proc.—2016 UKSim-AMSS 18th Int. Conf. Comput. Model. Simulation, UKSim 2016* 111–6

[92] Jalil Z, Mirza A M and Sabir M 2010 Content based zero-watermarking algorithm for authentication of text documents *Int. J. Comput. Sci. Inf. Security* **7** 212–7

[93] Al-nofaie S M, Fattani M M and Gutub A A 2016 Capacity improved arabic text steganography technique utilizing 'Kashida' with whitespaces *The 3rd Int. Conf. on Mathematical Sciences and Computer Engineering (ICMSCE2016) (Langkawi)* pp 38–44

[94] He L, Zhang L, Ma G, Fang D and Gui X L 2009 A part-of-speeach tag sequence text zero-watermarking *2009 Int. Symp. Comput. Sci. Comput. Technol. (ISCSCI 2009)* 187

[95] Rizzo S G, Bertini F, Montesi D and Stomeo C 2017 Text watermarking in social media *ASONAM '17: Proc. of the 2017 IEEE/ACM Int. Conf. on Advances in Social Networks Analysis and Mining* pp 208–11

[96] Yingjie M 2010 Chinese text zero-watermark based on sentence's entropy *2010 Int. Conf. on Multimedia Technology* pp 1–4

[97] Alotaibi R A and Elrefaei L A 2017 Improved capacity Arabic text watermarking methods based on open word space *J. King Saud Univ.—Comput. Inf. Sci.* **30** 236–48

[98] Jalii Z, Aziz H, Bin S, Muhammad S and Mirza A M 2010 A zero text watermarking algorithm based on non-vowel ASCII characters *2010 Int. Conf. on Educational and Information Technology* pp 503–7

[99] Ahvanooey M T, Mazraeh H D and Tabasi S H 2016 An innovative technique for web text watermarking (AITW) *Inf. Security J.* **25** 191–6

[100] Jalil Z, Mirza A M and Jabeen H 2010 Word length based zero-watermarking algorithm for tamper detection in text documents *2010 2nd Int. Conf. on Computer Engineering and Technology* (Piscataway, NJ: IEEE) pp 378–82

[101] Mir N 2014 Copyright for web content using invisible text watermarking *Comput. Human Behav.* **30** 648–53

[102] Jalil Z, Mirza A M, Iqbal T and Sciences E 2010 A zero-watermarking algorithm for text documents based on structural components *2010 International Conference on Information and Emerging Technologies* (Piscataway, NJ: IEEE) pp 1–5

[103] Alginahi Y M, Kabir M N and Tayan O 2014 An enhanced kashida-based watermarking approach for increased protection in Arabic text-documents based on frequency recurrence of characters *Int. J. Comput. Electr. Eng.* **6** 381–92

[104] Meral H M, Gu T and Sevinc E 2009 Natural language watermarking via morphosyntactic alterations *Comput. Speech Lang.* **23** 107–25

[105] Zhang Y 2010 A novel robust text watermarking for word document *Int. Congress on Image and Signal Processing* (Piscataway, NJ: IEEE) pp 38–42

[106] Topkara U and Lafayette W 2006 The hiding virtues of ambiguity: quantifiably resilient watermarking of natural language text through synonym substitutions *MM&Sec '06: Proceedings of the 8th workshop on Multimedia and security* pp 164–74

[107] Liu Y, Zhu Y and Xin G 2016 A zero-watermarking algorithm based on merging features of sentences for Chinese text *J. Chin. Inst. Eng.* **38** 391–8

[108] Jalil Z and Mirza A M 2010 An invisible text watermarking algorithm using image watermark *Innovations in Computing Sciences and Software Engineering* (Dordrecht: Springer) pp 147–52

[109] Zhong X and Shih F Y 2019 A high-capacity reversible watermarking scheme based on shape decomposition for medical images *Int. J. Pattern Recognit Artif Intell.* **33** 1950001

[110] Karajeh H and Maqableh M 2019 An imperceptible, robust, and high payload capacity audio watermarking scheme based on the DCT transformation and Schur decomposition *Analog Integr. Circuits Signal Process.* **99** 571–83

[111] Chaughule S S and Megherbi D B 2018 A robust secure and high capacity image watermarking scheme for information exchange in distributed collaborative networked intelligent measurement systems *CIVEMSA 2018–2018 IEEE Int. Conf. Comput. Intell. Virtual Environ. Meas. Syst. Appl. Proc.* 3528725544 (Piscataway, NJ: IEEE) 1–5

[112] Wu S, Huang J, Huang D and Shi Y Q 2005 Efficiently self-synchronized audio watermarking for assured audio data transmission *IEEE Trans. Broadcast.* **51** 69–76

[113] Chen Y, Li Z, Wang L, Wang N and Hong B 2019 High-capacity reversible watermarking algorithm based on the region of interest of medical images *Int. Conf. Signal Process. Proc., ICSP (2018–August)* (Piscataway, NJ: IEEE) 1158–62

[114] Cayre F, Fontaine C and Furon T 2005 Watermarking security: theory and practice *IEEE Trans. Signal Process.* **53** 3976–87

[115] Tašić J and Adamović S 2017 Digital image watermarking techniques and biometrics data security: a review *Int. Scientific Conf. on Information Technology and Data Related Research* pp 55–62

[116] Swanson M D, Kobayashi M and Tewfik A H 1998 Multimedia data-embedding and watermarking technologies *Proc. IEEE* **86** 1064–87

[117] Rana P, Mittal U and Chawla P 2020 Medical images security using watermarking, hashing and RGB displacement *ICRITO 2020—IEEE 8th Int. Conf. on Reliability, Infocom Technologies and Optimization (Trends and Future Directions)* (Piscataway, NJ: IEEE) pp 532–6

[118] Li D, Deng L, Bhooshan Gupta B, Wang H and Choi C 2019 A novel CNN based security guaranteed image watermarking generation scenario for smart city applications *Inf. Sci.* **479** 432–47

[119] Maier A, Lorch B and Riess C 2020 Toward reliable models for authenticating multimedia content: detecting resampling artifacts with Bayesian neural networks *2020 IEEE Int. Conf. on Image Processing (ICIP)* (Piscataway, NJ: IEEE) pp 1251–5

[120] Centeno M P, Van Moorsel A and Castruccio S 2018 Smartphone continuous authentication using deep learning autoencoders *Proc.—2017 15th Annual Conf. on Privacy, Security and Trust, PST 2017* (Piscataway, NJ: IEEE) pp 147–55

[121] Ferdowsi A and Saad W 2017 Deep learning-based dynamic watermarking for secure signal authentication in the internet of things *2018 IEEE International Conference on Communications (ICC)* (Piscataway, NJ: IEEE) pp 1–6

[122] Qiu X, Du Z and Sun X 2019 Artificial intelligence-based security authentication: applications in wireless multimedia networks *IEEE Access* **7** 172004–11

Chapter 8

New lightweight image encryption algorithm for the Internet of Things and wireless multimedia sensor networks

Amina Msolli, Abdelhamid Helali, Hassen Maaref and Ridha Mghaieth

The development of technologies is heading towards the Internet of Things (IoT). In recent years, connected objects have experienced real progress in our daily lives, in our homes, in our working environment and even in cities. Everything is becoming smart. Now, we note that the evolution of the IoT is generated by the origin of the wireless sensor network (WSN). The large-scale deployment of connected objects or sensors and transversal applications is integrating security needs. Cryptography can be used to provide authenticity, confidentiality and integrity. Using traditional security mechanisms can quickly deplete energy from objects due to limited resources. With this in mind, we present the following chapter: given the growing concerns relating to energy consumption and the limitation of the calculation of objects, it is important to provide security solutions that are less costly in terms of resource consumption while aiming to reduce the execution time. To this end, our main contribution relates to the realization of a lightweight encryption algorithm for the IoT and wireless image sensor networks (WISNs). We apply different modifications to the advanced encryption standard (AES) algorithm to make it lightweight and applicable to IoT. Thus, to validate our work and show the safety of our algorithm, we evaluate the simulation performances. We show that our proposed algorithm is safe and efficient.

8.1 Introduction

Recent evolutions in society are based on techniques increasingly oriented towards communication, image and mobility. All of this development could not be achieved without an evolution in the field of wireless communication and mobile computing is gaining more and more popularity. The advanced technologies of micro-electronics, micro-mechanics, and wireless communication in the development of sensors;

cheaper, more powerful, autonomous, with self-organizing capability and their large-scale uses, the aim of which is to disseminate in an open environment to capture, collect and route data to the base station, offers a new network called WSN. This network has realized several applications that are possible to implement in many fields such as the army, medicine, environment and home automation. The development of technologies is heading towards the IoT. In recent years, connected objects have experienced real progress in our daily lives, in our homes, in our working environment and even in cities. Everything is becoming smart and intelligent: objects, houses, buildings, factories, cities, etc. At the moment, we note that the evolution of the IoT is generated by its origin of the WSN.

The renovation and miniaturization of micro-cameras and microphones has evolved rapidly in recent years, similar to the evolution of mobile phones. These components increase the performance of speed and signal quality without increasing production cost. Today, we are considering complementary metal oxide semiconductor micro-cameras in the form of adaptable sensor boards with wireless nodes. WSNs are attracting more and more attention when the sensors are furnished with cameras and mouthpieces. In this case, the WSN can collect scalar information as well as picture, sound and video vectors. Thus, the WSN is alluded to as a wireless multimedia sensor network (WMSN) [1–7]. In general, instantaneous detection and transmission of images is more common than detection and transmission of video data streams in most applications, resulting in the reach of WISNs [6, 8]. The wireless picture sensor network, which collects vector information from a surveillance field, operates on similar standards to the WSN, however, the handling and transmission are more difficult because of the immense measure of data to process with respect to scalar data.

Multimedia data is largely stored in different media and exchanged over different kinds of networks (such as IoT and WMSN). Often, this data contains private or confidential data or sometimes even monetary interests. For instance, smartphone safety dangers can be countered by biometric distinguishing proof. Admittance to these smartphones will be restricted to proprietors who will be recognized by their identity picture. Therefore, picture encryption is a generally contemplated discipline.

Thus, there is large-scale deployment of connected objects or sensor nodes and transversal applications integrating security needs. Data security concerns in IoT and WISN networks are faced with objects or sensors with reduced volume, restricted storage capacity and most importantly, restricted battery power. The design of a cipher algorithm should meet these limitations, creating a tradeoff between safety on the one hand and rapidity and energy consumption on the other to increase the life of the networks. The sort of data gathered by wireless objects or sensors can be temperature, brightness or also an image that is a more complex entity to encrypt. Using traditional security mechanisms can quickly deplete energy from objects or sensors due to limited resources. Consequently, several fields of research have emerged in recent years offering security solutions capable of remedying the shortcomings of sensor nodes and the vulnerabilities of the communication medium. Cryptography can be used to provide authenticity, confidentiality and integrity. In the case of the image, the extra burden for the transmission of a lot of information ought to likewise be considered.

With this in mind, we present the following chapter: given the growing concerns relating to energy consumption and the limitation of the calculation of objects, it is important to provide security solutions that are less costly in terms of resource consumption while aiming to reduce the execution time. To this end, our main contribution relates to the realization of a lightweight encryption algorithm for the IoT and WISNs. We apply different modifications to the AES algorithm to make it lightweight and applicable to IoT and WISN. Thus, to validate our work and show the safety of our algorithm, we introduce various safety analyses, for which we evaluate the simulation performances. In addition, we show that our proposed algorithm is a safe, efficient and capable solution to integrate into the IoT.

After the introduction, the chapter begins with the study of cryptographic primitives, highlighting the attacks and the level of security in cryptanalysis. We then present the encryption systems to protect network communications. Two subsections are presented: we show symmetric cryptography by studying stream and block cipher. We explain the main solutions from the literature and the different encryption modes. Second, we demonstrate asymmetric encryption. In the third part, we present our proposal for a lightweight security encryption algorithm for IoT and WSN. We evaluate our proposal in terms of statistical, differential analysis and we compare it to the AES standard. We end the evaluation with a comparison of our proposal with the AES algorithm in terms of analysis of the computation speed. This chapter ends with a conclusion.

8.2 Cryptographic primitives

The lack of a security mechanism allows adversaries to carry out multiple attacks. These are augmented with a sensor network that relies on wireless communication in a hostile environment. Until now, most security mechanisms require cryptography as the most secure solution to protect data. Cryptography is to allow two entities to communicate via a public network so that a third party listening is unable to understand the content of the messages exchanged. The use of cryptographic means one must render illegitimate information collected on the public channel inoperative. The use of cryptography is fundamental when the confidentiality of communications must not suffer from any flaws. Nevertheless, there are attacks that take advantage of the vulnerabilities of cryptography systems to deduce clear data or to find the keys used, these attacks are part of the science of cryptanalysis. In this part, we introduce the science of cryptanalysis by indicating the various most well known attacks, and then we approach cryptographic systems.

8.2.1 Cryptanalysis

Cryptanalysis is the science (theoretical or technical) of reconstructing the plaintext without knowing the key with which the text was encrypted. The goal is to provide either the plain text or the key.

8.2.1.1 Cryptographic attacks

We indicate in this part the most well known attacks on cryptography. The cryptanalyst tries to retrieve as much information as possible about the cryptographic system used or the messages exchanged in order to exploit them in the attacks:

- ciphertext attack only;
- plaintext attack known;
- chosen plaintext attack;
- adaptive selected plaintext attack;
- chosen ciphertext attack;
- chosen key attack.

When the cryptanalyst does not have any information to implement the attacks mentioned above, they can try all possible combinations to find the encryption key. This is known as a 'brute force attack'.

8.2.1.2 Security level of an algorithm

The security level of encryption algorithms differs according to various criteria. We cite the most important criteria by grouping them under three categories:

- probably safe algorithm;
- unconditionally safe algorithm;
- algorithm invulnerable by calculation.

The choice of an encryption algorithm for a given application remains a problem to be solved before any security architecture proposal. This choice depends primarily on the level of security requested and the constraints of the WSN.

8.2.2 Cryptography system

In this section, we present the different cryptographic systems used to protect the communications of traditional wired and wireless networks. Cryptography is a technique that is essentially based on mathematical and algorithmic concepts. It allows one to transmit confidential data on an unsecured medium without an intruder being able to discover the content. This data will be decrypted only by the recipient or the one knowing the encryption key. Cryptography guarantees, among other things, various security services such as confidentiality, authenticity and integrity in data and communication schemes. We start with the symmetric cryptography system and then we detail the asymmetric cryptography system.

8.2.2.1 Symmetric cryptography

Symmetric cryptography is the oldest encryption algorithm. The problem with this kind of cryptography is that it uses a public encryption algorithm, that is, the key must be secret. The encryption applies at the level of the bits constituting the message by using an elementary logical operation (XOR or exclusive OR) of these bits and those of the key. We distinguish two types of algorithms: block cipher algorithms which take n bits as input and restore n bits, and stream cipher algorithms which work bit by bit.

Principle: Cryptography that is based on the use of a single encryption key is called 'symmetric', also called 'secret', to mean that the security of communicating entities is based on the fact that this key is known only by entities that communicate with each other. As an example of symmetric encryption, when the sender wishes to send a text to the recipient for this, it shares with them, a secret key. With this key, the sender will be able to encrypt the text to be sent to the recipient. In turn, the recipient will be able to decrypt the text using the same encryption algorithm and the secret key.

8.2.2.1.1 Stream encryption
Stream cipher algorithms convert plain text to cipher text, bit by bit by combining by an operation OR-exclusive the plain text bit stream with a random bit stream. On the decryption side, the bits of the cipher text are combined by the reverse of the operation OR-exclusive with the same random stream of bits to find the bits of the clear text. Stream encryption algorithms are often used in telecommunications because they do not propagate transmission errors unlike block encryption, they are fast and often have very compact implementations.

8.2.2.1.2 Block encryption
Block cipher algorithms are among the most widely used algorithms in cryptographic systems. Block encryption algorithms are characterized by a breakdown of data into blocks of generally fixed size. The blocks are then encrypted one after the other according to different modes (one can cite among the most used modes ECB (Electronic Code Book), OFB (Output Feedback) or CBC (Cipher Block Chaining) [9]). The two most well known examples of algorithms are DES (data encryption standard) and AES (advanced encryption standard).

8.2.2.1.3 Symmetric encryption algorithms
Symmetric key encryption solutions are exploitable within sensor networks and provide a real solution for network security [10]. However, if symmetric key encryption is possible within sensor networks [11, 12], the total security of this type of solution remains to be proven.

DES is a low complication encryption algorithm that utilizes a little 56-bit key [13]. Despite certain disadvantages, DES has been studied more extensively in scholarly world, and has enabled the development of current cryptanalysis systems. In addition, international data encryption algorithm (IDEA) is a block encryption algorithm intended to replace the DES algorithm [14]. IDEA exploits both confusion and diffusion of data, which define Shannon's principle, to produce the ciphertext using a 128-bit key. The algorithm performs the following operations: OR exclusive (XOR), modulo 2^{16} addition and modulo $2^{16} + 1$ multiplication. Since operations are done with 16-bit blocks, the algorithm is very capable in 16-bit microprocessors, the latter common to that of a sensor node.

In this section we present the standard block encryption algorithm AES, which is quite possibly the most famous symmetric cryptography algorithm. Otherwise called Rijndael, it is used in large-scale systems. The AES block cipher algorithm has been proposed as an encryption algorithm in the IEEE 802.15.4 standard to secure information at the MAC layer in transit over wireless sensor networks. However, this encryption is performed at the hardware level by the transceiver module.

There are other symmetric algorithms in the literature such as RC5 ('Ron's Code' or 'Rivest's Cipher'), TEA (Tiny Encryption Algorithm), Blowfish...

8.2.2.1.4 Encryption modes

Encryption modes are strategies for utilizing block encryption algorithms. The encryption algorithm is joined with a sequence of simple processes to improve security without penalizing the proficiency of the algorithm. This mix is known as a cryptographic mode.

- *Electronic Code Book (ECB)*
  This is the simplest mode, the plain message is subdivided into several blocks which are encrypted, applying the encryption algorithm, independently block by block. The big flaw of this method is that two blocks with the same content will be encrypted in the same way, formally, it comes as

$$C_i = E_k(M) \tag{8.1}$$

where C_i is the ith block of the ciphertext, E is the encryption algorithm, k is the key and M is the clear text. For these reasons, this mode is strongly discouraged in any cryptographic application. The only advantage it can provide is quick access to any area of the encrypted text and the ability to decipher only part of the data.

- *Cipher Block Chaining (CBC)*
  In this encryption mode, the blocks are linked together, hence the term 'chaining'. There is therefore an avalanche effect where each input block (clear text) is linked to the other (old encrypted output) by an exclusive OR. So for the first block, the initialization vector (VI) can be a password, a 'timestamp', etc. It is used in certain authentication phases.

- *Cipher Feedback (CFB)*
  The plain message is appended to the output of the encrypted block. The result serves as 'feedback' for the next step. The register can use any number of bits: 1, 8, 64 bits (most often 64 bits). It is used for stream encryption as well as for authentication.

- *Output FeedBack (OFB)*
  Feedback is independent of the clear message. Any mechanism is therefore independent of the m_i and c_i blocks where m_i is the ith block of the clear text and c_i is the ith block of the cipher text. This is a variant of a Vernam encryption with reuse of the key and the IV (vector initialization). It is used in the stream encryption frame on a noisy channel.

8.2.2.2 Asymmetric cryptography

Asymmetric cryptography or public key cryptography uses a pair of keys, not just one. It not only enables the encryption of information but also guarantees the authentication of the authors of the messages by using the digital signature using a private key encryption and the use of digital certificates. At the beginning of this part, we explain how asymmetric cryptography works.

Principle: Asymmetric cryptography, otherwise known as 'public key' cryptography, depends on the use of a pair of encryption keys to encrypt/decrypt, sign/ verify. The public key is extracted and then published through directories, for example, while the private key is kept secret with the user. A message encoded by the public key is decrypted by the private key, and vice versa. When the sender wants to send a text to the recipient, they will need their public key in order to encrypt the text. The recipient will be able to decrypt, using their private key, the received text using the same encryption algorithm used by the sender.

8.2.2.2.1 *Asymmetric encryption algorithms*

Some authors [7] contend for the utilization of symmetric encryption in WSNs rather than asymmetric encryption, because of the high computational overheads forced by asymmetric algorithms. However, some work has demonstrated that it will be possible to use asymmetric cryptography in a WSN [7, 15].

A short description of the most pertinent asymmetric encryption algorithms used in wireless sensor network applications is as follows:

- RSA (Rivest Shamir Adleman) [16]: The principle of RSA is based on the difficulty of decomposing a large number into its primary elements. The RSA key sizes recommended today to meet security requirements are at least 1024 bits (size of both the public key and the secret key). Note also that it is conceivable to build a signature algorithm based on the same principle, becoming one of the main innovations of public key cryptography [17].
- ECC (elliptic curve cryptography): is based on the trouble of inverting the discrete logarithm on an elliptical curve. As for RSA, cryptography based on elliptical curves allows the construction of encryption algorithms and signature schemes. One of the major advantages of using this form of cryptography is the small size of the keys used. Indeed, using a 160-bit key in an algorithm based on ECC is equivalent to an RSA key of size 1024 bits.

Typically, conventional asymmetric cryptography algorithms have high computational overheads, needing more handling time. Based on this hypothesis, according to [7, 18], the majority of the works appear to guarantee that public key cryptography is not possible for WSN applications. Nonetheless, through the long term, analyses, as carried out in [15, 19], have demonstrated the opposite, where proficient algorithms and with sensible key sizes show the achievability of asymmetric cryptography for wireless sensor networks.

However, there are several advantages to using symmetric encryption rather than asymmetric encryption. First, asymmetric encryption is slower than symmetric encryption [20, 21]. It requires a superior processing capability to encrypt and decrypt the contents of messages.

Moreover, for asymmetric encryption, the initial transmission of the public key on an unsecured channel exposes man-in-the-middle attacks (intercepting communications between two parties, without either party being able to suspect that the communication channel between them has been compromised). To guard against this risk, a public key infrastructure is generally used.

Also, for an equal degree of safety, the keys should be no longer than for symmetric encryption. Ease of implementation is more important in symmetric encryption because of the management of a single key [22, 23]. Finally, unlike symmetric encryption, asymmetric is vulnerable to a 'known clear text' attack, or even to an 'intermediary' attack (a hacker can substitute a public key with his own, interrupt and decrypt messages, then decrypt them with the right public key and send them back).

8.3 Proposed lightweight algorithm

The security concerns of multimedia data in IoT and WSN networks are confronted with objects and sensors with reduced volume, restricted storage capacity and most importantly, restricted battery power. The design of a cipher algorithm should meet these limitations, which creates a tradeoff between safety on the one hand and rapidity and energy consumption on the other. The solutions proposed in the literature use methods and standards in a way that does not fully meet the needs of these networks. We explain in this part the principle of our contribution of an encryption algorithms designed for images where we focused on modifying the standard AES algorithm in different location and block to maintain the introduction of operations broadcast and confusion and on the simplicity of the proposed algorithm. We demonstrate the effectiveness of our contributions: lightweight encryption algorithm with modified AES (shift-column transformation instead of mix column transformation), through a security analysis.

Our proposed encryption algorithm operates on a 16-byte internal state which consists of a 4 × 4 matrix. Initially, the input undergoes an Add-Round Key function. Then, the byte ordering relies mainly on a round function. This round function is divided into four sub-functions with the following organization:

- Shift-Columns (SC): Ensures the notion of broadcast, as defined by Shannon. Each byte of the column is shifted with an offset downwards: for the first column, there is an offset of three bytes. For the second column, the bytes in the column are shifted to two. For the third column, there is a single offset and there is no offset for the fourth column.
- Sub Bytes (SB) which ensures the notion of confusion as defined by Shannon. Each byte is processed independently of the others. Each byte is transformed by a non-linear function S (S-box) designed to withstand linear and differential cryptanalysis.
- Shift Rows (SR): Shifts each byte of row j by j steps to the left.
- Add Round Key (ARK) which adds a round key (derived from the initial key) to the current internal state.

The number of rounds as well as the derivation of round keys depends on the size of the key used for the AES, the 128-bit version being the most compact. However, in the last round there is no Shift-Column sub-function.

And finally, our lightweight algorithm proposal is installed in a Output FeedBack (OFB) Mode process to keep the streaming image transmission.

8.4 Safety assessment

8.4.1 Statistical analysis

A statistical analysis was acted to demonstrate the confusion and broadcast properties of the proposed approach, which permits it to powerfully resist statistical attacks. In particular, the histograms of the original images and the encrypted images are checked and the correlation coefficients of a few adjacent pixel pairs are calculated.

The experiments were carried out on three test images: clown, Panda, and an HD image. The results of images encryption with the proposed algorithm show a total invisibility of the images with different dimensions (320×200 pixels, 256×256 pixels and 1920×1080 pixels, respectively). Figures 8.1, 8.2 and 8.3 show a comparison of visibility between the proposed algorithm and the AES standard.

8.4.1.1 Uniformity analysis

The first metric to evaluate the robustness of the proposed algorithm against statistical attacks is the histogram. For a secure image encryption algorithm, it is essential that the histogram results of plaintext and ciphertext images are completely

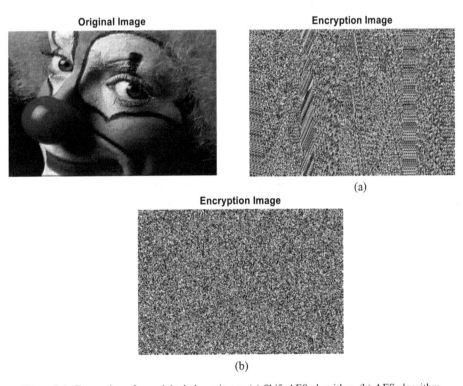

Figure 8.1. Encryption of an original clown image (a) Shift-AES algorithm, (b) AES algorithm.

algorithm

Figure 8.2. Encryption of an original panda image with (a) Shift-AES algorithm, (b) AES algorithm.

different from each other. Several clear images were chosen and their consistent encrypted images were calculated using diverse secret keys. All present comparative results, and it is displayed that the histograms of the encrypted images are quite uniform and that they are significantly different from those of the conforming original image. By way of example, in figures 8.4(b), 8.5(b) and 8.6(b), the standard images of clown, Panda and HD image defined by a matrix of 320 × 200 pixels, 256 × 256 pixels and 1920 × 1080 pixels, respectively, with its encrypted format with the proposed algorithm, and the corresponding histograms are shown in figures 8.4(a), 8.5(a) and 8.6(a).

8.4.1.2 Correlation analysis

Correlation analysis may reflect the diffusion effect of the encryption system knowing that a secure system reduces the correlation between pixels in the image. An image with its significant visual gratified is characterized by its strong correlation and redundancy between neighboring pixels, whether in horizontal, vertical or diagonal directions. A well-designed cryptosystem must hide such relationships between adjacent pixels and show zero correlation [24]. To assess the immunity of a given cryptosystem to this type of attack, the first N pairs of neighboring pixels are randomly selected from the clear image and its corresponding encryption version in

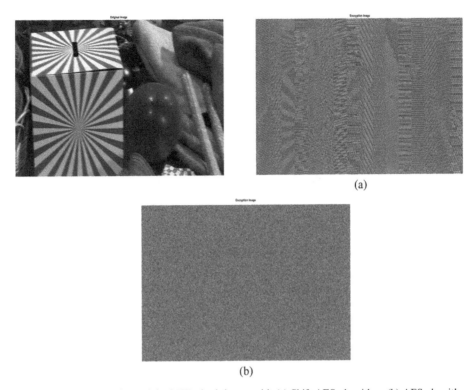

(a)

(b)

Figure 8.3. Encryption of an original HD cheek image with (a) Shift-AES algorithm, (b) AES algorithm.

each direction. Next, adjacent pixel correlations in a given image are quantified by calculating the r_{xy} correlation coefficient of each pair using the accompanying formulas (equations (8.2), (8.3), (8.4), and (8.5)):

$$r_{xy} = \frac{\text{cov}(x, y)}{\sqrt{D(x)} \times \sqrt{D(y)}} \tag{8.2}$$

$$\text{cov}(x, y) = \frac{1}{N} \sum_{i=1}^{N} (x_i - E(x))(y_i - E(y)) \tag{8.3}$$

$$E(x) = \frac{1}{N} \sum_{i=1}^{N} x_i \tag{8.4}$$

$$D(x) = \frac{1}{N} \sum_{i=1}^{N} (x_i - E(x))^2 \tag{8.5}$$

where x_i and y_i represent the gray level values of the ith pair of neighboring pixels chosen in the image, and N is the integer number of samples.

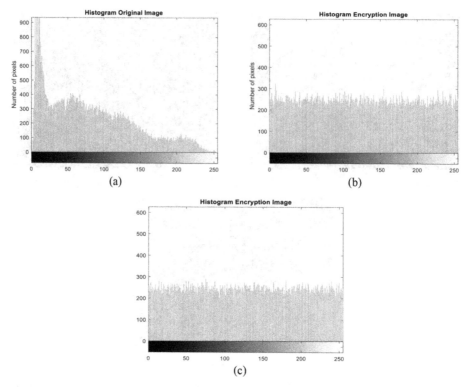

Figure 8.4. Histogram (a) of an original clown image (b) Shift-AES algorithm, (c) AES algorithm.

The results of r_{xy} calculation are given in table 8.1. It emerges from these results that the correlation coefficients for the clear images (clown, panda and HD) are close to 1, which means that the pixels are strongly correlated. However, for the encrypted images, the correlation coefficients are close to 0, which proves that there is a weak correlation and therefore no similarity.

Further, we used the Panda image to test the correlation between adjacent pixels in the vertical direction, in figure 8.7 for the first image and the encoded image separately. From the distribution diagram contrast, we see that on account of the original image, the adjacent pixels have solid correlations and line up with the first bisector, but in the case of the encrypted image, adjacent pixels are dissipated haphazardly. In general, the observation of profoundly dispersed pixels alludes to a robust algorithm for any statistical attack.

8.4.2 Sensitivity test: robustness against differential attacks

For the sake of secret key recovery, an attacker could attempt to distinguish any notable information between the normal image and its encryption version, by detecting the impact of a change of one pixel on the entire output of the encryption system. A well-designed cryptosystem is a system in which a minor change of its simple image results in a major transformation of its encrypted image and, therefore,

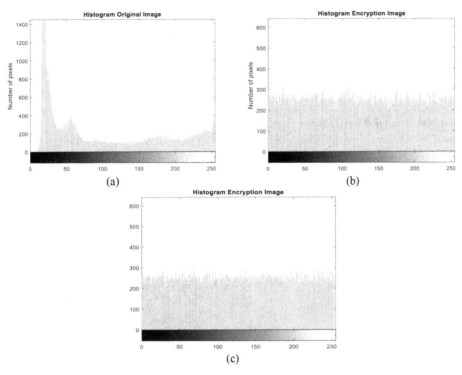

Figure 8.5. Histogram (a) of an original panda image (b) Shift-AES algorithm, (c) AES algorithm.

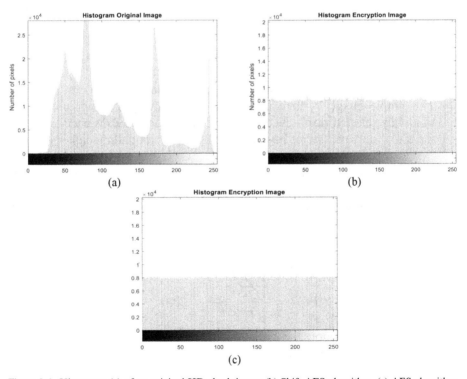

Figure 8.6. Histogram (a) of an original HD cheek image (b) Shift-AES algorithm, (c) AES algorithm.

Table 8.1. Correlation between pixels.

	Shift-AES algorithm					
	Clown		Panda		HD image	
	Original	Ciphered	Original	Ciphered	Original	Ciphered
Horizontal correlation	0.9428	−0.0391	0.9843	−0.0392	0.8046	0.0253
Vertical correlation	0.9785	−0.1169	0.9881	0.0982	0.9900	0.1131

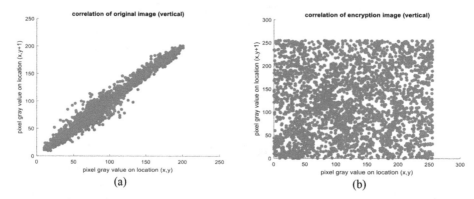

(a)   (b)

Figure 8.7. Vertical correlation (a) of an original panda image (b) of a panda image encrypted with the Shift-AES algorithm.

this type of attack is rendered null. To perform the experiment, the following procedure should be adopted:

- The clear image P_1 is encrypted to have a C_1 encryption image.
- The simple image P_2 here is obtained by applying a minor change to a randomly selected pixel, the corrupted ordinary image P_2 is encrypted under the use of the same secret key to produce the corresponding cipher image C_2.

Influence is measured quantitatively using the two commonly used metrics: NPCR and UACI.

- Number of pixel change rate (NPCR): It computes the number of pixel variances between two encrypted images below C_1 and C_2, using the following formula (equation (8.6)):

$$NPCR = \frac{\sum_{i=1}^{N}\sum_{j=1}^{M}D(i, j)}{H \times L} \times 100 \tag{8.6}$$

where N and M denote the length and tallness of the image, respectively, and $D(i, j)$ is defined as follows (equation (8.7)):

$$D(i, j) = \begin{cases} 0 & \text{if } C_1(i, j) = C_2(i, j) \\ 1 & \text{if } C_1(i, j) \neq C_2(i, j) \end{cases} \tag{8.7}$$

- Unified average change intensity (UACI): It calculates the average intensity of the differences between two numbered images C_1 and C_2, using the following formula (equation (8.8)):

$$UACI = \sum_{i=1}^{N}\sum_{j=1}^{M} \frac{|C_1(i, j) - C_2(i, j)|}{H \times L \times 255} \times 100 \tag{8.8}$$

To test the sensitivity of the key, two indexes are used: the NPCR and the UACI.

Table 8.2 presents the results obtained for the experimental secret key sensitivity values for the different encryption images, the NPCR and UACI values obtained by applying our Shift-AES approach compare with the AES algorithm. It should be noted that our satisfactory encryption approach is required to achieve the NPCR and UACI above 0.9949 and 0.3061, respectively, for the HD image. Based on the results shown in table 8.2, the NPCR and UACI values of the affected encrypted images verify the conditions.

8.4.3 Calculations speed analysis

In order to assess the difficulty of the computation, we simulate the encryption processing time using the proposed algorithm. Our simulation results are presented in table 8.3. To compare, we also list the coding processing time of the AES standard. As observed below, the proposed algorithm speed is a little more accelerated than the speed of AES standard, the reason is that the proposed

Table 8.2. NPCR and UACI to test key sensitivity.

	Shift-AES algorithm			AES algorithm		
	Clown	Panda	HD image	Clown	Panda	HD image
NPCR	0.9949	0.9949	0.9949	0.9959	0.9959	0.9960
UACI	0.3477	0.3734	0.3061	0.3480	0.3744	0.3065

Table 8.3. Operating time.

	Shift-AES algorithm			AES algorithm		
	Clown	Panda	HD image	Clown	Panda	HD image
Encryption time (ms)	1.366	1.482	8.794	8.517	8.504	15.948
Decryption time (ms)	1.288	1.283	8.645	8.372	8.353	16.601

algorithm includes a Shift-Column function block, which replaces the MixColumn function consuming more execution time. However, our algorithm is safer than the AES standard for the Iot and the WMSN, knowing that the computation speed of our proposed algorithm varies by 1/8 of the execution time of the AES standard. In other words, we simultaneously achieve security and speed resulting in longer network lifespan.

8.5 Conclusion

This chapter deals with the design and realization of a new encryption algorithm proposed in OFB mode for the preservation of image content during transmission and security at the same time. This proposal aims to improve the encryption performance compared to what exists in the scientific literature. Thus, a new approach is based on the modification of the MixColumn function by another transformation, in which its conditions retain the same Shannon principle and consume less computing time.

The robustness and efficiency of the proposed algorithm are evaluated against all commonly considered cryptographic attacks, including: differential attacks, statistical attacks in addition to other performance issues. Indeed, the in-depth analyses and tests validated the robustness of our algorithm compared to well-known cryptographic attacks, and highlighted the improvements in security obtained and the reduction in computation time compared to some existing methods.

References

[1] Kalaivani K and Sivakumar B R 2012 Surey on multimedia data security *Int. J. Model. Optim.* **2** 36–41

[2] Viral Patel and Krunal Panchal 2014 Survey on security in multimedia traffic in wireless sensor network *Int. J. Eng. Develop. Res. (IJEDR)* **2** 3906–10

[3] Akyildiz I F, Melodia T and Chowdhury K R 2007 A survey on wireless multimedia sensor networks *Comput. Netw.* **51** 921–60

[4] Misra S, Reisslein M and Xue G 2008 A survey of multimedia streaming in wireless sensor networks *Commun. Surv. Tutor., IEEE* **10** 18–39

[5] Xian T, Yu C and Chen F 2014 Secure MQ coder: an efficient way to protect JPEG 2000 images in wireless multimedia sensor networks *Signal Process. Image Commun.* **29** 1015–27

[6] Aziz S M and Pham D M 2013 Energy efficient image transmission in wireless multimedia sensor networks *IEEE Commun. Lett.* **17** 1084–7

[7] Guerrero-Zapata M, Zilan R, Barcelo-Ordinas J M, Bicakci K and Tavli B 2010 The future of security in wireless multimedia sensor networks *Telecommun. Syst.* **45** 77–91

[8] Almalkawi I, Zapata M, Al-Karaki J and Morillo-Pozo J 2010 Wireless multimedia sensor networks: current trends and future directions *Sensors* **10** 6662–717

[9] Douglas S 2002 *Cryptography: Theory and Practice* 2nd edn (Boca Raton, FL: CRC/C&H)

[10] Nour El Deen Mahmoud K N E, Taha M H N, Mahdy H E N and Saroit I A 2013 A Secure energy efficient schema for wireless multimedia sensor networks *CiiT Int. J. Wirel. Commun.* **5** 235–46

[11] Wang Y, Attebury G and Ramamurthy B 2013 Security issues in wireless sensor networks: a survey *Int. J. Future Gen. Commun. Netw.* **6** 97–116

[12] Wang Q X, Xu T and Wu P 2011 Application research of the AES encryption algorithm on the engine anti-theft system *Proc. of IEEE Int. Conf. on Vehicular Electronics and Safety (Beijing, China)* pp 25–9

[13] Mandal A K, Parakash C and Tiwari A 2012 Performance evaluation of cryptographic algorithms: DES and AES *Proc. of IEEE Students' Conf. on Electrical, Electronics and Computer Science (Bhopal, India)* pp 1–2

[14] Modugu R, Yong-Bin K and Minsu C 2010 Design and performance measurement of efficient IDEA (Int. Data Encryption Algorithm) crypto-hardware using novel modular arithmetic components *Proc. of IEEE Instrumentation and Measurement Technology Conf. (Austin, TX, 3–6 May)* pp 1222–7

[15] Sen J 2009 A survey on wireless sensor network security *Int. J. Commun. Netw. Inf. Secur.* **1** 55–78

[16] Al-Hamami A H and Aldariseh I A 2012 Enhanced method for RSA cryptosystem algorithm *Proc. of Int. Conf. on Advanced Computer Science Applications and Technologies (Kuala Lumpur, Malaysia, 26–28 2012 November)* pp 402–8

[17] Al-Haija Q A, Tarayrah M A, Al-Qadeeb H and Al-Lwaimi A 2014 A tiny RSA cryptosystem based on Arduino microcontroller useful for small-scale networks *Procedia Comput. Sci.* **34** 639–46

[18] Gaubatz G, Kaps J P, Ozturk E and Sunar B 2005 State of the art in ultra-low power public key cryptography for wireless sensor networks *Proc. of IEEE Int. Conf. on Pervasive Computing and Communications Workshops (Kauai Island, HI, 8–12 March 2005)* pp 146–50

[19] Lenstra A K and Verhuel E R 2001 Selecting cryptographic key sizes *J. Cryptol.* **14** 255–93

[20] Msolli A, Helali A and Maaref H 2018 New security approach in real-time wireless multimedia sensors network *Int. J. Comput. Electr. Eng.* **72** 910–25

[21] Msolli A, Ameur H, Helali A and Maaref H 2017 Secure encryption for wireless multimedia sensors network *Int. J. Adv. Comput. Sci. Appl.* **8** 330–37

[22] Msolli A, Helali A and Maaref H 2016 Image encryption with the AES algorithm in wireless sensor network *2nd Int. Conf. on Advanced Technologies for Signal and Image Processing - ATSIP'2016 (March 21–24 2016)* pp 41–5

[23] Msolli A, Helali A and Maaref H 2016 Symmetric encryption algorithm image for wireless multimedia sensor network *Proc. of Engineering & Technology (PET) IPCO-2016* pp 107–13

[24] del Rey A M and Sanchez G R 2015 A protocol to encrypt digital images using chaotic maps and memory cellular automata *Log. J. IGPL* **23** 485–94

Chapter 9

Applying the capabilities of machine learning for multimedia security: an analysis

Suja Cherukullapurath Mana and T Sasipraba

The advancements in information communication technologies pave the way for tremendous usage of multimedia. Media communication has a huge impact on our lives nowadays. Due to the growth of electronic media and internet technologies, all our daily life activities are highly influenced by the media. Also there are huge amounts of public data available on the internet and keeping these data secured is a challenge of the era. Social networks also pave the way for a huge amount of multimedia data available on internet. Safekeeping this data is crucial to avoid any misuse. As the usage of multimedia increases, so do the illegitimate activities to bypass the security. So security of multimedia is an important research area and many advancements are happening to ensure the security of multimedia systems.

Traditional security mechanisms are insufficient in ensuring the security of multimedia data. This chapter analyzes how we can utilize the capabilities of machine learning algorithms to ensure media security. Machine learning (ML) algorithms are highly capable of detecting any malicious activities happening on the web. Both supervised and unsupervised algorithms are available to detect various security threats. These algorithms can effectively analyse the network traffic and classify it. Multimedia network intrusion detection also can be efficiently done by ML based implementations. Due to the robust feature extraction capability of such algorithms, the amount of preprocessing needed also can be effectively reduced. Scalability and adaptability are also a point of consideration while selecting the suitable security mechanisms. This chapter discusses the effectiveness of machine learning in ensuring multimedia security. Various ML based security mechanisms applicable for multimedia are being studied in detail and the advantages of using ML based techniques over traditional security mechanisms are also analysed.

doi:10.1088/978-0-7503-3735-9ch9

9.1 Introduction

Multimedia is being used in every field of life nowadays. Some of the key application areas of multimedia are in business, education, the entertainment field, transportation field etc. Most of the companies depend on the capabilities of multimedia to connect with their customers. Advertisements are the key way to promote the products. The influence of multimedia on promoting the business is huge. Similarly, in the education field multimedia is also being used to a great extent. Due to this prevailing pandemic situation, most of the educational institutions are working in an online mode. Educational institutions are exploring the capabilities of multimedia for the better dissimination of their content.

In the entertainment area multimedia animation features are heavily utilized to better entertain viewers. By applying capabilities of various graphics software, better visual experience can be achieved. In the transportation industry multimedia is also being utilized to create interactive maps and navigation systems. The diagram given below (figure 9.1) displays some of the application areas of multimedia systems.

As the amount of data handled by multimedia systems is huge and it is sensitive, security is an important point of consideration [1]. Various security measures are in place to safely store the data being used by multimedia systems. Various security algorithms are utilized to ensure that no unauthorized access to the multimedia data is occurring. This chapter performs an analysis on how various ML and deep learning algorithms can be utilized to provide better security for multimedia systems.

In the following sections the authors discuss ML, various ML algorithms and how effectively they can be utilized for multimedia security. Further, the chapter reviews how effectively ML algorithms can be applied for ensuring security in multimedia.

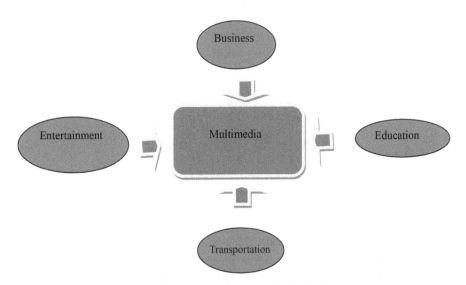

Figure 9.1. Application areas of multimedia.

9.2 Overview of machine learning

ML is a fast-growing field of data science. ML aims at providing machines with the capability to predict without being explicitly programmed. Scientists have developed a variety of ML algorithms. These algorithms are capable of automatically modeling and finding similarity patterns in datasets. This knowledge acquired by the ML system will then be utilized to predict the test data. The capabilities of ML algorithms can be effectively utilized to ensure multimedia data security. In this section the authors provide an overview of some of the ML algorithms which can be utilized for implementing multimedia security. In further sections we analyze how some of these algorithms can be utilized to ensure the security of multimedia systems.

ML algorithms are briefly classified into supervised ML algorithms and unsupervised ML algorithms. In supervised algorithms some labeled data set is already available. Some information about the system is already available and that information will be utilized to make future predictions. On the other hand in unsupervised algorithms no prior information about the system is already available. No labeled data will be there. The system has to learn from the data and make the prediction. For example, consider a scenario of classifying fruit based on the shape. In a supervised ML system some labeled data will be already available like long fruit with yellow color is banana, round red color is apple, small round shape with red or green color is grapes etc. So when new test data comes, the system will utilize these already known factors to classify the input. But in the case of unsupervised algorithms no such prior knowledge is there. The system has to learn and make the predictions. Examples for supervised learning algorithms are classification and regression. An example of unsupervised learning algorithms is clustering

There is also one more type of learning called reinforcement learning [2]. Through reinforcement learning the machine is being trained to make decisions in various environments. It helps the machine to make a sequence of decisions [2]. This model will employ agents who will consider the measure of rewards and punishment possible and try to maximize the number of rewards. Reinforcement learning helps to make good decisions in large complex environments.

The below given diagram (figure 9.2) displays the various categories of ML algorithms

Examples for supervised ML algorithms are classification and regression. Clustering is an example of unsupervised algorithm.

9.2.1 Classification

Classification is a process where the input data is divided into number of classes. Classification algorithms define models which can effectively classify the input data into various classes. Email spam detection is a classic example of classification algorithm. In this model it is trained on the basis of a large number of emails and that knowledge is utilized to classify the upcoming emails to spam or non-spam classes [3]. The primary function of classification algorithm is to find a mapping function that can effectively classify the input data into different output classes. They can be utilized to classify data into malicious and benign data. Classification

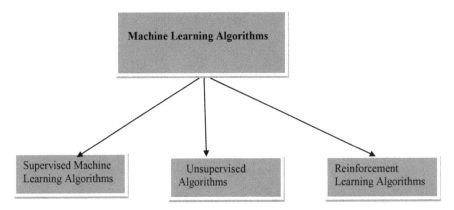

Figure 9.2. Types of ML algorithms.

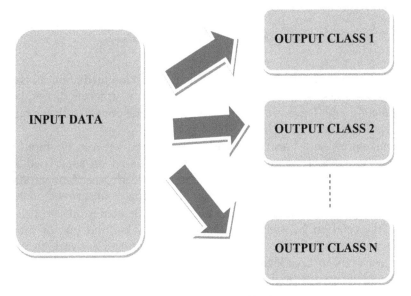

Figure 9.3. Overview of classification.

algorithms can be utilized in multimedia networks to classify the data. Support vector machine, K nearest neighbors, decision tree and naïve Bayesian are some of the famous classification algorithms.

Figure 9.3 displays an overview of classification. As shown in the figure, the input data will be classified into different output classes by the application of different classification algorithms. These classification algorithms can be utilized to classify malicious and benign multimedia data.

9.2.2 Regression

Regression mainly applies on continuous variables. It is used to find correlation between dependent and independent variables. Regression analysis can be effectively

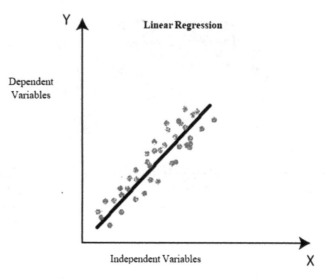

Figure 9.4. An illustration of linear regression.

applied on continuous data. It is highly efficient in making predictions in the case of continuous variables. Some of the applications are in weather prediction [4], house price prediction etc. There are different types of regressions like linear regression, logistic regression etc.

In linear regression a linear relationship is assumed between the input variable and output variable. It is an algorithm which is based on supervised learning. Through a linear relation it shows a relation between dependent variables and independent variables. Figure 9.4 shows an illustration of linear regression.

Logistic regression is used when the dependent variable is binary. It is used to illustrate the relation between one dependent variable and one or more independent variables. Generally, it is used to predict categorical variables. Logistic regression usually utilizes logic function to predict the result. Sigmoid function model is widely used in logistic regression. Figure 9.5 shows an illustration of logistic regression.

9.2.3 Deep learning

Deep learning is a subdivision of ML in which the model simulates the working of the human neural network. Deep learning networks imitate the working of human brain neurons to process data and make selections. Deep learning is an artificial intelligence (AI) function and it is used heavily in medical image processing, recommendation systems, animal species recognition etc. Deep learning is a subpart of AI and ML. Deep learning uses algorithms inspired by human neural network to process large amounts of data and make decisions. A deep learning network has many hidden layers which will extract the features and those features will be utilized to make the classifications. The name deep learning came from the presence of these deep layers.

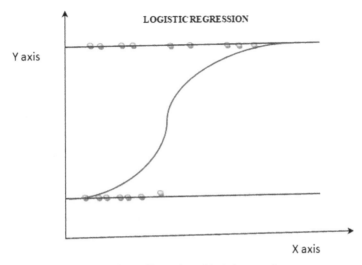

Figure 9.5. An illustration of logistic regression.

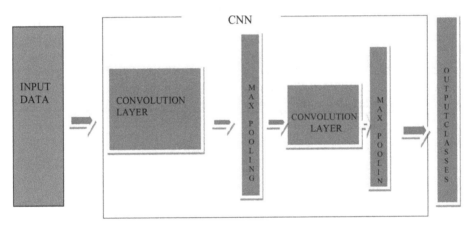

Figure 9.6. CNN architecture.

Convolution neural networks, recurrent neural networks, generative adversial networks, and back propagation are some of the efficient deep learning algorithms. All these deep learning algorithms have the capability of processing large amounts of unstructured data and extracting features from these unstructured data. Convolution neural networks are very efficient in image processing applications [5]. They can effectively extract features from the images through various hidden layers and can effectively perform the classification [6]. Maxpooling layer can be used to effectively extract features using maximum pooling.

Figure 9.6 shows the convolution neural network architecture consisting of convolution layers and maxpooling layers. Neural networks prove to be efficient in multimedia security implementations [7].

The next section of the chapter studies various ML and deep learning algorithms that can be applicable for multimedia security.

9.3 Machine learning algorithms for multimedia security

This section analyses how ML algorithms can be effectively utilized to provide security for multimedia systems. ML algorithms are highly capable of detecting anomalies that may be happening to multimedia systems and can predict any possibilities of security breach [8–10]. The ability of ML algorithms to make accurate prediction can be utilized to monitor the trends in multimedia systems and to identify any possible security threats [11]. This section reviews some of the studies which describe how ML and deep learning algorithms can be effectively implemented to provide security mechanisms in multimedia systems.

In one study named 'Retrival of illegal and objectionable multimedia' [12], the authors describe how support vector machine (SVM) algorithm and an X media analysis system can effectively detect illegal contents in multimedia. This paper [12] refers to X as illegal multimedia elements. This study implements a multimedia security system which provides an efficient system to monitor multimedia contents, digital rights monitoring and also ensures that the multimedia content is safe and appropriate to watch [12–14]. The architecture diagram of the proposed system [12] consists of three important components, namely code analyser, feature extractor and classifier. The authors [12] claim that the proposed system can effectively detect illegal contents in the multimedia transmitting through the internet and it is safe for kids. The architecture diagram is shown in figure 9.7

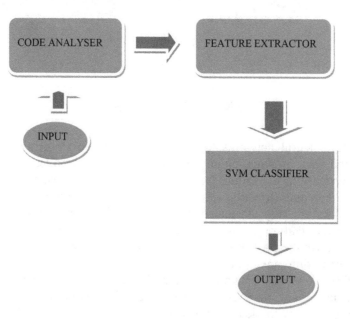

Figure 9.7. Architecture of an SVM based multimedia security system [12].

This proposed model in figure 9.7 utilizes MPEG 7 visual descriptor for feature extraction. The SVM algorithm is used for classification [12, 13]. The SVM algorithm will effectively classify the legitimate and illegitimate contents.

Another study [15] applies ML algorithms to detect anomalous messages in session initiation protocol (SIP) messages. These anomalous messages are capable of crashing the servers and can launch malicious activities remotely. All messages will be scanned by the ML algorithms by extracting features. From these extracted features the ML algorithm will decide whether the message is benign or malicious [15]. The system has been tested with real world data set and claims to obtain a high level of accuracy in prediction. This application is capable of detecting anomalies in SIP messages. The important steps involved in this proposed system are analysis of SIP messages, extracting features from this message, removing redundancy in features, and applying the ML algorithm to identify any malicious messages. Different machine learning algorithms like SVM, naïve Bayesian algorithm, inductive rule learner algorithm are being used by this system [15]. The high level architecture discussed in the paper [14] is shown in figure 9.8

In another study [16], the authors proposed a deep learning based anomaly detection method for software defined networks (SDNs). A hybrid deep learning based anomaly detection model is proposed in this study [16]. The paper suggests a solution for social multimedia network related anomalies. An ensemble approach with SVM and restricted Boltzmann machine is being used here. Improvement in the SVM algorithm is achieved by gradient descent approach. An SDN assisted routing scheme has been designed for the distribution of contents. The anomaly detection module of the proposed system [16] utilizes two phases, namely feature selection and classification. An improved restricted Boltzmann machine (RBM) algorithm is used to perform dimensionality reduction. RBM follows a stochastic approach to perform this. It consists of one visible layer and one invisible layer. The visible layer is used to represent data and hidden layer is used to increase the learning capability [16]. Then the feature extraction classification is performed by using gradient based SVM algorithm. SVM uses a weighted mixed kernel function. SVM tries to find out a hyper plane which separates various classes. The report produced by this ML based anomaly detection module will be then sent to an SDN controller through a secured channel. This ML based anomaly detection architecture is very efficient in detecting anomalies. Figure 9.9 shows the steps in the anomaly detection module.

In a study by Qiu *et al* the authors implemented a multimedia network security mechanism based on deep learning [17]. They also utilized the capabilities of neural network at the data collection unit in order to characterize data at the input point itself. A multimedia systems utilizes a huge number of sensors which can be an entry point of intruders [18, 19]. Malicious sensors can provide false and dangerous messages to the system [18, 19]. An AI assisted lightweight security mechanism is applied to ensure multimedia security. Lightweight physical layer authentication (LPLA) is performed with the help of ML algorithms [17]. An ML based anomaly detection method by exploiting the lightweight physical layer attributes are considered here. An AI based model is designed to extract attributes and then it is

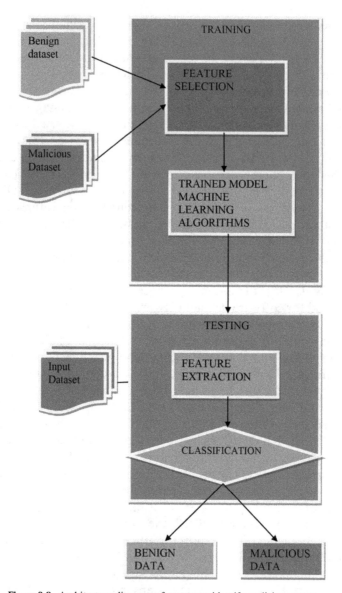

Figure 9.8. Architecture diagram of system to identify malicious messages.

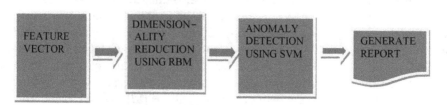

Figure 9.9. Steps in the anomaly detection module.

viewed as a classification system which is easy to train using physical layer parameters [17]. In this model the multidimensional characteristics are collected first. An intruder can be effectively be detected by this mechanism with the help of the ML algorithm. In a nutshell the AI based algorithm will generate the authenticator for the datacenter and thereby increase security [17]. The authenticator generated by the SVM algorithm will increase the security of the system. Since this mechanism is working on the basis of channel characteristics, no separate key generation and management is needed. The amount of computational overheads is also less in this system

In the paper [20] by Tamy *et al*, the authors evaluate various ML algorithms in terms of their efficiency in detecting attacks in SCADA networks. Four ML algorithms SVM, naïve Bayes, tree J48 and random forest are compared based on the evaluation measures like recall, accuracy and time of execution etc [20]. These ML algorithms are tested against 10% random sample gas pipeline dataset [20]. The naïve Bayesian is based on the simplified Bayesian probability model [20]. In the naïve Bayes algorithm probability of one variable does not affect the probability of other variables [20, 21]. SVM utilizes a hyperplane to separate different classes. Random forest algorithm is based on a model aggregation concept [22]. Tree J48 algorithm utilizes a decision tree for classification [23]. As per the analysis, random forest has an accuracy of 99.3, J48 has an accuracy of 99.16, naïve Bayes algorithm has an accuracy of 94.15 and SVM has an accuracy of 94.2 in predicting malicious attacks. Prediction accuracy gives the percentage of correctly classified instances. Prediction accuracy is calculated as the count of correctly identified instances divided by total number of instances in the data set [20]. Another evaluation parameter is the sensitivity of the model which is the ratio of true positive classes to the predicted true positive results by the model. The true negative rate is given by the ratio of true negative to the total of true negative and false positive [20]. Precision is the percentage of accurately classified elements for a given class. From the analysis it is clear that naïve Bayes algorithm will take the least amount of time to build the model, whereas random forest will take the most amount of time. This study provides an effective way to compare various algorithms in detecting attacks in SCADA networks [20].

In a study authored by Zang *et al* [24], the authors proposed a deep reinforcement learning based root mutation scheme for multimedia [24]. The authors propose a deep Q learning method to detect the attacks in a multimedia network. Root mutation works by changing the roots of multiple flows in the network in order to prevent attacks [24]. The main goal of the deep Q root mutation system is to change the routing frequently which will create a difficult situation for the intruder. By adopting deep reinforcement learning algorithms, selection strategy will be learned from the nature of attacks and attack strategies [24]. Intrusion detection systems can also be implemented efficiently with ML techniques [7]. Neural networks and SVM algorithms can be used to implement intrusion detection systems for multimedia networks [7]. Using these algorithms optimal features can be identified and any possible intrusions can be identified and classified [7].

9.4 Advantages of using ML based security mechanism for multimedia

This section performs a comparison between traditional security mechanisms and ML based mechanisms. In traditional security mechanisms like key management based cryptographic methods the amount of computational resources and capabilities required is very high [25]. These types of mechanism are inefficient for multimedia networks [17]. Also, there are possible vulnerabilities in the procedures like key distribution which are unavoidable in most of the traditional security mechanisms. But in the case of ML based multimedia security mechanisms, these types of breach points are comparatively less.

Most of the multimedia networks utilize a lot of sensors, so traditional key based mechanisms may invite a lot of security problems under this dense network scenario [17]. The economic aspect of implementing key based traditional security mechanisms for these dense sensor networks is also a point of consideration [17]. These aspects support ML algorithms better than the traditional security mechanisms. The use of a public key may also be a point of vulnerability for key based security techniques. The intruder may utilize this publically available key to do the malicious activity. Overall ML based security mechanisms outperform the traditional key based mechanisms in the case of a multimedia network. The simplified architecture of an ML based security mechanism is given below (figure 9.10).

Efficient feature extraction is also another point of consideration. In the case of traditional key based security systems the feature extraction process leads to high latency in the network [17]. This latency is not acceptable in multimedia networks. ML and deep learning algorithms are highly efficient in feature extraction even in complex networks. This feature makes it beneficial for complex multimedia networks. Security authentication is also a key requirement of a multimedia

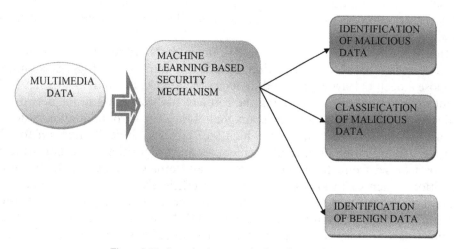

Figure 9.10. Steps in the anomaly detection module.

Table 9.1. Comparison between traditional and ML based security mechanisms Advantages of using ML based security mechanisms are pictorially represented in figure 9.11.

Traditional approach	ML based approach
Traditional methods require more resources	ML based methods require comparatively less amount of computational resources
Key distributions can be vulnerable to various attacks	Number of breach points are comparatively less
Less economical	More economical
Feature extraction process may lead to high latency	Feature extraction can be efficiently done without causing much latency in the network
Less adaptable	More adaptable

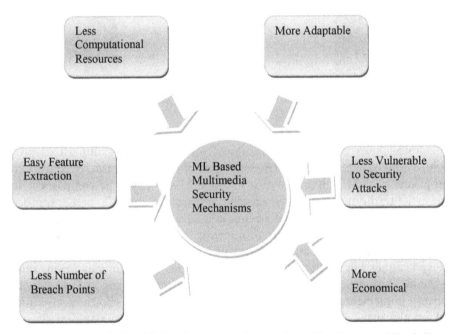

Figure 9.11. Advantages of using ML based security mechanisms for multimedia; some of the challenges of traditional security mechanisms are depicted in figure 9.12 [17].

network which is a little hard to implement using traditional key based security mechanisms [17]. ML based methods provide an intelligent authentication approach which is highly beneficial for multimedia networks. Adaptability is also more for the ML based approach, whereas in a traditional key management based approach adaptability is much less. Table 9.1 shows the comparison between traditional key based methods and ML based methods

From this analysis it is clear that ML based methods outperform traditional multimedia security mechanisms

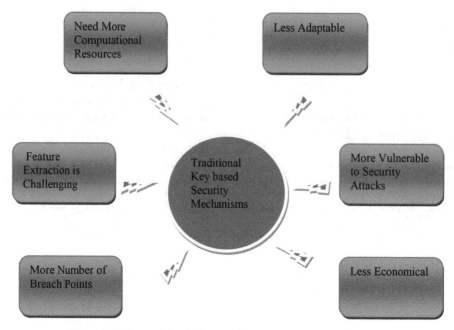

Figure 9.12. Some of the challenges of traditional security mechanisms.

9.5 Conclusion

This chapter reviews how ML algorithms can be effectively utilized to prevent malicious attacks in multimedia. The main goal of this chapter is to effectively study the application of ML algorithms for multimedia security. The comparison study between the traditional key based security approaches and ML based approaches shows that ML based methods have better adaptability, less latency and can provide better security authentication for multimedia networks. The classification and detection capability of ML and deep learning algorithms can be effectively utilized to prevent attacks in multimedia networks. Various algorithms like svm, random forest, convolution neural network, reinforcement learning algorithms etc can be effectively implemented to ensure multimedia security. The choice of algorithm is based on the particular application scenarios. In most of the studies these ML algorithms outperform other traditional security mechanisms. The performance of these ML and deep learning algorithms is measured in terms of precision, recall, root mean square errors and f score etc. In all these measures ML algorithms provide promising results. In a nutshell, by wisely choosing the correct ML algorithm based on particularities of the multimedia application malicious attacks can be pre-identified and prevented to a great extent.

References

[1] Rahman H U, Rehman A U, Nazir S, Rehman I U and Uddin N 2019 Privacy and security limits of personal information to minimize loss of privacy *Proc. of the Presented at the Future of Information and Communication Conf. (New York)*

[2] Jeerige A, Bein D and Verma A 2019 Comparison of deep reinforcement learning approaches for intelligent game playing *IEEE 9th Annual Computing and Communication Workshop and Conf. (CCWC) (Las Vegas, NV)* 0366–71 pp

[3] Alurkar A A *et al* 2017 A proposed data science approach for email spam classification using machine learning techniques *Internet of Things Business Models, Users, and Networks (Copenhagen)* pp 1–5

[4] Saha G and Chauhan N 2017 Numerical weather prediction using nonlinear auto regressive network for the Manaus region, Brazil *Innovations in Power and Advanced Computing Technologies (i-PACT), (Vellore)* pp 1–4

[5] Liu J, Yuan H and Li M 2017 Hidden information recognition based on multitask convolution neural network *6th Int. Conf. on Computer Science and Network Technology (ICCSNT) (Dalian)* pp 194–8

[6] Yue G and Lu L 2018 Face recognition based on histogram equalization and convolution neural network *10th Int. Conf. on Intelligent Human-Machine Systems and Cybernetics (IHMSC) (Hangzhou)* pp 336–9

[7] Hui L and Yonghui C 2010 Research intrusion detection techniques from the perspective of machine learning *Int. Conf. on Multimedia and Information Technology (Kaifeng)* pp 166–8

[8] Qiu X, Du Z and Sun X 2019 Artificial intelligence-based security authentication: applications in wireless multimedia networks *IEEE Access* **7** 172004–11

[9] Garg S, Kaur K, Kumar N and Rodrigues J J P C March 2019 Hybrid deep-learning-based anomaly detection scheme for suspicious flow detection in SDN: a social multimedia perspective *IEEE Trans. on Multimedia* **21** 566–78

[10] Xiao L, Jiang D, Xu D, Su W, An N and Wang D Oct. 2018 Secure mobile crowdsensing based on deep learning *China Commun.* **15** 1–11

[11] Chen S 2019 Is artificial intelligence new to multimedia? *IEEE MultiMedia* **26** pp 5–7

[12] Choi B, Kim J and Ryou J 2008 Retrieval of illegal and objectionable multimedia *2008 Fourth Int. Conf. on Networked Computing and Advanced Information Management (Gyeongju)* pp 645–7

[13] Manjunath B S, Salembier P and Sikora T 2002 Introduction to MPEG-7: multimedia content description *Interface* (New York: Wiley)

[14] Hsu C W, Chang C C and Lin C J 2007 *A Practical Guide to Support Vector Classification* (Taipei: National Taiwan University)

[15] Rafique M Z, Khan Z S, Khan M K and Alghatbar K 2011 Securing IP-Multimedia Subsystem (IMS) against anomalous message exploits by using machine learning algorithms *2011 Eighth Int. Conf. on Information Technology: New Generations (Las Vegas, NV)* pp 559–63

[16] Garg S, Kaur K, Kumar N and Rodrigues J J P C March 2019 Hybrid deep-learning-based anomaly detection scheme for suspicious flow detection in SDN: a social multimedia perspective *IEEE Trans. Multimedia* **vol 21** 566–78

[17] Qiu X, Du Z and Sun X 2019 Artificial intelligence-based security authentication: applications in wireless multimedia networks *IEEE Access* **7** pp 172004–11

[18] Wu D, Si S, Wu S and Wang R Aug. 2018 Dynamic trust relationships aware data privacy protection in mobile crowd-sensing *IEEE Internet Things J.* **5** 2958–70

[19] Wu D, Deng L, Wang H, Liu K and Wang R Oct. 2019 Similarity aware safety multimedia data transmission mechanism for Internet of vehicles *Future Gener. Comput. Syst.* **99** 609–23

[20] Beaver J M, Borges-Hink R C and Buckner M A 2013 An evaluation of machine learning methods to detect malicious SCADA communications *12th Int. Conf. on Machine Learning and Applications (Miami, FL)* pp 54–9

[21] Mukherjee S and Sharma N 2012 Intrusion detection using naive Bayes classifier with feature reduction *Procedia Technol.* **4** 119–28

[22] Breiman L 2001 Random forests *Mach. Learn.* **45(1)** 5–32

[23] Ali J *et al* 2012 Random forests and decision trees *Int. J. Comp. Sci. Issues (IJCSI)* **9**(5) 272

[24] Zhang T *et al* 2020 DQ-RM: deep reinforcement learning-based route mutation scheme for multimedia services *Int. Wireless Communications and Mobile Computing (IWCMC) (Limassol)* pp 291–6

[25] Qiu X, Jiang T, Wu S and Hayes M 2018 Physical layer authentication enhancement using a Gaussian mixture model *IEEE Access* **6** 53583–92

Chapter 10

Assistive communication technology options for elderly care

Marjo Rissanen and Antti Rissanen

Covid-19 pandemic has fundamentally changed health care practices and protocols in organizations. The current situation has been seen as especially problematic in relation to elderly care because there are not opportunities for family members to meet with elderly residents at a hospital or nursing home care in the usual way. This has inspired development of methods for appropriate information sharing. This chapter discusses future service models for patient monitoring on the hospital–home axis in the context of elderly care as well as related security issues and ethical responses. In the presented model, family members could be better informed of a patient's health status through a home video connection during the patient's hospital stay, especially during time periods when normal visiting protocols and co-operation are restricted. Video services and cameras have been included in many service chains in the medical field, and new kinds of service models can be built with reasonable costs. Advancements in security infrastructure will offer possibilities to implement new kinds of healthcare service models in the future.

10.1 Introduction

New environmental situations change ordinary practices in health organizations, leading to a need for new kinds of service models to ensure appropriate communication and connection between patients at the hospital and family members at home. Restrictions to hospitals' visiting policies due to the global Covid-19 pandemic not only worsen patients' well-being but also cause stress to the patients' families. As many IT technologies have become cheaper, the healthcare field has aimed to increase its effectiveness by applying them. At the same time, with new operating models, connected security, privacy, and data protection requirements create new challenges to be considered.

Telemedicine, including camera surveillance and video conferencing, have long been used in healthcare in different contexts. Video recording has a solid place in, for example, medical training, e-care, and elderly care [1]. In many medical specialties, healthcare professionals connect with their patients 24/7 via webcam-enabled computers [2]. During the Covid-19 pandemic, healthcare providers have increasingly shifted from traditional care to virtual co-operation with health consumers with suitable technologies. In many contexts, these virtual experiences are seen as a positive development. In Tamil Nadu around 90% of healthcare professionals and 87% of the general population found teleconsultations to be useful during the pandemic [3]. Wright *et al* [4] noticed that mental healthcare providers appreciated televideo visits, and some found them to be more satisfactory than (voice-based) telephone visits. In general, health consumers perceive online video consultations to be flexible and professional [5]. During the coronavirus pandemic, a telemedicine system was utilized in China to monitor the progression of patients who had only mild symptoms and were sent home by physicians to recover. This system was beneficial for optimizing resources and preventing cross-infections [6]. Video technology has also been used for supervision within clinical teams and clinical education during the pandemic [7]. As a result of the exceptional circumstances faced in healthcare, care institutions have, to varying extents, developed practices for mutual communication between a patient at a hospital and family members at home using, for example, tablet computers [7].

However, doctors around the world are worried about the lack of protection of technology, e.g., for the privacy of patient information, and 60% of healthcare professionals agree that teleconsultation lacks confidentiality [3, 8]. Security problems related to Internet connections as well as the use of public networks and neglected security updates are some reasons for this concern [2]. The current period and its challenges have led to the development of visions for extending the monitoring of a patient treated in a hospital or nursing home to their family members at home. Thus family members can be more aware of the patient's status and well-being at hospital care in spite of decreased possibilities for contact. Principles, treatment policies, and security issues related to these kinds of timely service models will be discussed in the following sections.

10.2 Cameras for patient monitoring in hospitals

10.2.1 Cameras for patient supervising in elderly care

Cameras are gaining more emphasis in all aspects of elderly patient monitoring in healthcare settings. Monitoring technologies have increased flow among elderly people who live independently in their home. Monitoring technologies are used for elderly care in different ways. In the Växjö municipality of Sweden [9], cameras were installed in a patient's house so that the bed or another selected part of the house could be seen. Once a day, care professionals utilized the video footage to see if the patient was where they were supposed to be. If they were not, the professionals checked again after a while, and if the patient could still not be seen, they visited the patient physically [1, 9].

Some home monitoring systems for elderly people who live independently at home include a web camera that can be used for monitoring and communication. Systems employing Internet of Things (IoT) technologies can use diverse kinds of sensors to directly monitor the elderly person's physiological signals and identify daily activities [10].

In a nursing home in Olofström, Sweden, camera technology was tested on patients with the approval of their close relatives. Three times a night, the staff checked the camera to make sure everything was in order. One reason this technology was tested was because when staff had to walk into the patient's room, the patient often woke up and sometimes faced difficulties falling back asleep [1, 11].

10.2.2 Extending camera monitoring from the hospital to the home

Camera surveillance of hospital patients for relatives at home has become more common in healthcare and the social sector. In kindergartens, there are commercial multimedia platforms and home monitoring practices that allow parents to follow their child at kindergarten while the parents are at work.

Video monitoring practices in which family members at home follow their child receiving hospital care have been implemented in the newborn intensive care unit (NICU), with mainly positive experiences. Parents' written consent was obtained before a web camera was installed by the baby's bed [12]. Parents at home securely viewed real-time video of their child via an encrypted Internet browser or mobile phones by using a child-specific confidential password [12]. Recently, bedside webcams have been used in intensive care units (ICUs) for adults during the Covid-19 pandemic to offer families an opportunity to contact their critically ill family member [7]. Clinical psychologists prepare the family by declaring the situation before making a video call. Staff in the ICU recognized that all patients' families benefit from the availability of video calls [7].

A situation in which a camera is used to allow family members at home to follow an elderly patient during a hospital stay is not fundamentally different. Indeed, 'in the future health care providers may see live video feeds at any patient's bedside, young or old' [13]. The global Covid-19 pandemic has created an especially ripe time to implement such practices. Such service models can be very helpful and advantageous in all standard types of care if the protocols are carefully planned and defined.

10.2.3 Home-access video service as experienced by family members

Several studies have investigated the use of video in neonatology units to provide parents at home with direct access to their child. In the study by Kerr *et al* [14], parents had direct access to a neonatal unit via video, and they considered this to be an essential improvement. Access to video recording at home stimulated emotional bonding in early phases and reduced the separation anxiety and stress of parents [14–16]. Also, Hawkes *et al* [17] reported that parents described a sense of emotional well-being, and 92% were confident in the security of the webcam system. Likewise, Yeo *et al* [12] found that webcams were easily accepted and adopted by parents.

Nearly all families found the safety and security of online access to be acceptable (97% of parents), and all families found this service to be useful and were interested in recommending it to potential users [12]. However, sometimes the cameras were turned off by staff, and if parents were not aware of the reasons, this caused concern [14, 18].

10.2.4 Home-access video service as experienced by staff

Healthcare staff considered video recording to be essential progress in the field of neonatology [14] and home-accessible online video to be an additional monitoring option [15]. This practice was seen as an acceptable approach if its use is supervised and if it does not disturb professionals' behavior and practice [15]. However, healthcare professionals were concerned that videos could be utilized for legal purposes in adverse clinical cases [15, 19]. In addition, in Hawkes *et al*'s study [17], 68% of nurses were concerned about privacy risks. Further, they thought that a webcam system could increase stress among staff [17, 20]. In total, 82% of nurses felt that the system could lead to an increase in the number of phone calls by parents to the unit [17].

A few years ago, most healthcare staff members were not familiar with webcam use [17]. Ways to overcome general security issues, data protection, and intense cooperation between the IT professionals and health staff at hospitals were seen as essential prerequisites for the practice [15]. In addition, in some studies, staff reported an increased workload and difficulties with the technology [21]. It is seen as important to ensure motivation and offer versatile training sessions to nursing staff before deployment in order to create a constructive attitude toward the web camera service [20]. It has been argued that each hospital should create a policy that is suitable for families, staff, and the legal department [13]. In addition, intense collaboration with nurses is required to implement live-streaming cameras in standard care [21].

10.2.5 New contexts and possibilities for camera surveillance in elderly care

When daily visits to hospitals and other health organizations are limited in terms of the number of visitors and duration of stay, home monitoring is a good option. Video connection, which allows family members to monitor a hospital patient from home 24/7, creates completely new opportunities for unrestricted access to relatives: family members can thus follow the patient's situation and well-being from home with the intensity they want, depending on the consent of the patient.

This kind of a supervision model does not provide possibilities for two-way communication between the patient and their relatives. Symmetric protocols for mutual communication during periods of restricted access to patients have already been arranged to varying degrees in healthcare [7], and the promotion and productization of those solutions as a normal part of health service platforms is also desirable. One possibility for mutual communication is via standard mobile phones, if they are allowed in the hospital or nursing home and the patient in question is able to use them to communicate with family members via video calls. Therefore this kind of a model mainly serves family members by providing them with an everyday view of the patient's situation without requiring them to ask the hospital unit about the patient's well-being.

10.3 Home-access monitoring and security

In principle, the technological solution for this type of home-access approach does not necessarily require new, application-specific demands or protocols. The system involves a web camera installed at the patient's hospital bed and a secure data communication connection with a virtual private network (VPN) and pertinent safety protocols. The employed communication infrastructure and security policy dictate which practices are used to ensure the process is as secure as possible. The security infrastructure also dictates which device protocols are applied (i.e., is this service implemented using hospital equipment that is borrowed for home use, or is a home computer safe enough?). As is known, increasing the complexity of the end point in a healthcare context increases security risks [22]. Thus, the selected device security protocols require special attention in deployment strategies.

For security reasons, the IT unit of any hospital or care organization must supervise the Internet traffic, and if problems or disturbances are detected, the connection can be smoothly disconnected from the care organization. Detected security problems must be immediately reported to the customer by the hospital's IT department, and the customer will be notified when the connection is determined to be secure again. Authentication with passwords or another secure method is required for a high degree of security. Sensitive medical data, like video material, typically requires specific encryption and anonymization techniques [23]. Reduction of information (e.g., some kind of audio editing and video resolution) may be applied if requested by the person being monitored. Spatialization of sound and attenuation of unwanted signals create a large number of transfer functions. As this is a different monitoring mechanism for communication, consideration of audio signals and acoustic conditions is not initially on the priority list. For ethical reasons, any video recording requires the consent of the patient and the relative(s) observing them. Because the relative decides when to observe the patient, it makes sense that the camera is on and active only when the relative is actually monitoring.

A webcam should be placed in the patient's room so that it is aligned with the patient (e.g., above the bed). When positioning the camera, the installer should ensure that it does not interfere with any care processes or normal routines in the hospital. Importantly, the patient can only be observed while staying in their own bed in the hospital. (see figure 10.1).

10.4 Benefits of the service

10.4.1 Benefit for the hospital patient

In this model, the hospital patient is the only target of the monitoring. The decision regarding utilization lies with the patient. The benefit for the patient is awareness of a complementary monitoring option by relatives, which can increase their feeling of safety during the hospital stay.

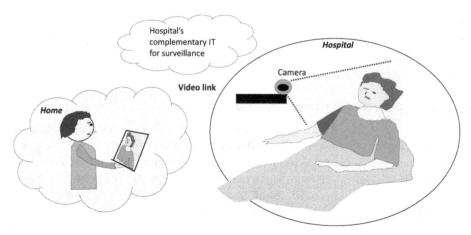

Figure 10.1. Visualization of the service, in which a family member at home can see a patient at the hospital 24/7.

10.4.2 Benefit to the patient's relatives

During periods like the Covid-19 pandemic, patients' family members can experience fear and distress related to the patient's well-being [24]. Unrestricted access to the patient via 24/7 home monitoring offers a new type of information channel for the patient's family. Family members usually want to be aware of the patient's condition on a daily basis during the hospital stay. Uninterrupted or on-demand camera monitoring can offer for relatives constant information about the patient's situation. Thus, visits to the hospital do not have to be made daily, which is especially important when the required travel time is long or when visiting opportunities are restricted. Also, relatives do not have to inquire about the patient's health status via phone or e-mail as often.

10.4.3 Benefit to the organization

Only a few hospitals or care institutions have continuous or on-demand camera surveillance in patient rooms. In most cases, supervision takes place at certain time periods defined by routines or when the patient independently alerts staff that they need help. To ensure safety, units use a mechanical button on the bed or arm band that allows a patient to easily alert when help is needed. However, this does not necessarily help in all emergency situations. Nowadays, this situation has, to some extent, been rectified with the help of various sensor detectors. The home-access model can be considered a complementary monitoring option to increase patient safety (see figure 10.2).

The method creates additional security for the patient but at the same time frees up staff resources because relatives do not have to constantly inquire about the status of the patient at the hospital ward. If a relative notices something strange in the patient's condition or behavior, he or she can report it to the hospital. The relative may also be able to follow the progress of patient's daily routines. If the routines for care, for example, differ significantly from the normal home routines,

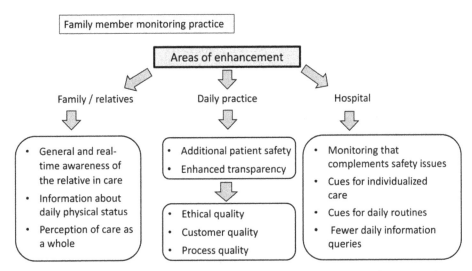

Figure 10.2. Principles of monitoring with a remote connection for safety and better mood.

the relative can contact the hospital and inform the department. Even small details can have a positive effect on compliance with treatment among elderly patients. A relative may also present cues that may be useful in improving the quality of overall activities. This type of insight may be valuable and is easier to detect when daily clinical routines are more clearly traceable because of greater transparency. This kind of service model may increase random contacts at the hospital department, but on the other hand, with the possibility of independent monitoring, the number of daily routine calls may decrease at the same time, especially in situations when daily visits to hospital are somehow restricted.

10.5 Requirements for the service model

10.5.1 When is a home-access camera a facet of quality?

Even limited home surveillance makes sense in situations when pandemics disturb or stop normal visiting opportunities in hospitals. Usually, patients in long-term care and their relatives benefit from such arrangements. Even in typical circumstances, the opportunities for patients' relatives to visit in emergency units are generally restricted, which may cause stress among family members. In addition, pandemic restrictions, which are usually set throughout the hospital and apply to all departments, strictly limit or do not allow visits. In this context, 24/7 live video monitoring of patients for family members at home may be helpful.

When more experience with video surveillance can be gained, it makes sense to extend such practice models also to all normal clinical practice. The extension of home-access monitoring practices to other specialty areas among all adult patients of care might also thus be useful. When such monitoring possibilities become more widespread, this will represent a major step toward greater security, improved transparency, and enhanced customer quality in healthcare.

10.5.2 Conditions for practice

A connection from a hospital to the patient's home requires a high level of security protection based on specific principles, which may differ from conventional tele-communication principles. After all, this is not just a connection between a doctor and patient, but one involving a person in the hospital, who is under constant surveillance and in a potentially vulnerable state, as they are separated from family. The patient's consent is a requirement for adopting the practice. In the case of young children, parental consent is always required.

A positive attitude toward such services among hospital management and staff improves the adaptation of the practice. The intensity of monitoring depends on the consent of the family members who use the service.

This type of service model should be organized in a way that does not increase the staff's workload or disturb normal clinical routines. The service should be integrated with normal clinical practices so seamlessly that health professionals could totally forget its presence. Also, any manipulative procedures should be completely within the control of IT professionals who control the transmission of online traffic. In some studies [17, 20], nurses were involved in some technical procedures related to this technology. Such additional work should be eliminated so that health professionals could concentrate only on their routine clinical duties. Camera positioning is also a critical task. Cameras should also not disturb any physical activities. Thus, the best place for camera installation is above the bed, focused on the patient's face.

Some studies [17, 20] indicated increased stress among staff when this type of service was implemented in neonatal units. It is crucial that any additional stress or disturbance experienced by staff is handled immediately, corrective implementations are designed, and further developmental work is organized (see figure 10.3). Most new technologies are challenging to fully implement at once [20]. Therefore, gradual deployment and contextual institution-specific experiences in some medical specialty areas are useful before full implementation in an organization. Organizations have

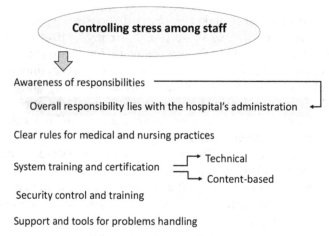

Figure 10.3. Controlling stress among staff in their working environment.

Conditions for the family member monitoring practice

- Common acceptance of the practice in the organization
- Security management for the utilization of the practice
- Definition of standards and specifications including security
- Does not disturb any care practices
- The activity has the consent of the patient or parents of the child
- The intensity of the monitoring is decided by the family member
- The practice does not shift any responsibility in any way

Figure 10.4. List of conditions for successful monitoring.

service-related security management policies. This kind of service model must also have its place in such management plans. The UK Information Commissioner's Office has provided advice to support patients when they communicate with their relatives by video conferencing [7, 25]. Common guidelines and policy recommendations for these kinds of asymmetric video services are also desirable (see figure 10.4).

10.6 Security issues in networked health infrastructure

10.6.1 Information security at the strategic level

New service protocols must be implemented in organizations' information security frameworks, and these in turn should be aligned with organizational values and IT strategic plans [26, 27]. Managerial support is generally necessary when launching an information security management system and a group of professionals with versatile knowledge is needed to ensure that the system is functional. This group defines the goals, content, and systems for information protection [28]. New service protocols require typically special attention. The administration of the organization must be committed and involved in such novel processes and create a climate of readiness for change.

ISO 27799:2008 standard guides information security in healthcare [29]. Information security relates to the necessary policies, processes, and organizational formations for functional software and hardware. Guidelines take into account the risk management policy, compliance with laws and regulations, and strategies for information security. It is emphasized that the consistency of the risk-related goals of business and IT must be taken into account. Risk assessment must be understandable to hospital management and suitable based on the hospital's cost policy and risk acceptance levels [28, 29].

Addressing security considerations in information systems design generally starts with analysis of requirements and threat modelling of a new technology [30]. Then, it continues with cycles of risk management, security testing and security maintenance [30]. Even if the same application and connected platforms are used in different organizations, institution-specific security policies and contextual features dictate the way in which (and the scope at which) they will be implemented.

10.6.2 Different layers of security

Trust plays a significant role in human–computer interaction [31]. Yan *et al* have identified three direct determinants of human–computer trust interaction (HCTI): interaction intention, computer system trust, and communication trust. *Interaction intention* refers to users' eagerness to interact with a computer system, which contains aspects like motivational tasks, perceived usefulness, and ease of use. *Computer system trust* refers to the trustworthiness of a computer system, which is based on system quality and information quality. *Communication trust* covers aspects like perceived privacy, identity, and the security of communication channels [31].

As is well known, security problems may occur in any layer of IT. The *application layer* covers areas like data access, recovery attacks, and issues of authentication. The *network layer* concerns issues related to network protocol problems, and the *perception layer* relates to various other security aspects. [32]. Security aspects are also considered [33] at various levels of security design. At the *platform level*, focus is placed on protection of system authentication and authorization as well as file integration management. At the *applications level*, protections are built into applications themselves. Database login, authorization, transaction management, and database recovery are key issues at this level. At the *record level*, protections are invoked after a user accesses an application and connects specific records. Threat models must cover software-centric, asset-centric, and attacker-centric perspectives. The software-centric model starts at the design phase of the system. The asset-centric model takes into account the identified assets of an organization or a system (e.g., collections of sensitive personal information). Attacker-centric models require profiling of an attacker's characteristics, related skill sets, and motivations [33].

Webcam solutions have known vulnerabilities at the application and network layers [29]. It is critical to address these issues for broad adoption policies of contextual webcam-related healthcare informatics. It has been remarked [32] that security and privacy are less important than convenience in the context of newer technologies. However, people are not eager to utilize useful innovations in healthcare if they do not trust their security. For example, the low adoption rate of personal health records in healthcare is thought to arise from low trust in security issues [34].

10.6.3 Key elements of safe IT infrastructure in healthcare in the future

10.6.3.1 Security and trust with future networks

The growing volume of data has revealed the limits of existing telecom networks' capacities. Wireless communication standards—5G/B5G—are designed to counter this overload [35]. However, 5G is also seen as subject to uncertainties and risks, which should be minimized by reducing possible weaknesses [35]. For instance, 5G networks encompass many stakeholders with different security requirements that lead to several security threats and challenges [36]. This requires the interplay and interaction of many tools to secure networks for the future [35, 37]. Future networks, such as 6G standards, will produce even more opportunities, like AI-driven communication technologies [38] and an intelligent Internet of Healthcare Things

(IoHT) that can offer more comprehensive healthcare service models [39]. However, this means that security threats will become more challenging [39].

10.6.3.2 Internet architecture and new advances

The prevailing Internet architecture should meet the requirements for efficiency, scalability, extensibility, and deployability [40, 41] especially in healthcare. Currently, the Internet is evolving at a fast rate in terms of applications and services, but the elements of core protocols have remained the same for decades [40]. The Internet Protocol (IP) enables (data) packets to be forwarded, but it has drawbacks, like lack of transparency and control [40, 41]. Border Gateway Protocol (BGP) is a routing protocol that is used to connect systems. It has some shortcomings, like slow updates and low scalability. Other serious threats to current Internet protocols include spoofing, distributed denial-of-service (DDoS) attacks, and hijacking [40, 41]. New defense mechanisms are only problems to solve for new kinds of attackers [41, 42].

'Scalability, Control, and Isolation on Next-Generation Networks' (SCION) is a novel enhanced Internet architecture that can replace IP and wide-area routing. Its purpose is to solve various security issues, from route control up to end-to-end communication [43, 44]. Compared to the current Internet, it offers enhanced security, reliability, and performance [40, 41]. Isolation domains (ISDs) are the core of SCION. These shape various autonomous systems (ASs) into sovereign routing planes [41]. In contrast to the current BGP system, in which Internet servers determine the path of data and make all routing decisions, control of the flow of data through SCION lies with the terminal device [35, 41]. Therefore, end hosts know about obtainable network paths, chain them according to their own preferences, and insert forwarding information into the packet headers [43, 44]. This allows any manipulation attempts or security gaps to be instantly flagged [35].

SCION aims to simplify complex source codes [35]. Deployment of SCION is straightforward and involves the addition of only slight complexity to the prevailing infrastructure [44]. Recently, several institutions in Switzerland have implemented SCION for commercial operations [45]. Solutions like SCION could represent promising technologies in future healthcare environments, where security concerns could be a serious barrier to the adoption of new kinds of innovations. It has been remarked [46] that there is no reason why health organizations' database computers should be stuck on the Internet; there is a general misconception that there are no other end-to-end networks besides IP or that one could not be built conveniently and with reasonable costs.

10.6.3.3 VPNs and security issues

The purpose of VPNs is to share information between two entities on the Internet through a protected channel [47, 48]. However, VPNs may face security issues like DDoS attacks. Because of these problems, VPN architectures are secured by, for example, intrusion prevention systems. They require configuration procedures and protocols for validating authentication between the client and VPN server (testing, configured firewalls). Even if attacks on various VPN servers can be blocked by various intrusion prevention systems, there are still possibilities for new types of attacks [47].

10.7 Deploying novel surveillance services in healthcare

10.7.1 Underlining the basics

During the production of information systems, particularly innovation policy in healthcare, specific principles should be included in the design strategy. The benefits of innovation without any ethical compromises are central to these principles. It is essential that the result of research and development is a product or service that effectively serves the target process or replaces the existing process in a more efficient way. Strategies for the development of information systems must align with the organization's operational strategy, infrastructure, and mission [49]. Changes in the environment create their own boundary conditions that inspire future strategies. To achieve a good care outcome, the goal should be optimal synergy between all the influences through the entire service chain; this means a seamless 'whole' between the innovation, the service process, health professionals involved in care, and the health consumer [50]. Achieving such a seamless whole [51] is not always straightforward. It requires consumers to have flexible channels to report their experiences with new service models. Then feedback of health professionals' view of the functionality of new innovations should also reach system designers. Clinical normal process auditing also should focus on attention on the general acceptability and functionality of new innovations (figure 10.5). Evidence-based information, shared decision-making, and creative leadership are principles that are emphasized in translational innovation policy.

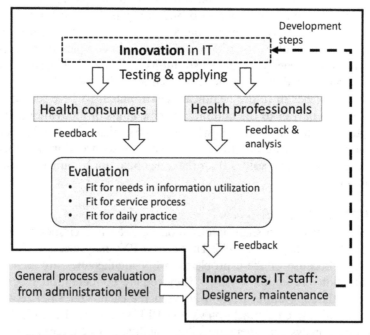

Figure 10.5. Successful development work in IT innovations deployment.

Nowadays, security policy is a critical requirement for new innovations and their deployment in health informatics. Thus, advances in security management and possibilities for new inventions in this area go hand-in-hand. Consumer-targeted applications are often part of the customer's care environment and form a significant supporting area in terms of care intensity, service availability, and overall quality optimization.

Understanding the need for knowledge is an essential starting point for embracing new thinking models in health informatics. The planning process starts with awareness of problems [52]. In the field of IT innovation, new applications are produced for both known problems (improvement) and new problems (invention) [53]. However, not all emerging problems can be solved with the existing knowledge base and design frameworks. The healthcare sector, like other organizations, must apply experience, intuitive skills, and a trial-and-error methodology-synergies between relevance and rigor [54]. New parameters that affect operations include those introduced by global pandemics, which pose completely new types of challenges to operational quality control and innovation policy in general. Such situations create new, critical areas of improvement.

Patients and their families are aware of many problems that are not addressed by normal healthcare quality monitoring [55]. For this reason, innovation can start with gaining an improved understanding of consumers' experience. Thus, organizations should be outward-looking and willing to hear and respond to feedback from customers when trying to enhance the relevance of design practices. This feedback can provide information about knowledge gaps, inspire design activities, and, potentially, improve the innovation capacity of organizations and designers. New innovations have then their impact on the organization's operating models [56]. Thus flexible channels for user experience are needed also further on.

10.7.2 Design cycles and relevant frames for design

Patient safety is ensured by a combination of quality services and products, which are developed based on relevant supporting frames of design practice. In health informatics, identification of design areas is helpful for perceiving design-related questions and complexities. Design questions focus on the *target environment* (relevance cycle; requirements and testing), *actual design practices* (design cycle; design activities and evaluation), and *supporting knowledge bases* that serve design practice (rigor cycle) [54]. The operationalization of design challenges in each design cycle in the health service context improves the understanding of the critical design connected complexities.

When camera surveillance and new kinds of technologies are implemented in healthcare, analysis of *environmental requirements* is essential. Such an analysis needs to answer e.g., the following questions: Where and in which contexts are more advanced monitoring models the answer to perceived problems? How can consumers be served in a satisfactory way with this technology? In the *design phase*, the importance of the creative concept and 'sources of creative insights' [54, 57] is central to the innovation policy. As digitalization and artificial intelligence become more widespread, service protocols are rapidly changing and new opportunities are opening up. In addition, changing environments, such as global pandemics, necessitate continuous creative design. A creative perspective does not only mean original implementation of service content; it is equally essential for technical implementation. Combating security threats is an essential creative process in various technology infrastructures, and it requires not only knowledge and expertise but also creative and original solutions, as well as the coordination and anticipation of many risk factors.

The benefits of design practice should be assessed in terms of how the designed products ultimately fit their intended use (referred to as product fitness)-how successfully problem and solution spaces interact [58]. New innovations in healthcare need their own context-specific evaluation methods. Such *evaluations* may represent observational, analytical, experimental, testing, descriptive, or other arrangements [59]. Suitable evaluation combinations are also a way to a mature quality policy and respectively streamline new types of services.

10.7.3 Shared leadership

At the core of leadership and design policy are an understanding of the importance of synergistic thinking and appreciation of different perspectives. By scenarios is aimed to demonstrate the utility and significance of new types of products [60] but complex health environments create their own boundaries. Innovations are often produced with a participatory design orientation [61]. New developments should be understandable to different stakeholders [62].

The primary stakeholders in innovation development in health informatics are IT designers and end users (i.e., customers). Shared decision-making involves consideration of patients' values and preferences [63]. Shared decision-making is recommended in IT design due to its versatility and overall quality requirements. The key stakeholders are subscribers of the applications and systems and the personnel (medical, administrative, technical) operating them. Stakeholders in healthcare should be aware of their own role in the development, utilization, and evaluation of customer-oriented IT. Organizations should also support realization of this cooperation. Naturally, different understandings, skills, and differences of opinion between different groups may complicate the development and deployment of new innovations. In many cases, the difficulty of a common language and communication may hinder effective cooperation. Despite these difficulties, novel innovation paths, like new kinds of surveillance strategies in healthcare, represent shared challenges that should be overcome by equally listening to and taking into account the views of different parties.

10.7.4 Challenges of innovation adaptation

Adoption of new innovations may be challenging in healthcare. Rapid changes in the field of informatics often involve new types of problems and research needs [53]. Specific *customization* procedures are sometimes a way for better adaptation. While very advanced customization is not always possible, customization procedures to a certain degree at different levels of healthcare may be needed for better 'fit'. There are a number of different organizations involved in healthcare, so a solution that works on the same principle and under the same conditions is rarely an ideal and adaptable solution for all actors.

The importance of a *people-driven foundation* for any transformation is essential in spite of technology-driven innovations and environments [64], especially in clinical healthcare practice. Acceptance and suitability for human processes should dictate which innovations are valuable for daily practice. Individual perceptions should be noticed, as not all innovations are targeted at or suitable for every health consumer. Use of the newest innovations should always be optional in healthcare.

The influence of digital change on the staff and culture of organizations should not be underestimated [64]. Adoption policies often emphasize alignment with the norms, culture, and operational processes of the target organization. However, novel solutions do not always fit smoothly in well-established and traditional organizations without profound clarification of their justification and ethical acceptability. Training and coaching programs that concentrate on new behaviors and mindsets help to develop required capabilities in new environments, and they are a key area of smart adoption policies (see figure 10.6) [64].

10.7.5 New service models and translational design challenges

It is essential to evaluate novel camera surveillance practices in healthcare from the perspective of translational design challenges and various quality frames. The deployment policies for innovations form one focus area in translational research and design [65, 66]. In healthcare, versatile quality perspective gives added value, including ethical, organizational, economic, and social meanings as well as needed cognitive aspects [67].

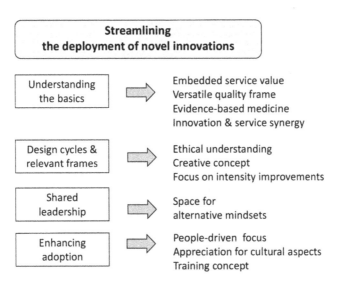

Figure 10.6. The main requirements for monitoring.

Table 10.1. Evaluation of new service models involving camera surveillance

Theme & Practices	Translational Design Emphasis	Quality Frame Emphasis
Design practice:		
–Security emphasis	–From ideas to practice with	Customer
Design frames:	ethical considerations	Process
–Ethical emphasis		Ethics
Design environment:	–Evidence-based design	Product
–Customer adaptation		Innovation
–Staff adaptation	–Process-system synergy	
Shared leadership:	–Team synergy	
–Shared mission	–Multidisciplinary approach	Process
–Shared duties	–Customers' voice	
Innovation adaptation:		Customer
–Customization	–Value for customer	Process
–Training programs	–Smoothing way from design to practice	Image
–Focus on people	–Customer service as a primary mission	Mission

In the health sector, customer-targeted services primarily involve profoundly evaluating the *customer perspective*. In other words, does the customer benefit from the service? How? Did identified problems with the quality of customer service inspire the innovation? *Product quality* issues are identified by reflection on whether a product is a functional and convenient tool to seamlessly support operations in a health service process. In a healthcare context, the focus of *innovation quality* should be issues such as whether the product is useful and ethically acceptable in addition to its pure novelty value [68]. From the point of view of *process quality*, it is essential to consider how well a product or service promotes or supports the intensity of care and overall quality of the target process in healthcare. Focus should also be placed on quality issues of design processes and implementation policy of innovations.

Positive change with a good cost–benefit ratio is a common goal of designing and adapting innovations in healthcare. Thus, the value of IT applications in healthcare is generally considered from a *cost–benefit* perspective, which connects to an ethical perspective, as it is also a matter of prioritization policy [50]. Intensity thinking is related to the degree and appropriate availability of services. IT-innovations are nowadays a tight part of service entities. Professional service entities form thus one part of ethical responsibility in health organizations. Novel IT-innovations and their compliance with security requirements are an important part of this intensity scheme and ethical responsiveness.

Generally, in healthcare, *ethical thinking* should be performed throughout the entire service process, not only for individual attributes, like privacy, confidentiality, and product security. In addition to having overall utility value, the product should support the care process without ethical compromises. *Mission quality* in the health context includes reflection on whether a product has a clear mission for health improvement or health-related service support. In other words, is it possible to reach this essential goal through the innovation in question? Is the innovation aligned with the overall operations and values of an organization? *Image quality* concerns, for example, the reality of the image of the product created through marketing reflecting also ethical aspects of this criterion [68]. Evaluating an image also involves defining whether a novel innovation will create positive image value for a health organization (see table 10.1).

10.8 Conclusion

Video monitoring is a common practice in different healthcare contexts. However, here are few examples of such services for the family members of patients in current healthcare practice. Visiting routines may be disturbed in hospitals and care organizations due to, for example, pandemic situations. Home-access monitoring practices can decrease the stress experienced by family members in such situations. With the possibility for daily monitoring, they can be aware of the patient's status in spite of restrictions. However, according to some studies, these types of practices may cause stress for the nursing staff in hospitals. However, if all the reasons for this additional burden are discussed and staff members are carefully taught to understand the positive aspects of such services for their daily clinical practice, this mindset may change and the technology adoption process may become smoother. It is essential to understand that this kind of monitoring service does not change responsibility in any way; the hospital remains responsible for patient safety, and this service merely complements safety efforts. Healthcare organizations can significantly increase their image value through these types of visionary practices. In addition, they can demonstrate their eagerness to change, achieve greater transparency, and ensure service quality. Connected security factors may pose challenges to these types of services, but new advances in the security of IT infrastructure may lessen these barriers.

References

[1] Nilsson F and Lee Y-S 2020 Assistive technology within elderly care: a study of professional's attitudes towards using assistive technology *BA Thesis* Linnaeus University, Faculty of Technology, Department of Informatics

[2] Kichloo A *et al* 2020 Telemedicine, the current COVID-19 pandemic and the future: a narrative review and perspectives moving forward in the USA *Fam Med Community Health* **8** e000530

[3] Kannuchamy S, Kesavelu D and Rai R 2020 Evaluation of telemedicine among healthcare professionals and general population-a cross sectional study *NOVYI MIR Res. J.* **5** 190–202

[4] Wright J, Dewan S, Hilty D and Dewan N A 2020 Health care providers' perceptions of quality, acceptance, and satisfaction with telebehavioral health services during the COVID-19 pandemic: survey-based study *JMIR Mental Health* **7** e23245

[5] Sølling I K, Carøe P, Mathiesen K S and Lindgren K 2020 When the physical presence in the citizen's home is replaced by online video consultations; a citizen perspective *Nordisk sygeplejeforskning* **10** 70–85

[6] Xu H, Huang S, Qiu C, Liu S, Deng J, Jiao B, Tan X, Ai L, Xiao Y and Belliato M 2020 Monitoring and management of home-quarantined patients with COVID-19 using a WeChat-based telemedicine system: retrospective cohort study *J. Med. Internet Res.* **22** e19514

[7] Igra A, McGuire H, Naldrett I, Cervera-Jackson R, Lewis R, Morgan C and Thakuria L 2020 Rapid deployment of virtual ICU support during the COVID-19 pandemic *Future Healthc. J.* **7** 181

[8] Langarizadeh M, Moghbeli F and Aliabadi A 2017 Application of ethics for providing telemedicine services and information technology *Med. Arch.* **71** 351

[9] Anon 2019 *Hemtjänst, Senior Guide* (Växsjö, Sweden: Kommun)

[10] Deepa K and Saravanaguru R 2020 Context-aware elderly people monitoring based on IoT *J. Xi'an Univ. Arch. Technol.* **3** 5797–804

[11] Billing S 2018 Äldreboende i Olofström testar kameraövervakning *SVT Nyheter* https://www.svt.se/nyheter/lokalt/blekinge/aldreboende-i-olofstrom-infor-kameraovervakning

[12] Yeo C L, Ho S K, Khong K C and Lau Y Y 2011 Virtual visitation in the neonatal intensive care: experience with the use of internet and telemedicine in a tertiary neonatal unit *Perm. J.* **15** 32

[13] Rhoads S J, Green A L, Lewis S D and Rakes L 2012 Challenges of implementation of a web-camera system in the neonatal intensive care unit *Neonatal Netw.* **31** 223–8

[14] Kerr S, King C, Hogg R, McPherson K, Hanley J, Brierton M and Ainsworth S 2017 Transition to parenthood in the neonatal care unit: a qualitative study and conceptual model designed to illuminate parent and professional views of the impact of webcam technology *BMC Pediatr.* **17** 158

[15] Le Bris A, Mazille-Orfanos N, Simonot P, Luherne M, Flamant C, Gascoin G, ÓLaighin G, Harte R and Pladys P 2020 Parents' and healthcare professionals' perceptions of the use of live video recording in neonatal units: a focus group study *BMC Pediatr.* **20** 1–9

[16] Guttmann K, Patterson C, Haines T, Hoffman C, Masten M, Lorch S and Chuo J 2020 Parent stress in relation to use of bedside telehealth, an initiative to improve family-centeredness of care in the neonatal intensive care unit *J. Patient Exp.* **7** 1378–83

[17] Hawkes G A, Livingstone V, Ryan C A and Dempsey E M 2015 Perceptions of webcams in the neonatal intensive care unit: here's looking at you kid! *Am. J. Perinatol.* **32** 131–6

[18] Gibson R and Kilcullen M 2020 The impact of web-cameras on parent-infant attachment in the neonatal intensive care unit *J. Pediatr. Nurs.* **52** e77–83

[19] Gelbart B, Barfield C and Watkins A 2009 Ethical and legal considerations in video recording neonatal resuscitations *J. Med. Ethics* **35** 120–4

[20] Joshi A, Chyou P-H, Tirmizi Z and Gross J 2016 Web camera use in the neonatal intensive care unit: impact on nursing workflow *Clin. Med. Res.* **14** 1–6

[21] Kilcullen M L, Kandasamy Y, Evans M, Kanagasignam Y, Atkinson I, van der Valk S, Vignarajan J and Baxter M 2020 Neonatal nurses' perceptions of using live streaming video cameras to view infants in a regional NICU *J. Neonatal Nurs.* **26** 207–11

[22] Jalali M S and Kaiser J P 2018 Cybersecurity in hospitals: a systematic, organizational perspective *J. Med. Internet Res.* **20** e10059

[23] Abugabah A and Nizamuddin N 2020 Smart healthcare ecosystem for elderly patient care *2020 43rd Int. Convention on Information, Communication and Electronic Technology (MIPRO)* 365–70

[24] Flint L and Kotwal A 2020 The new normal: key considerations for effective serious illness communication over video or telephone during the coronavirus disease 2019 (COVID-19) pandemic *Ann. Intern. Med.* **173** 486–8

[25] Information Commissioner's Office (UK) 2020 Health, social care organisations and coronavirus—what you need to know

[26] Bowen P, Hash J and Wilson M 2006 *Special Publication 800-100 Information Security Handbook: A Guide for Managers* (Gaithersburg, MD: National Institute of Standards and Technology)

[27] Johnson A M 2018 The strategic value of participating in information security research: evidence from the finance, healthcare, and insurance industries *J. Southern Assoc. Inf. Syst.* **5** 1

[28] Velibor B 2020 Managing information security in healthcare *Oraşe Inteligente Şi Dezvoltare Regională* **4** 63–83

[29] Bernik I 2014 Information security management in health care according to ISO/IEC 27799 Standard *Medicine 2.0 Conf. (Toronto, Canada)* (JMIR Publications Inc.)

[30] Yeng P, Wolthusen S and Yang B 2020 Comparative analysis of software development methodologies for security requirement analysis *Towards Healthcare Security Practice 13th Int. Conf. in Information Systems (Sofia)*

[31] Yan Z, Kantola R and Zhang P 2011 A research model for human-computer trust interaction *2011 IEEE 10th Int. Conf. on Trust, Security and Privacy in Computing and Communications* (Piscataway, NJ: IEEE) pp 274–81

[32] Spriggs B 2018 *Survey of Security in Home Connected Internet of Things* (Portland, OR: Portland State University)

[33] Paudel S 2014 *Security engineering and software development for critical infrastructure IT in the cloud PhD Thesis* (Wien: Technical University)

[34] Gabel M, Foege J N and Nüesch S 2019 The (in)effectiveness of incentives: a field experiment on the adoption of personal electronic health records *ICIS Proc. Fortieth Int. Conf. on Information Systems (Munich)*

[35] Kamasa J 2020 Securing future 5G-networks *Policy Perspect.* **8** 4

[36] Moudoud H, Khoukhi L and Cherkaoui S 2020 Prediction and detection of FDIA and DDoS attacks in 5G enabled IoT *IEEE Netw.* **35** 194–201

[37] Siriwardhana Y, Gür G, Ylianttila M and Liyanage M 2020 The role of 5G for digital healthcare against COVID-19 pandemic: opportunities and challenges *ICT Express* **7** 244–52

[38] Nayak S and Patgiri R 2020 6G communication technology: a vision on intelligent healthcare *arXiv* preprint arXiv:2005.07532

[39] Kaiser M S, Zenia N, Tabassum F, Al Mamun S, Rahman M A, Islam M S and Mahmud M 2021 6G access network for intelligent internet of healthcare things: opportunity, challenges, and research directions *Proc. of Int. Conf. on Trends in Computational and Cognitive Engineering* (Berlin: Springer) pp 317–28

[40] Chandrashekar D 2020 *Performance Comparison of SCION with Routed IP on Virtual Machines* (Espoo: Aalto University)

[41] Perrig A, Szalachowski P, Reischuk R M and Chuat L 2017 *SCION: A Secure Internet Architecture* (Berlin: Springer International Publishing)

[42] Perrig A 2020 Global communication guarantees in the presence of adversaries *Proc. of the 15th ACM Asia Conf. on Computer and Communications Security* pp 4–5

[43] Barrera D, Chuat L, Perrig A, Reischuk R M and Szalachowski P 2017 The SCION internet architecture *Commun. ACM* **60** 56–65

[44] Anon 2021 SCION (Internet architecture) *Wikipedia*

[45] Etlinn A 2019 A secure internet isn't science fiction

[46] Kantola R A 2020 Lukijan mielipide | Terveystiedot turvalliseen verkkoon *Helsingin Sanomat* [Reader's opinion Health information on a secure network] https://www.hs.fi/mielipide/art-2000007605968.html

[47] Ghebadne J, Dossou M, Vianou A, Yatakpo H and Assogba M 2019 Using secure virtual private networks for increasing the patient prviacy in case of telemonitoring services *Int. J. Comput. Inf. Technol.* **8** 8–11

[48] Ogbu M N, Onoh G N and Okafor K C 2017 Cloud based virtual private networks using IP tunneling for remote site interfaces *2017 IEEE 3rd Int. Conf. on Electro-Technology for National Development (NIGERCON)* (Piscataway, NJ: IEEE) pp 30–41

[49] Henderson J C and Venkatraman H 1999 Strategic alignment: leveraging information technology for transforming organizations *IBM Syst. J.* **38** 472–84

[50] Rissanen M 2020 Translational health technology and system schemes: enhancing the dynamics of health informatics *Health Inf. Sci. Syst.* **8** 1–10

[51] Meadows D 1991 System dynamics meets the press, an excerpt from the global citizen *The Global Citizen* (Washington DC: Island Press) pp 1–12

[52] Vaishnavi V K and Kuechler W 2015 *Design Science Research Methods and Patterns: Innovating Information and Communication Technology* (Boca Raton, FL: CRC Press)

[53] Gregor S and Hevner A R 2013 Positioning and presenting design science research for maximum impact *MIS Q.* **37** 337–55

[54] Hevner A R 2007 A three cycle view of design science research *Scand. J. Inf. Syst.* **19** 4

[55] Levtzion-Korach O, Frankel A, Alcalai H, Keohane C, Orav J, Graydon-Baker E, Barnes J, Gordon K, Puopolo A L and Tomov E I 2010 Integrating incident data from five reporting systems to assess patient safety: making sense of the elephant *Jt. Comm. J. Qual. Patient Saf.* **36** 402–AP18

[56] Choo C W 2006 *The Knowing Organization: How Organizations Use Information to Construct Meaning, Create Knowledge, and Make Decisions.* 2nd edn (New York: Oxford University Press)

[57] Csikszentmihalyi M 1997 *Flow and the Psychology of Discovery and Invention* (New York: Harper Perennial)39

[58] Hevner A, vom Brocke J and Maedche A 2019 Roles of digital innovation in design science research *Bus Inf Syst Eng* **61** 3–8

[59] Arnott D and Pervan G 2010 An assessment of DSS design science using the Hevner, March, Park and Ram guidelines *Information Systems Foundations: The Role of Design Science* (Canberra: ANU E Press) pp 255–84

[60] Hevner A R, March S T, Park J and Ram S 2004 Design science in information systems research *MIS Q.* **28** 75–105

[61] Fishman B J, Marx R W, Best S and Tal R T 2003 Linking teacher and student learning to improve professional development in systemic reform *Teach. Teach. Educ.* **19** 643–58

[62] Sigmund H and Kristensen F B 2009 Health technology assessment in Denmark: strategy, implementation, and developments *Int. J. Technol. Assess. Health Care* **25** 94–101

[63] Hoffmann T C, Legare F, Simmons M B, McNamara K, McCaffery K, Trevena L J, Hudson B, Glasziou P P and Del Mar C B 2014 Shared decision making: what do clinicians need to know and why should they bother? *Med. J. Aust.* **201** 35–9

[64] Scheurwater M, Voster R and Koorn R 2019 Technological progress: people or robot driven? *Compact* **3** 7–9

[65] Buntin M B, Burke M F, Hoaglin M C and Blumenthal D 2011 The benefits of health information technology: a review of the recent literature shows predominantly positive results *Health Affairs* **30** 464–71

[66] Carr K M and Bradley-Levine J S 2016 Translational research design: Collaborating with stakeholders for program evaluation *Qual. Rep.* **21** 44

[67] Goes P B 2014 Design science research in top information systems journals *MIS Quart.* **38** iii–viii

[68] Rissanen M 2015 Ethical quality in eHealth4: a challenge with many facets *Health Information Science Lecture Notes in Computer Science* ed X Yin, K Ho, D Zeng, U Aickelin, R Zhou and H Wang (Cham: Springer International Publishing) pp 146–53

Chapter 11

Deep learning approach for scenario-based abnormality detection

M Suresha, S Kuppa and D S Raghu Kumar

The immense growth of the world population creates many problems, which are maintaining law and order, urbanization, internal security, healthcare etc. Recently several nations have been focusing on research in the security domain; it shows how to combat some critical security issues through enriching the technology. Especially in the security domain, surveillance systems play a major role, hence increase of security cameras generating huge amounts of video data, published and spread explosively. This data can be used to solve a wide variety of security issues. In this chapter, we discuss two major stages of research aiming to stimulate scenarios of videos with deep learning approaches, i.e. scenario understanding and abnormality detection. In the first stage, scenario understanding concentrates on automatically understanding video clips, by labelling clips based on their semantic contents like human actions or complex events, key frame extraction, artifacts modelling and action attention for spatio-temporal feature modelling. Evaluating these core spatio-temporal features using hybrid models helps to classify and caption video content, further, it enhances to a group of labels to capture prominent informative dynamics in videos. In the second stage, abnormality detection could be achieved by identifying common and uncommon behaviors using learned knowledge base markers and natural abnormality translation techniques. Further, the authors also provide a review on popular competitions and benchmarks, which helps to evaluate the growth of this vibrant security domain.

11.1 Introduction

The twenty-first century has created a digital revolution in the world. Research communities have introduced a huge amount of advanced electronic devices; these devices produce huge amounts of data; recently Forbes approximates 2.5 quintillion bytes' data produced per day. Using this big-video data [1] could achieve a great

doi:10.1088/978-0-7503-3735-9ch11

smart city concept by introducing different kinds of smarter [2] and secure devices. Information storage devices in every security domain are regularly needed to deal with a massive amount of different layers of data. In smart and safe city projects fluctuating sizes become more predominant. Figure 11.1 shows the rapid growth of surveillance nodes by the usage of high-definition monitoring, and figure 11.2 shows how the amount of data involved increases within a short period time. Efficient collection and analysis of these data is a more critical job and also designing a video knowledge stream, by all accounts, is an inescapable, industry-wide objective in the security industry.

Security clients trust that their investment in new technology and smart products [2–6] will bring significantly more advantages than simply tracking and tracing people [7]. The new technology achieved collects both real-time information and evidence before a security event happens. Some advantages like reducing the huge amount of workforce required to search surveillance footage, finding anomalous data, and detecting an even more robust way to enhance surveillance systems to transfer from post-security event tracing to pre-security event alerts or even alerts during security events may happen. Hence these demands are satisfied by recognizing actions [8], activity [9], behaviors [10] and video description generation [11]. These ways replace traditional surveillance setups with a more intelligent one. Also, this setup has evolved to produce new applications in business environments, like demographic evaluation, which helps targeted advertisement and dense traffic management [2].

Abnormality [12], anomalies [13], suspicious human movement detection [4] have improved traditional surveillance systems to become an intelligent surveillance system. Intelligent video surveillance has been accessible for a long time, with the

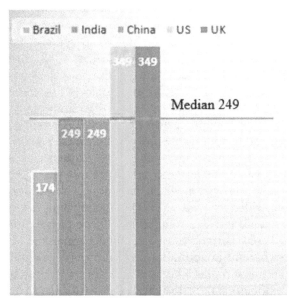

Figure 11.1. Median number of cameras reported for all organizations in different countries.

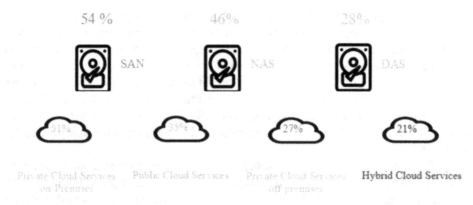

Figure 11.2. Growth of data changing over a twelve month period.

multimedia research community engaged to identify specific suspicious activity detection using some grammar-based approaches [14], which detect abnormality in a specific scenario. Apart from a specific scenario, it is difficult to find abnormalities, and it becomes one of the challenging tasks, because in each scenario abnormalities may differ. It is difficult to generalize the same grammar-based model in all scenarios. For example, what is required in front of an office door or in a playground scenario differ widely. For these kinds of situations, to build a standard generalized framework for abnormal activities is the biggest challenge faced by the research community.

Traditional intelligent algorithms have strong requirements for a scenario background because recognition accuracy and analysis in different scenarios remains inconsistent. This is fundamental because of the way that the conventional intelligent video analysis [15] model still has numerous imperfections. Scenario variations are a common problem to generalize an abnormal activity framework, but this would be achieved by understanding video content. Each scenario with different kinds of scenario-based activity would be generated, therefore, the activity contains commonly known computer vision descriptors such as objects and motions. Understanding of each scenario activity with objects association is possible by classification and captioning of video content. The important factors of video classification are spatial and temporal clues [16]. Spatial clues are static features in the scenario like objects, and temporal clues are motions in the scenario to classify video content or understand a scenario; using these two features successfully classifies a scenario. After successfully understanding a scenario one needs to generate a description on the same scenario, in which descriptions are captioned [17] in a video content. Captioning video content takes spatio-temporal features but here are considered every sequence in video content from the sequence of frames to generate descriptions. With these descriptions, one can find normal and abnormal events in each scenario using natural abnormality translation. This requires state-of-the-art deep neural computational models, because it performs accurate results with lower error rate, good computational power with fewer feature mechanisms compare to handcrafted [16] methods.

Visual analytics have move from low-level image feature representation to a significant high-level activity understanding approach. It can be classified into three main steps: identification of objects and their abstraction agents [18], monitoring of those objects and similarity indicators from frame to frame, and assessment of estimate results to describe and inter-semantic events [19] and concealed phenomena. This analogy can reach out to a different set of applications with movement-based action recognition [20], access control, video ordering [21], human–machine interaction [22], and traffic management and navigation. Intelligent video surveillance has been accessible for a long time. However, the results of its applications have not been perfect. The rise of deep learning has empowered these requests to become reality.

Scenario based abnormality detection first concentrated on preprocessing and improving the accuracy of the model. In this regard, first to be improved was spatial features evaluation, hence calculated key frames based on clear background with the help of instance segmentation [23]. When clear background key frames are extracted, it improves the classification accuracy. Because the neural model easily computes spatial objects without any motion occlusion [24]. State full artifacts modelling is similar to object detection [25], first are detected all objects in particular key frames then extracted spatal features. Finally, in spatial optimization one captures the key attention actions frames in a video sequence, further all these key components are merged with a two-stream hybrid model for spatio-temporal feature extraction [26, 27]. The two-stream multi-model contains all these spatial frames and temporal optical flow frames for modelling of spatio-temporal patterns. After successful evaluation of spatio-temporal features, one classifies video content or a scenario using sequences of a long-short-term-memory (LSTM) [22] network. Then one needs to generate descriptions or captions of video content [17]. This can be achieved by a deep description-understanding network [28, 29]. After successful classification and captioning of video content, it can be organized into the knowledge base from each successfully classified scenario. The knowledge base has different metrics, standard rules or standard abnormality, scenario specific abnormality and scenario captioned routine activity. Scenario captioned routine activity can be achieved by different levels of natural abnormality translation. Natural abnormality translation contains different phases to convert video to mining a text. Further levels are associated with categorizing normal and abnormal behavior in video content.

Organization of this chapter is as follows. There is a brief literature review in section 11.2. Section 11.3 gives an overview of scenario understanding, then we introduce basic preprocessing stages to improve efficiency of the deep network and a hybrid model for extracting spatio-temporal patterns. Detailed discussions on key frame extraction using instance segmentation, state full artifacts modelling, action recognition and attention of key action generation, hybrid multi-model for spatio-temporal patterns are presented in sub-sections 11.3.1, 11.3.2, 11.3.3, 11.3.4 respectively. Then we discuss the abnormality detection under natural abnormality translation in section 11.4, section 11.5 provide details about abnormality detection datasets in different scenarios, challenges are discussed in section 11.6, trends and strengths are discussed in section 11.7 followed by the conclusion.

11.2 Literature study

The primary goal of this literature study is to highlight innovative research on an abnormality or anomaly detection and tracking by identifying objects abstraction and its agents, analyzing long-term and short-term motion, and extracting key component frames from video streams automatically. On the other hand, we focus on efficiency of intelligent video surveillance systems with outstanding new machine learning and deep learning methods to analyze video content and control the system automatically. We discuss different machine and deep learning techniques with continual knowledge transfer mechanism to solve intelligence, and automated monitoring.

Some recent surveys found in [22, 25, 30–32] described intelligent video analysis systems, human activity recognition, motion analysis, suspicious activity detection and applications of activity recognition systems. These surveys predominantly focused on three major tasks: detection, tracking and understanding the content. Human action recognition and detection involves short and long-term motion segmentation and objects association classification. Hence, background extraction, statistical techniques, spatio-temporal differencing and optical flow address the motion segmentation.

Some works are particularly focused on specific abnormal activity. The authors of [33] proposed a security system based on suspicious behavior detection for only trespassing of imaginary lines, scrimmage, running people or riots. In [34], the authors proposed a method to detect suspicious movement like loitering activity and track an object by using a color histogram method. In [35], they proposed an event detection approach in indoor scenarios for object misleading and in [36], multi-object tracking is porposed that uses common feature descriptors like color, texture, shape and temporal properties to track multiple objects both in indoor and outdoor scenarios. In [37], they focused only on a particular scenario to find suspicious human activity recognition in ATM by using background subtraction methods, and in [4] to detect suspicious activity in an examination hall by taking head pose gestures and object exchange. There is a different set of methodologies used to detect abnormality and suspicious human activity [12] using level set method for abnormal event detection and localization to extract some features and using an local binary fitting model for detection which gives excellent performance for only specific scenarios. Using grammar-based [14] real-time suspicious human movement detection only focused on a few scenes in a particular scenario. In [38] the authors proposed a suspicious activity detection framework by using behavior interpretation algorithm (BIA) [38], which compares both ongoing activity and activity in general, uncommon or unknown. The findings anticipate suspicious actions [39] by setting some thresholds then evaluating actions.

Recently, a neural network [40] based hidden Markova model (HMM) was used for action recognition. In this method, a sequence of star skeletons was generated based on an action over a period of time. Then, time-sequential image frames convert into feature sets and these feature sets translate into sequential symbols. Further, it isused as input to a neural network model for action recognition, which categorizes whether a particular action is suspicious or not. In [41], the authors use a deep neural network (DNN) for suspicious activity detection by using a combination of convolution neural network (CNN) and deep belief network (DBN). They first extracted common features from CNN then fed these features to DBN for classification and detection of different classes of suspicious actions. The extended version of deep 3D CNN [42] is also used for human action recognition to find suspicious events using template-matching techniques. Some suspicious activities are pre-trained then predicted in the real world.

Human action recognition (HAR) plays a major role in visual understanding, especially in abnormality detection [8]; in this way different frameworks are designed to understand abnormality by analyzing human action recognition in outdoor scenarios and action recognition based on uniform segmentation [43]. Human detection is done with the combination of Euclidean distance and joint entropy-based methods. By these combination techniques a two-phase [44] method is designed for finding human action using a skeletonized images matrix which can be extended to single- and two-person action recognition methods using silhouette [45] of a frame class and optical point descriptors. Some finite state models like a machine recognizer [46] were also proposed for human activity recognition using a basic general set of actions. Usage of multiple frames gives motion estimation [47] and object detection. Using these two techniques, human activity detection is carried out from traditional background subtraction methods. In the sequence of frames, comparing the inter frame by using centroid and aspect ratio [48] is used to recognize the actions using common statistics to compute the trajectory paths without modelling the HMM, or coupled hidden Markov models (CHMMs) to find human activity. Recognition of human activities in a group was made using category feature vectors (CFVs) [49] with a combination of Gaussian mixture models (GMMs). GMMs can represent the distribution over the CFVs and improve the accuracy of recognition. In [9, 50], the authors proposed human activity detection using a hardware based approach using different sensors for human activity detection. For human activity recognition based on an image classification method, the authors of [39] chose a particular image from the set of frames and classification using various machine-learning methods such as Bag of Features model, Support Vector Machine, K-Nearest Neighbors. In [51], they proposed a rule-based classifier method to detect human activity. First, they extracted some common features like silhouette and spatial-temporal patterns using these features to generate activity then detected using rule-based classifiers. Further, in [52], the authors proposed a unique approach for action recognition based on combinational knowledge-based reasoning. The evolution of handcrafted methods to modern machine vision techniques based on sensible features allowing creation of computer vision aided artificial intelligence has produced promising results in action recognition techniques, which can be given a path to contextual and scenario independent implementation with outperforming modern vision methodologies.

Video understanding is important for scenario-based abnormality detection. This can be achieved by video representation learning, video classification and captioning of the video content. Learning of video representation is harder because encoding of abstract spatial-temporal patterns is a challenging task. In this way some recent surveys found [16, 53] encoding spatio-temporal patterns. Spatio-temporal features are a core component of video understanding. In [54], the authors proposed a method called Local Nearest Neighbor Distance (LNND) descriptors for anomaly detection, which can evaluate spatio-temporal patterns in crowd scenes to find multiple events or a single event. In [27], spatio-temporal clues were used for motion capture interpretation using 3D marker. Usage of spatio-temporal patterns to learn and recognize actions overcomes the view dependency problem by defining skeleton oriented centric technique, which improves the recognition accuracy. In [55], a descriptor was designed by combining both spatial-temporal features points 3D gradient with a textural symmetry for human activity recognition. This can be improved to fuse two CNNs, the first of which has spatial patterns and the second has temporal patterns [56]. Fusing these two motion features then takes a fusion score value to predict human action. In two-stream fusion technique, it is difficult to model long-term patterns. In [29], the authors proposed a method for video recognition using both CNN and LSTM network in a recurrent neural network (RNN) model. It takes long-term temporal information then describes a video. The LSTM networks are used with different combinations of networks. In [17], the authors proposed a method where temporal pooling is done using 3D CNN for extracting optical flow features. Further, these features are modelled by LSTM networks to classify video content.

Introduction of sequence-to-sequence learning uses an LSTM network for captioning video content. It has taken a stack of two LSTM layers concatenated into word padding and LSTM outputs. These pipelines [57] consist of feature extraction, filtering, shot clustering and labelling stages which produces both scene detection and annotation. Annotation of dynamic action is a difficult process, therefore, action classification helps to solve annotation in a dynamic action problem using an extreme learning machine (ELM) [58] algorithm for single hidden layer feedforward neural networks trained with test action instances. These action instances form small groups based on nearest action instances. The action instances groups are subsequently mapped to new feature sets. Based on these features set dynamic actions are annotated. In some scenarios, modelling action sequences with intra- and inter-class is essential. Therefore, modelling within-class and between-class actions similarity graphs generated using Grassmann manifolds [59] which gives promising results. It can be achieved by reproducing kernel Hilbert spaces and then discriminant analysis on each manifold. In [60], the authors propose a large-scale video classification network using different fusion techniques based on frame sequence and network architecture. The first network has taken more than 1 million videos and 487 different classes. Using CNN, they extracted the relationship between inter features and inter classes [61] by evaluating different network architecture and different classes. In [61], the authors proposed a method for categorization of videos using deep networks and [27] modelling spatio-temporal clues using hybrid deep neural network CNN, RNN with both spatial frames and stacked motion optical flow images for video classification. The detailed results and outcomes are discussed [62] with state-of-the-art deep learning networks for feature extraction techniques and outcomes for video classification and captioning.

11.3 Scenario understanding

Scenario understanding advances the autonomous security surveillance system to solve single scenario restricted problems to multiple scenario problems. Each security case has scenario dependent and independent problems concerning with time. An intelligent algorithm needs to be designed to solve this problem. This can be achieved using advances of deep neural networks [63]. State-of-the-art techniques are discussed in each section on how to design scenario-understanding framework to solve this problem. Figure 11.3 shows the overview of the scenario based abnormality detection model. First spatio-temporal features are extracted then we fuse these features to classify and caption video content. Finally, we translate the abnormality with a knowledge base.

11.3.1 Key frame extraction using instance segmentation

Currently, the main area of research aims to optimize the deep neural network. In this context reduction of parameters, selective allocation of channels at the time of training and visual attention generation are the predominantly served core areas, but before going attending to optimization problems the preprocessing of a huge amount of raw data is important to achieve the best result. Here key frames extraction is one of the techniques to reduce complexity in raw data. The key frames extracted are based on a lower number of moving instances in each frame.

Segmentation is an important task to look at every object, which helps to classify contents in video frames. In a video segment each instance is based on its pixel-level or object of interest. Generally, segmentation is focused on dividing images into sets of pixels and each set is derived based on similarity in texture, color or use some

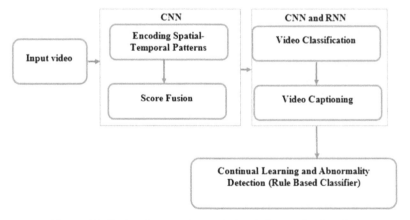

Figure 11.3. Typical diagram of scenario-based abnormality detection.

specific requirements. There are different types of segmentations available in the real world such as schematic segmentation [64], instance segmentation [23] etc. Instead of semantic segmentation, we use instance segmentation because it does not categorize each pixel in an image. It is primarily focused on object interest and creates a mask around every object in an image instead of bounding boxes. A pre-trained mask-RCNN [65] network performs instance segmentation of each frame. It shows generalized tasks like detection of objects, human pose with a precise segment of every instance.

Optimization of algorithms and reduced the computing resource is a well-known common problem in every research area. The work proposed in [66] extracts key frames in video content, and then evaluates selected key frames. In this method, they select frames by taking each neighbor as a surrogate for evaluating optical frames in video content. Key frames, or super frames in a video can form first level narration subset frames used to represent video content. Deep neural networks can learn the context of neighbors of key frames by selecting each key frame region and finding temporal activity in a video sequence. Some activity requires fewer frames and some complex activity requires more frames. The main advantage is to improve the network productivity by training selected frames instead of all frames in a video sequence.

In this method, one identifies key frames based on motion stillness and optical flow [67] with displacement values between consecutive frames. The function of time [68] is calculated using optical flow and then magnitude of every motion clue is evaluated using a motion metric, after estimation of aggregating optical flow in a vertical and horizontal direction in each frame represented in equation (11.1)

$$M(t) = \sum_i \sum_j |O(Fx(i, j, t))| + |O(Fy(i, j, t))| \qquad (11.1)$$

where $O(Fx(i, j, t))$ here i, j are pixels in a frame t at x component of optical flow and similarly for y component. Optical flow is an apparent motions pattern of an object in consecutive video frames. Hence, local maxima and minima would represent important activities or stillness between action sequences because the gradient values of this function changes according to motion and consecutive video frames. We select two frames when the temporal constraint in fast-moving activities is applied during selection [70] with number of instances. The frames are selected dynamically based on video content. Hence, simpler ones may have more, whereas more complex motion events would have fewer key frames. Introduction of key frame selection, instead of using all frames or a random representation of video content, makes this method computationally more efficient.

11.3.2 State full artifacts modelling

Modelling of important factors in natural data is an important task to achieve better results. Artifacts are core components in data like image, video and audio. Especially in video data, to perform video understanding [16], abnormality detection and action recognition etc, artifacts play a major role, where concentrated on region of interest of every object with its attention mechanism. Instead of choosing all components, attention mechanism is focused on problem-specific best artifacts. In abnormality detection, we choose salient objects, objects moving with action and static spatial contents. This can be achieved by pre-trained networks like region proposal network (RPN) [71] and generative adversarial network (GAN) [22].

11.3.3 Action recognition and attention of key action

A video contains several frames based on its length, it is computationally expensive to consider all frames and degrade the relationship among the sequence because all frames are not required. This issue motivates one to find attention of key action to identify important spatio-temporal information that is directly related to the specific class. Kar *et al* [72] proposed automated human action attention, which is an important component for abnormality detection. Key action frames can be extracted based on action attention. Action attention in video sequences produces consecutive action annotations for every short-term or long-term motion; from this production, they adopted multi-armed bandits to explore maximum exploitation and maximum exploration with local minima and maxima values, respectively.

11.3.4 A hybrid model for spatio-temporal features

Spatio-temporal clues are core features to classify and caption a video content. The spatiotemporal clues contain short-term, long-term motions. Modelling these features used two-stream, hybrid deep neural designs. Instead of using two-stream approach, a hybrid multi-model approach derives effectively both long-term and short-term motion compared to the two-stream [56] approach. In two-stream, the first stream evaluates spatial features and the second extracts short-term motions but hybrid models evaluate long-term motion clues effectively. It is possible using an LSTM network [13]. To extract these long-term motions, hybrid deep networks [16, 73] explore spatial, short-term and long-term clues with abstract semantics, also fusing both spatial and short-term motion clues from LSTM and novel regularized fusion networks. In figure 11.4, the overview of the framework is shown. First, spatial and short-term motion features are extracted from two-stream CNNs, and then input into LSTM [13] for long-term feature modelling. Video-level local spatial and global motion features are extracted and pooled using regularized feature fusion

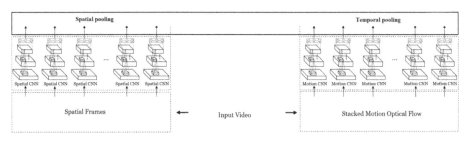

Figure 11.4. Overview framework for spatio-temporal clue modelling.

network [74]. Finally, all outputs of the feature fusion network are fused with sequence-based LSTM for final predictions.

11.3.5 Classification and captioning

Video classification automatically categorizes video contents based on classes such as human actions and complex activity. After successful modelling of spatio-temporal clues, it is easy to classify video content combining the spatial and temporal (short-term and the long-term) motion features. This can be achieved using regularized feature fusion networks [75–77] instead of using direct classification. Figure 11.5 shows the detailed architecture of a classification network, here regularized feature fusion takes both spatial-temporal features and evaluates correlations between these features (e.g., a person related to some specific visual features and their body movement), and it maintains better fusion representations. In fusion, inputs are taken followed by pooling and aggregating of each frame-level feature to video level. The input features are mapped in a non-linear way to next layer and then fused with a feature fusion layer, then regularization factors are applied to the network weights. Fusing the features with sequence-based LSTM provides good complementarity. Table 11.1 shows the classification accuracy with different abnormality detection datasets and comparative performance of CNN and LSTM, and both spatial and motion are shown in table 11.2, depicting the classification accuracy of two different approaches, i.e. LRCN and efficient large convolutional neural network (EL-CNN).

After successful classification of video content, one needs to annotate the movement of objects concerning static visual features. This task is more complex and it requires more knowledge to design a description production model because it generates action or activities in video content and scenes, and is capable of expressing how these activities/scenes/objects related to each other in a natural sentence instead of only capturing and recognizing the objects. The proposed framework is based on [29] deep video description and it extends to using generated

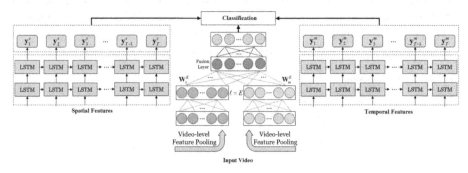

Figure 11.5. Overview of classification framework.

Table 11.1. Video classification accuracy of CNN and LSTM with spatio-temporal features.

Serial no.	Dataset	Spatial + motion CNN	Spatial + motion LSTM	CNN + LSTM (spatial + motion)	Background
1	UCSD	69%	70%	**82%**	Dynamic
2	UMN, Web	71%	72%	**84%**	Dynamic
3	Subway	62%	69%	**81%**	Dynamic
4	U-Turn	64%	79%	**87%**	Static
5	MIT PLIA1	65%	70%	**82%**	Dynamic
7	QMUL	67%	76%	**85%**	Static
8	CAVIAR	60%	70%	**80%**	Dynamic

Table 11.2. Video classification comparison with different models.

Serial no.	Dataset	LRCN [29]	EI-CNN [78]	CNN +LSTM (spatial + motion)	Background
1	UCSD	82.9%	44.4%	**88%**	Dynamic
2	UMN, Web	88.7%	52.3%	**89%**	Dynamic
3	Subway	79.5%	60.1%	**85%**	Dynamic
4	U-Turn	85.3%	58.5%	**86%**	Static
5	MIT PLIA1	82.2%	56%	**89%**	Dynamic
7	QMUL	81.4%	56%	**87%**	Static
8	CAVIAR	80%	44%	**84%**	Dynamic

descriptions for abnormality detection using spatio-temporal patterns. The authors of [29], as shown in figure 11.6, proposed a deep description-understanding network, which can be used to generate sequences of sentences with pretrained weights. Table 11.3, shows the accuracy of captioning with different datasets.

11.4 Abnormality detection

Abnormality detection using scenario understanding is possible after successful classification and captioning of video content. We categorize video content based on different scenarios with their spatial semantics and object abstraction. Once the scenario is classified, we then generate a description of activity on a particular scenario with the help of video captioning. In each scenario, a constant spatial background with some common activity, exists where in each case a pre-trained model generates a caption of every activity in a scenario, and it generates description over time. These descriptions are stored in the semantic knowledge base. A semantic knowledge base contains generated text records of each scenario within a specific time. The knowledge base further divides using standard NLP technique [79] to classify normal activity and abnormal activity.

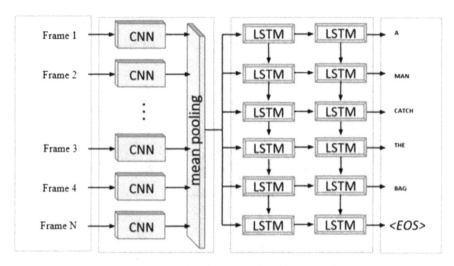

Figure 11.6. Overview framework for video captioning.

Table 11.3. Results of video captioning using LRCNN model.

Serial no.	Dataset	Video	Results	Background
1	UCSD	98	67.2	Dynamic
2	UMN, Web	16	70.6	Dynamic
3	Subway	08	70.2	Dynamic
4	U-Turn	01	74.5	Static
5	MIT PLIA1	—	72.2	Dynamic
7	QMUL	1	80.6	Static
8	CAVIAR	55	74.7	Dynamic

11.4.1 Natural abnormality translation

Natural abnormality translation extends some core techniques and some predefined rules like commonly known abnormalities situated in all scenarios, classified as common, unknown, time-variance and scenario specific. Common abnormalities are common in all scenarios for example abundant objects, gunfire etc. Unknowns are scenario-based understanding abnormalities that vary from scenario to scenario, for example a person running in the playground is normal but in some shops or malls that is abnormal. Time-variance events are sometimes normal and sometimes abnormal. These events can be differentiated with time constraint. For example, in bank scenarios activity during day hours is normal but abnormal at night, which directly depends on the time. Scenario specific sets some rules on a specific time, for example in the same class normal days and examination days may lead to many abnormalities. These are all compound evaluated using a natural abnormality detection module. The proposed model learns to solve all kinds of problems using a knowledge base, which is designed using classification and captioning of video

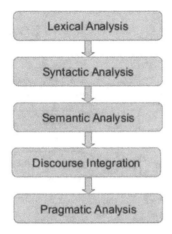

Figure 11.7. Abnormality translation phases with typical example.

content. Each sequence of descriptions is sorted and stored concerning each scenario using sentiment analysis techniques. This can be achieved with different translation techniques such as (figure 11.7) lexical analysis, syntactic analysis, semantic analysis, and discourse integration followed by pragmatic analysis. In lexical analysis, we organize description generated by captioning of each object with spatial coordination output of the lexical analysis input to syntactic analysis. It reorganizes each activity into a particular segment parse and stored in a temporary knowledge base. The temporary knowledge base is evaluated by semantic analysis and this compares the description and gives scores to overall comparison, and it can be performed using pre-computed description. Based on computed score the integration called discourse integration is performed to categorize different abnormalities. The pragmatic analysis finally produces an alert at a particular scene related with time. Figure 11.8, shows the results of scenario based abnormality detection, anchor boxes have been used to mask an abnormality event in a video sequence on particular frame captured by activity-based captions. Table 11.4 shows the accuracy of the proposed method compared to some abnormality detection models and frameworks.

11.5 Datasets

Table 11.5 shows the abnormality detection datsets available in the real world, it can be categorized based on static and dynamic background.

11.6 Challenges

Real-time monitoring of video content faces lot of problems, in this context the problem of variability is one of the most important areas. In visual understanding the system needs to generalize multiple variations in object appearance such as viewpoint, facial expressions, pose, conditions of lighting, image quality and occlusions [16, 83]. Besides, this task should preferably be performed in real time

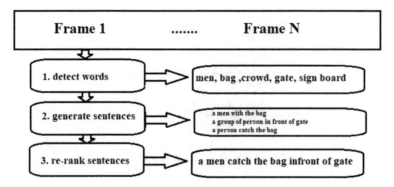

Figure 11.8. Scenario based abnormality detection results on AVENUE dataset.

Table 11.4. Results of abnormality detection on different methods.

Serial no.	Methods	UCSD	UMN	CAVIAR	AVENUE
1	MPPCA [80]	59%	64.%	52%	45%
2	Social force (SF) [81]	67.5%	52.8%	56%	52%
3	Conv AE [22]	82%	85.7%	67.2%	65%
4	MPCC+SF [82]	68.2%	67.3%	62.8%	63%
5	**OURS**	**96.5%**	**92.2%**	**95.8%**	**97.2%**

Table 11.5. Datasets for scenario-based abnormality detection.

Serial no.	Dataset	Video	Images	Number classes	Released year	Background
1	UCSD	98		2	2013	Dynamic
2	UMN, Web	16		4	2011	Dynamic
3	Subway	08		1	2010	Dynamic
4	U-Turn	01		1	2008	Static
5	MIT PLIA1	—	2.5M	205	2017	Dynamic
7	QMUL	1	9K	1	2008	Static
8	CAVIAR	55		2	2004	Dynamic
9	AVENUE	48		1	2013	Dynamic

compared to conventional computing platforms and find each semantics context with interrelationship. In video data, a huge amount of semantics context and multiple classes of actions need to be classified, such as interaction with human-to-human, human-to-object, human-to-animal and group of activities etc. Modelling these spatial and temporal clues in a video is one of the biggest and most challenging tasks. Some motions and actions are continuously occurring over time and then the model detects different classes of activities formed by an individual or a set of groups according to time, classifies and captions this based on semantic context, further differentiating each activity as an important task. Representation of normal regions in video streams is quite difficult. Therefore, preparing a robust fully optimized statistical model is required for achieving good accuracy. The exact notion of abnormal behavior is either subjective or changes over different applications if the possibility of an ambiguity boundary between normal or anomalous behavior.

11.7 Trends and strengths

In autonomous surveillance systems, there is no generalized tool for abnormality detection. The research community found some grammar-based abnormalities fixed on some specific scenarios. Apart from this a lot of abnormal events can happen in different scenarios so there are a lot of things to find out to fulfil the complete autonomous surveillance system. In a real world scenario, we observe different activities like theft, suspicious persons, trespassing, person re-identification, tracking, tracing and multiple objects etc. The proposed work extracts first level abstraction in autonomous surveillance and is applicable for all scenarios. Here is the first video content understanding model for detecting abnormalities.

Intelligent video understanding systems are aimed at automated tracking of individuals, crowd monitoring and recognizing their activities [16]. This includes the detection of abnormal, suspicious or criminal activities and reporting to concerned law and enforcement agents or authorities to take immediate action. Using these state-of-the-art technologies reduces the workload of security personnel and alerts will be signaled security events, which can help to prevent dangerous situations:

- first, it detects all kinds of abnormality in different scenarios in general;
- usage of transfer learning technique helps applicability to different scenarios;
- invigilation works are made easy in an examination center;
- film certification process made easy by examining video content.

11.8 Conclusion

In this chapter, we discussed state-of-the-art scenario based abnormality detection technique on two key approaches that are related to classification and captioning of video content. Given a huge amount of video data generated every day, it remains challenging to model video features using handcrafted mechanisms that are costly to design. Based on these observations a new way to model features and their mechanisms has been found using deep neural models that also maintains the proposed model with less computational power and more accurate results by substantial evaluation of key frames using instance segmentation, artifacts modelling and attention generation. These are all inputs to evaluate core abundant spatio-temporal patterns; the essence of deep network successful modelling of these features provides promising results. Therefore, modelled spatio-temporal features are fused to understand a scenario or classify a particular scenario and description is generated through deep description understanding of the neural model for captioning. A successful evaluation of video text abnormality translation is introduced to learn abnormalities. The abnormality translation generates a natural sentence, categorizes sentences, ranks and re-ranks sentences in different levels to predict abnormality in all scenarios. This chapter will be useful to shed light on the insights of intelligence surveillance in security domain research.

References

[1] Najafabadi M M, Villanustre F, Khoshgoftaar T M, Seliya N, Wald R and Muharemagic E 2015 Deep learning applications and challenges in big data analytics *J. Big Data* **2** 1–21

[2] Hatcher W G and Yu W 2018 A survey of deep learning: platforms applications and emerging research trends *IEEE Access* **6** 24411–32

[3] Ko T 2011 A survey on behavior analysis in video surveillance applications *Video Surveillance* 280–93

[4] Gowsikhaa D, Manjunath and Abirami S 2012 Suspicious human activity detection from surveillance videos *Int. J. Internet Distrib. Comput. Syst.* **2** 141–9

[5] Liu H, Chen S and Kubota N 2013 Intelligent video systems and analytics: a survey *IEEE Trans. Ind. Informatics* **9** 1222–33

[6] Federal Highway Administration 2015 *Video Analysis Research Projects* (US Department of Transportation)

[7] Sanoj C S, Vijayaraj N and Rajalakshmi D 2013 Vision approach of human detection and tracking using focus tracing analysis *Int. Conf. Inf. Commun. Embed. Syst. ICICES* pp 64–8

[8] Niu W, Long J, Han D and Wang Y 2004 Human activity detection and recognition for video surveillance *IEEE Int. Conf. on Multimedia and Expo (ICME) (IEEE Cat. No. 04TH8763)* vol 1 (Piscataway, NJ: IEEE) pp 719–22

[9] Damarla T, Kaplan L and Chan A 2007 Human infrastructure & human activity detection *FUSION 2007 10th Int. Conf. Inf. Fusion*

[10] Zhang B, Wang L, Wang Z, Qiao Y and Wang H 2016 Real-time action recognition with enhanced motion vector CNNs *Proc. of the IEEE Conf. on Computer Vision and Pattern Recognition* pp 2718–26

[11] Ullah A, Ahmad J, Muhammad K, Sajjad M and Baik S W 2017 Action recognition in video sequences using deep bi-directional LSTM with CNN features *IEEE Access* **6** 1155–66

[12] Kangwei L, Jianhua W and Zhongzhi H 2018 Abnormal event detection and localization using level set based on hybrid features *Signal Image Video Process* **12** 255–61

[13] Naseer S *et al* 2018 Enhanced network anomaly detection based on deep neural networks *IEEE Access* **6** 48231–46

[14] Rajenderana S V and Fei K 2014 Real-time detection of suspicious human movement *Int. Conf. on Electical, Electronics, Computer Engineering and their Applications*

[15] Mathur G and Bundele M 2017 Research on Intelligent Video Surveillance techniques for suspicious activity detection critical review *2016 Int Conf Recent Adv Innov Eng ICRAIE 2016* vol 2016 pp 1–8

[16] Suresha M, Kuppa S and Raghukumar D S 2020 A study on deep learning spatiotemporal models and feature extraction techniques for video understanding *Int. J. Multimed. Inf. Retr.* **9** 81–101

[17] Sun J, Wang J and Yeh T-C 2017 Video understanding: from video classification to captioning *Computer Vision and Pattern Recognition* (Stanford, CT: Stanford University) pp 1–9

[18] Shi Y, Tian Y, Wang Y, Zeng W and Huang T 2017 Learning long-term dependencies for action recognition with a biologically-inspired deep network *Proc. IEEE Int. Conf. Comput. Vis.* **2017** 716–25

[19] Hu S H, Li Y and Li B 2016 Video2vec: learning semantic spatio-temporal embeddings for video representation *Proc.—Int. Conf. Pattern Recognit.* pp 811–6

[20] Bulbul M F, Islam S and Ali H 2019 3D human action analysis and recognition through GLAC descriptor on 2D motion and static posture images *Multimed. Tools Appl.* **78** 21085–111

[21] Li Q, Qiu Z, Yao T, Mei T, Rui Y and Luo J 2017 Learning hierarchical video representation for action recognition *Int. J. Multimed. Inf. Retr.* **6** 85–98

[22] Alom M Z *et al* 2019 A state-of-the-art survey on deep learning theory and architectures *Electronics* **8** 292

[23] Kuncheva L I, Yousefi P and Almeida J 2018 Edited nearest neighbour for selecting keyframe summaries of egocentric videos *J. Vis. Commun. Image Represent* **52** 118–30

[24] Basit A 2019 *Dynamic Matrix Decomposition for Action Recognition* arXiv:1902.07438

[25] Tripathi R K, Jalal A S and Agrawal S C 2018 Suspicious human activity recognition: a review *Artif. Intell. Rev.* **50** 283–339

[26] Chu W S, De La Torre F and Cohn J F 2017 Learning spatial and temporal cues for multi-label facial action unit detection *Proc—12th IEEE Int Conf Autom Face Gesture Recognition FG 1st Int Work Adapt Shot Learn Gesture Underst Prod ASL4GUP 2017 Biometrics Wild Bwild 2017 Heteroge* pp 25–32

[27] Wu Z *et al* 2018 Modeling multimodal clues in a hybrid deep learning framework for video classification *IEEE Trans. Multimed.* **20** 3137–47

[28] Chen K, Kovvuri R, Gao J and Nevatia R 2018 MSRC: multimodal spatial regression with semantic context for phrase grounding *Int. J. Multimed. Inf. Retr.* **7** 17–28

[29] Donahue J *et al* 2017 Long-term recurrent convolutional networks for visual recognition and description *IEEE Trans. Pattern Anal. Mach. Intell.* **39** 677–91

[30] Shekhar S *et al* 2015 Spatiotemporal data mining: a computational perspective *ISPRS Int. J. Geo-Inf.* **4** 2306–38

[31] Santosh K K, Dogra D P and Roy P P 2019 Anomaly detection in road traffic using visual surveillance: a survey *ACM Comput. Surv.* **53** 1–26

[32] Popoola O P and Kejun Wang 2012 Video-based abnormal human behavior recognition: a review *IEEE Trans. Syst. Man Cybern. Part C Applications Rev.* **42** 865–78

[33] Bermejo E, Déniz O and Bueno G 2010 Security system based on suspicious behavior detection *Buran* **17** 12–16

[34] Patil S and Talele K 2015 Suspicious movement detection and tracking based on color histogram *Proc.—2015 Int. Conf. Commun. Inf. Comput. Technol. ICCICT 2015*

[35] Rahangdale K 2016 Event detection using background subtraction for surveillance**1** 25–8

[36] Takala V and Pietikäinen M 2007 Multi-object tracking using color texture and motion *Proc. IEEE Comput. Soc. Conf. Comput. Vis. Pattern Recognit.* pp 1–7

[37] Rasheed K and Amin I 2010 Detection of suspicious activity through video surveillances *J. Independent Stud. Res. Comput.* **8** 12–6

[38] Neelima D, Jaideep G and Priyadharsani G I 2013 An intelligent suspicious activity detection framework (ISADF) for video surveillance systems *Int. J. Comput. Appl.* **84** 26–30

[39] Baptista R, Antunes M, Aouada D and Ottersten B 2018 Anticipating suspicious actions using a small dataset of action templates *13th Int. Joint Conf. Comput. Vision Imaging Comput. Graph. Theory Appl.*

[40] Singh D, Yadav A K and Kumar V 2014 Human activity tracking using star skeleton and activity recognition using HMMs and neural network *Int. J. Sci. Res. Publ.* **4** 2250–3153

[41] Scaria E, Abahai A T and Isaac E 2017 Suspicious activity detection in surveillance video using discriminative deep belief network *Int. J. Control Theory and Appl.* **10** 261–8

[42] Arunnehru J, Chamundeeswari G and Bharathi S P 2018 Human action recognition using 3D convolutional neural networks with 3D motion cuboids in surveillance videos *Procedia Comput. Sci.* **133** 471–7

[43] Sharif M, Khan M A, Akram T, Javed M Y, Saba T and Rehman A 2017 A framework of human detection and action recognition based on uniform segmentation and combination of Euclidean distance and joint entropy-based features selection *Eurasip J. Image Video Process* **2017** 89

[44] Mliki H, Zaafouri R and Hammami M 2018 Human action recognition based on discriminant body regions selection *Signal Image Video Process* **12** 845–52

[45] Islam S, Qasim T, Yasir M, Bhatti N, Mahmood H and Zia M 2018 Single- and two-person action recognition based on silhouette shape and optical point descriptors *Signal Image Video Process* **12** 853–60

[46] Noorit N and Suvonvorn N 2014 *Proc. of the First Int. Conf. on Advanced Data and Information Engineering (DaEng-2013)* vol 285 pp 379–80

[47] Dhulekar P A, Gandhe S T, Shewale A, Sonawane S and Yelmame V 2017 Motion estimation for human activity surveillance *2017 Int Conf Emerg Trends Innov ICT ICEI 2017* pp 82–5

[48] Albukhary N and Mustafah Y M 2017 Real-time human activity recognition *IOP Conf. Ser. Mater. Sci. Eng.* **260** 012017

[49] Lin W, Sun M T, Poovandran R and Zhang Z 2008 Human activity recognition for video surveillance *Proc.—IEEE Int. Symp. Circuits Syst.* pp 2737–40

[50] Gabriel I V and Anghelescu P 2015 Vibration monitoring system for human activity detection *Proc. 2015 7th Int. Conf. Electron Comput. Artif. Intell. ECAI 2015* pp AE41–4

[51] Sugimoto M, Zin T T, Toriu T and Nakajima S 2011 Robust rule-based method for human activity recognition *Int. J. Comput. Sci. and Netw. Sec.* **11** 37–43

[52] Del Rincón J M, Santofimia M J and Nebel J C 2013 Common-sense reasoning for human action recognition *Pattern Recognit. Lett.* **34** 1849–60

[53] Geetha R, Sumathi N and Sathiabama D 2008 A survey of spatial temporal and spatio-temporal data mining *J. Comput.* 31–3

[54] Song X, Lan C, Zeng W, Xing J, Sun X and Yang J 2019 Temporal-spatial mapping for action recognition *IEEE Trans. Circuits Syst. Video Technol.* **30** 748–59

[55] Melfi R, Kondra S and Petrosino A 2013 Human activity modeling by spatio temporal textural appearance *Pattern Recognit. Lett.* **34** 1990–4

[56] Simonyan K and Zisserman A 2014 Two-stream convolutional networks for action recognition in videos arXiv:1406.2199

[57] Lee S, Kim H G and Ro Y M Stan: spatio-temporal adversarial networks for abnormal event detection *Image and Video Systems Lab School of Electrical Engineering KAIST South Korea*

[58] Iosifidis A, Tefas A and Pitas I 2013 Dynamic action recognition based on dynemes and extreme learning *Machine Pattern Recognit. Lett.* **34** 1890–8

[59] Harandi M T, Sanderson C, Shirazi S and Lovell B C 2013 Kernel analysis on Grassmann manifolds for action recognition *Pattern Recognit. Lett.* **34** 1906–15

[60] Karpathy A, Toderici G, Shetty S, Leung T, Sukthankar R and Li F F 2014 Large-scale video classification with convolutional neural networks *Proc. of the IEEE Computer Society Conf. on Computer Vision and Pattern Recognition* vol 2014 pp 1725–32

[61] Ye H, Wu Z, Zhao R, Wang X, Jiang Y and Xue X 2015 Evaluating two-stream CNN for video classification *Proc. of the 5th ACM on Int. Conf. on Multimedia Retrieval* pp 435–42

[62] Wu Z, Jiang Y, Wang J, Pu J and Xue X 2014 Exploring inter-feature and inter-class relationships with deep neural networks for video classification *MM14 2014* pp 167–76

[63] Lecun Y, Bengio Y and Hinton G 2015 Deep learning *Nature* **521** 436–44

[64] Qiu Z, Yao T and Mei Learning T 2018 Deep spatio-temporal dependence for semantic video segmentation *IEEE Trans. Multimed.* **20** 939–49

[65] Ouyang W *et al* 2017 DeepID-Net: object detection with deformable part based convolutional neural networks *IEEE Trans. Pattern Anal. Mach. Intell.* **39** 1320–34

[66] Gharbi H, Bahroun S and Zagrouba E 2016 A novel key frame extraction approach for video summarization vol 3 Visigrapp, pp 146–153

[67] Lai W-S, Huang J-B and Yang M-H 2017 2 Virginia Tech 3 Nvidia Research 1 vol 1 no Nips, pp 1–11 2017

[68] Bobick A F and Davis J W 2001 The recognition of human movement using temporal templates BT *Pattern Anal. Mach. Intell. IEEE Trans.* **23** 257–67

[69] Lu C, Shi J and Jia J 2013 Abnormal event detection at 150 FPS in MATLAB *Proc. IEEE Int. Conf. Comput. Vis.* 2720–7

[70] Loukas C, Varytimidis C, Rapantzikos K and Kanakis M A 2018 Keyframe extraction from laparoscopic videos based on visual saliency detection *Comput. Methods Programs Biomed.* **165** 13–23

[71] Ren S, He K, Girshick R and Sun Faster J 2017 R-CNN: towards real-time object detection with region proposal networks *IEEE Trans. Pattern Anal. Mach. Intell.* **39** 1137–49

[72] Kar A, Rai N, Sikka K and Sharma G 2017 AdaScan: adaptive scan pooling in deep convolutional neural networks for human action recognition in videos *Proc.—30th IEEE Conf. Comput. Vis. Pattern Recognition CVPR 2017* vol 2017 pp 5699–708

[73] Wang Y, Long M, Wang J and Yu P S 2017 Spatiotemporal pyramid network for video action recognition *Proc.—30th IEEE Conf. on Computer Vision and Pattern Recognition CVPR 2017* vol 2017 pp 2097–106

[74] Singh T and Vishwakarma D K 2019 A hybrid framework for action recognition in low-quality video sequences

[75] Wu Z, Wang X, Jiang Y, Ye H and Xue X 2015 Modeling spatial-temporal clues in a hybrid deep learning framework for video classification *MM15 Proc. of the 23rd ACM Int. Conf. on Multimedia* pp 461–70

[76] Dai Q, Wu Z, Jiang Y G, Xue X and Tangz Fudan-Njust J 2014 Violent scenes detection using deep neural networks *CEUR Workshop Proc.* vol 1263

[77] Wu Z, Jiang Y, Wang X, Ye H, Xue, X and Wang, J 2015 Fusing multi-stream deep networks for video classification arXiv:1509.06086

[78] Varadarajan B, Toderici G, Vijayanarasimhan S and Natsev A 2015 Efficient large scale video classification arXiv:1505.06250

[79] Yin W, Schütze H, Xiang B and Zhou B 2016 ABCNN: attention-based convolutional neural network for modeling sentence pairs *Trans. Assoc. Computat. Linguistics* **4** 259–72

[80] Kim J and Grauman K 2009 Observe locally infer globally: a space-time MRF for detecting abnormal activities with incremental updates *2009 IEEE Comput Soc Conf Comput Vis Pattern Recognit Work CVPR Work 2009* vol 2009 pp 2921–8

[81] Mehran R, Oyama A and Shah M 2009 Abnormal crowd behavior detection using social force model *IEEE Comput. Soc. Conf. Comput. Vis. Pattern Recognit. Work CVPR Work 2009* vol 2009 no 1, pp 935–42

[82] Mahadevan V, Li W, Bhalodia V and Vasconcelos N 2010 Anomaly detection in crowded scenes *Proc. IEEE Comput. Soc. Conf. Comput. Vis. Pattern Recognit. No May 2014* pp 1975–81

[83] Guo Y, Liu Y, Georgiou T and Lew M S 2018 A review of semantic segmentation using deep neural networks *Int. J. Multimed. Inf. Retr.* **7** 87–93

IOP Publishing

Advanced Security Solutions for Multimedia

Irshad Ahmad Ansari and Varun Bajaj

Chapter 12

Ear recognition for multimedia security

**Sagar G Sangodkar, Niranjan Suthar, Akash Palde,
Parmeshwar Birajadar and Vikram M Gadre**

The ear as a biometric modality has various application possibilities in areas such as forensics, multimedia security and surveillance. The ear has a unique anatomical structure and appearance that differs from person to person and is a stable biometric trait that does not change much over time. Also, the ear image acquisition process is contactless and non-intrusive. In this work, we implement various components of an ear recognition system. First, we propose a deep learning approach for detection of ears based on YOLO (you only look once) object detection architecture. We then propose two different approaches for feature extraction. The first approach is based on multi-resolution scattering wavelet network, whereas the second approach is based on convolution neural networks (CNNs). The proposed feature extraction approaches outperform several techniques existing in the literature on standard ear datasets. Finally, we conclude with the potential applications of ear recognition and research directions further in the area.

12.1 Introduction

Biometrics [1] is the science of identifying an individual based on one or more intrinsic physical or behavioral traits. The physical traits involve fingerprints, iris, ear, face, finger knuckles, palm prints, hair etc, whereas behavioral traits involve speech accent, tone, signature, keystroke recognition, gait etc, which are unique for every individual. A biometric system takes physical or behavioral or both the attributes of an individual, processes them and identifies and/or verifies the identity of the individual. Hence, the biometric based authentication is much more reliable as compared to the traditional ways of token-based (ex. driver's license) or knowledge-based (ex. passwords) authentication systems.

12.1.1 Components of a biometric system

A typical biometric system consists of the following four basic building blocks, as shown in figure 12.1:

Sensor: A biometric sensor captures the biometric data of a user in a raw format. It is essential to build a suitable human–machine interface for the biometric system. A robust sensor module is necessary to build a successful biometric system.

Feature extraction: It generates a digital representation (template) of the biometric data captured by the sensor module. The template (sometimes also referred to as feature vector) should contain discriminatory information essential for recognizing the user. This module also includes appropriate preprocessing of the data to remove any noise or artifacts added by the sensor module while capturing the data.

Database: The biometric templates of all the users interacting with the system are stored securely in one place in the database. The templates are then accessed and used accordingly for identification or verification.

Matcher: A matcher compares the query template with the template stored in the database and generates a match score which is a measure of similarity between the two templates. The match scores generated by the matcher are either used to provide a ranking of the enrolled identities or to validate a claimed identity.

12.1.2 Modes of operation

A biometric system is first used to enroll users in the database. In this enrollment phase, biometric template of all the users is generated and stored in the database for later matching. The biometric system is then operated in either of the two modes: identification or verification as illustrated in figure 12.2.

(A) **Identification**: In the identification mode, a user presents their biometric input to the system to get identified among the identities enrolled in the system. This is done by matching the input template with all the templates stored in the database on a one-to-many basis. The system then outputs the identity of the person whose template has the highest match with the input template. Sometimes a classifier can also be employed which can directly classify the input template into one of the enrolled identities.

(B) **Verification**: In the verification mode, the system verifies the identity claimed by a user presenting his biometric input. This is done by matching the input biometric data provided by the user with the template stored in the database corresponding to the claimed identity on a one-to-one basis.

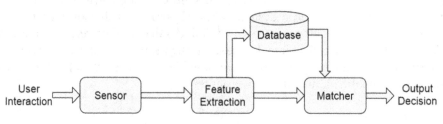

Figure 12.1. Components of a biometric system.

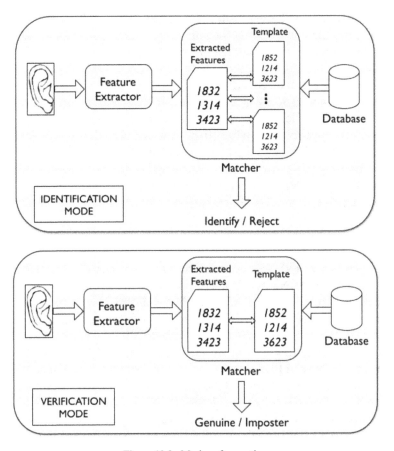

Figure 12.2. Modes of operation.

If the match score is above a certain threshold, the claim is accepted as 'genuine', otherwise the claim is rejected and the user is considered an 'impostor'.

12.1.3 Performance evaluation metrics

Biometric performance measures give an idea about the accuracy and efficiency of a biometric system which can be used to access the performance of various systems.

Identification mode performance metrics

When the system is used in identification mode, the metrics commonly used to evaluate the system performance are as follows:

- **Recognition accuracies at various ranks**: Rank-1 accuracy corresponds to the fraction of cases where the identity is correctly identified by the system. Similarly Rank-n accuracy corresponds to the fraction of instances when the correct identity is among the top-n identities predicted by the system.

- **Cumulative match characteristics (CMC) curves**: CMC curves are generated by plotting the accuracies at various ranks, with the ranks along the x-axis and the corresponding accuracies along the y-axis.

Verification mode performance metrics

The output of a biometric system operating in the verification mode is binary, i.e. output is either labelled as positive (genuine) or negative (imposter), which is a binary classification problem in which there can be four possible scenarios:

- True positive (TP): A genuine person is truly labelled as a genuine person.
- False positive (FP): An imposter is falsely labelled as a genuine person.
- True negative (TN): An imposter is truly labelled as an imposter.
- False negative (FN): A genuine person is falsely labelled as an imposter.

The verification system performance is typically evaluated using the following metrics:

- **False negative rate (FNR)**: Also referred to as false reject rate (FRR) or false non-match rate (FNMR). It corresponds to the probability of a biometric system rejecting a genuine subject. $FNR = FN/(FN + TP)$.
- **False positive rate (FPR)**: Also referred to as false acceptance rate (FAR) or false match rate (FMR). It corresponds to the probability of a biometric system declaring an impostor as a genuine subject. $FPR = FP/(FP + TN)$.
- **True positive rate (TPR)**: Also referred to as genuine acceptance rate (GAR), sensitivity or recall. It corresponds to the probability of a biometric system accepting a genuine subject. $TPR = TP/(TP + FN) = 1 - FNR$.
- **True negative rate (TNR)**: Also referred to as specificity or selectivity. It corresponds to the probability of a biometric system rejecting an imposter subject. $TNR = TN/(TN + FP) = 1 - FPR$.
- **Equal error rate (EER)**: If the FAR and the FRR values are plotted against various thresholds, there exists a point where the FAR and FRR values are equal. The value of FAR (or FRR) at this point is called the equal error rate.
- **Receiver operating characteristics (ROC)**: The plot of FAR versus GAR is referred to as the ROC curve.
- **Area under curve (AUC)**: It is the area under the ROC curve. The more the AUC, the more accurate is the system.

12.2 Ear recognition

The human ear starts developing during the early days of pregnancy and gets completed by the time of birth. Various anatomical structures such as tragus, antitragus, helix, antihelix, incisura, lobe, etc, as shown in figure 12.3, differ in shape and appearance from person to person and do not change much over time. It is also observed that the left and right ears of most people are close to bilateral symmetric [2], although it is different for some. The ear is thus a potential biometric candidate that can be efficiently used to build a successful biometric system.

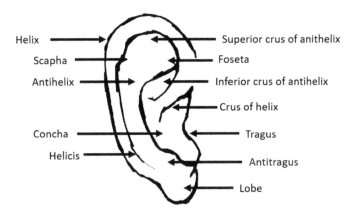

Figure 12.3. Ear anatomy.

Figure 12.4. A typical ear recognition pipeline.

The advantage of using the ear is that the ear image acquisition process is contactless and non-intrusive. The ear can be used alongside other biometric modalities (such as face) in multimodal biometric systems, where even when the face is not properly captured, the ear can be used to identify the person. There have been significant contributions to this field recently, but there are still some open research problems which hinder large-scale deployment of ear recognition technology.

A typical ear recognition pipeline consists of the following steps, as shown in figure 12.4:

- Acquisition of a digital image containing ear biometrics using an appropriate sensor;
- Detection and segmentation of image containing the ear followed by ear normalization or alignment so as to bring it to a standard configuration;
- The ear image is then represented using a feature vector using a robust feature extraction technique which captures discriminative information required for recognition;
- Finally, the feature vector of a query image is then matched with the features vectors stored in the database to either identify the person from a known set of identities or verify the identity claimed by the person.

We shall explore in detail each of these steps in this work.

12.3 Ear detection

We use the YOLO object detection algorithm for this task where the object of interest is the ear. The first version of the YOLO algorithm [4] was proposed by

Redmon *et al* in 2016, and was a new approach to solving the object detection problem. Previously, object detection was performed by first obtaining several region proposals in an image using a region proposal network which that were then fed to a classifier to classify the objects contained in it along with bounding box regression. These two-stage detectors such as RCNN, Fast-RCNN and Faster-RCNN perform classification several times on numerous region proposals and are thus slow in operation, whereas YOLO passes an input image only once through a fully convolutional neural network (FCNN) and performs detection along with classification in a single shot. Specifically, it divides the input image into $n \times n$ grids and then for each grid, it obtains bounding boxes along with class probabilities of objects contained in those bounding boxes using a single CNN. Thereafter, various versions of YOLO [5] were proposed with significant improvements in accuracy and speed. We have used YOLOv3 [6] in this work which is a multi-scale object detector and especially beneficial to detect ears at various scales.

Advantages of YOLO
- It is extremely fast and achieves real-time speed with good precision.
- While making predictions it considers the image globally, which is not the case in region proposal and sliding window-based techniques.
- It performs detection at different scales by using output at various FCNN layers which helps to overcome the issue of detecting small objects.

Network architecture
Feature extractor and detector are two major parts in which the network can be divided. An input image first passes through the feature extractor to obtain features at various scales. In the case of YOLO v3, the feature extractor used is Darknet-53 which is made up of several convolutional layers and residual blocks, as shown in figure 12.5

YOLO v3 is designed to detect objects at multiple scales by using features obtained from multiple layers. Specifically, the features from the last three residual blocks are all used by the detector part to obtain bounding boxes and the corresponding object class. The detector has a structure similar to feature pyramid networks [24], where the features at one scale are integrated with another scale features using 1×1 convolutions.

Assuming the input size is 416×416, the size of the feature vector at the last three layers would be $13 \times 13 \times 1024$, $26 \times 26 \times 512$ and $52 \times 52 \times 256$. They are then manipulated using 1×1 convolutions by the detector to obtain outputs of size $13 \times 13 \times 30$, $25 \times 26 \times 30$ and $52 \times 52 \times 30$, where $5 \times (NUM\_CLASS + 5) = 30$ and $NUM\_CLASS = 1$, which is the ear. We can interpret it as if the input image is divided into grid cells of size 13×13, 26×26 and 52×52 and corresponding to every grid cell, we obtain 30 values. That is, each cell is responsible for 5 bounding box predictions and for each bounding box prediction, we have 6 entries corresponding to objectness score (o_s), x-y coordinates (b_x, b_y), height (b_h) and width (b_w) of bounding boxes and the probability for ear class (p_ear) as illustrated in figure 12.6.

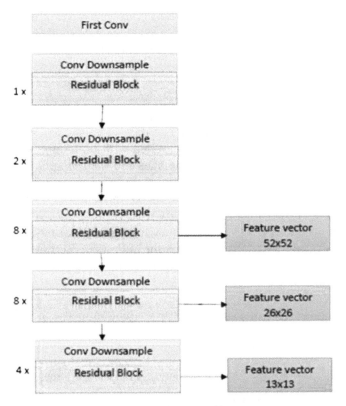

Figure 12.5. Darknet-53 architecture.

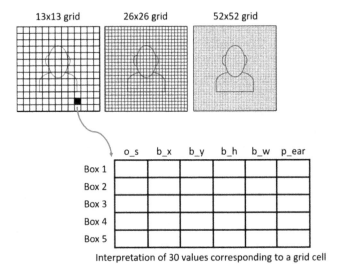

Interpretation of 30 values corresponding to a grid cell

Figure 12.6. Interpretation of YOLO network output.

The large number of redundant predicted bounding boxes are reduced by first discarding the boxes that have detected a class with a score value less than a threshold. Thereafter, we use non-max suppression method [6], in which we discard overlapping bounding boxes, which gives us our final detections.

Training procedure

The single CNN network consisting of feature extractor and detector is trained end-to-end using the AWE dataset [3]. The dataset consists of 1000 profile face images containing the ear which are annotated with bounding boxes for the ear region. The training set consists of 750 images and the remaining 250 images are used for testing.

During training, we use fixed size input images having 416 × 416 pixels, with a batch size of 8. Confidence loss, probability loss and IOU loss are the three losses that contribute to the total loss which we try to optimize during training. The loss functions are the same as that proposed by the authors of YOLO [6]. The model is then trained for a total of 150 training epochs with an initial learning rate of 10–4.

Evaluation and results

MAP (mean average precision) is used as an evaluation metric in order to measure the accuracy and performance of an object detection model. YOLO v3 gives MAP of 97.79% on the AWE dataset using a score threshold of 0.3 and IOU threshold of 0.45.

12.4 Ear feature extraction

Once the ears are detected and tightly cropped out from the image captured by a camera, the next step is to obtain a feature vector using a robust feature extraction technique which can then be used for later matching. This is the most crucial step of the ear recognition pipeline. The generated biometric template should contain the necessary discriminative information required for building an accurate biometric system.

Several feature extraction techniques in the literature [3] can be classified as follows:

- **Geometric**: These approaches focus on the geometric features of the ear such as edges, ear curvature, morphology and so on.
- **Holistic**: These approaches compute global ear features. Examples of holistic approaches include principal components analysis, non-negative matrix factorization, discriminant analysis, force field transform and so on.
- **Local**: These approaches try to encode the textural information present in an image by extracting features from local image regions. The widely used local approaches are binarized statistical image features (BSIF), Gabor, histogram of orientated gradients (HOG), local binary pattern (LBP) and local phase quantization (LPQ).
- **Hybrid**: Hybrid approaches use representations obtained from multiple techniques.

Recently deep-learning based approaches have significantly outperformed the classical feature extraction techniques due to their ability to produce discriminative and powerful ear features which are directly learned from the data [7, 8].

12.4.1 Multiresolution technique for feature extraction

We use wavelet filters based deep convolutional network, also referred to as scattering wavelet convolution network (ScatNet) [11, 12], to extract ear features at multiple resolutions. A ScatNet is built by cascading wavelet transforms, obtained using various scales and orientations of wavelets, with nonlinear modulus and averaging operators.

Mathematically, we can write wavelet transform as in equation (12.1):

$$\widetilde{W}x = \{x * \varphi_{2^J}, \ |x * \psi_\lambda|\}_{\lambda \in P}$$
$$= \{S[\varnothing]x, \ U[\lambda]x\}_{\lambda \in P} \quad (12.1)$$

where $P = \{\lambda = 2^{-j} r: r \in G+, j \leqslant J\}$, J is the number of scales, φ and ψ are the averaging low pass filter and the wavelet filter, respectively.

For any $p = (\lambda_1, \lambda_2, ..., \lambda_m) \in P^m$, let $U[p]x = U[\lambda_m] ... U[\lambda_2]U[\lambda_1]$ and $S[p]x = U[p]x \times \varphi_2^J$. Each layer m of the network stores the propagated signals $\{U[p]x\}_{p \in P^m}$. $\widetilde{W}$ is then applied to all the propagated signals $U[p]x$ of layer m, as shown in equation (12.2), to produce the output scattering signals $\{S[p]x\}_{p \in P^m}$ and all the propagated signals $U[p + \lambda]$ on which $\widetilde{W}$ is again applied in the $(m + 1)$th layer, thereby obtaining a convolution type network as illustrated in figure 12.7.

$$\widetilde{W}U[p]x(u) = \{S[p]x, \ U[p + \lambda]x\}_{\lambda \in P} \quad (12.2)$$

The ScatNet thus obtained has a very specific architecture and is different from CNNs in a variety of ways. Output coefficients are produced at each layer of

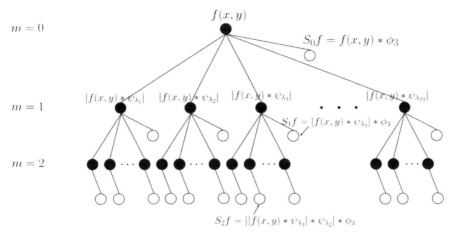

Figure 12.7. Scattering wavelet network with three scales ($J = 3$) and eight orientations ($L = 8$). White and black circles represent the scattering coefficients and wavelet modulus, respectively.

ScatNet as opposed to the last layer in CNNs. Filters are fixed predefined wavelets and are not learned from the data. For appropriate wavelets, first-order coefficients $S[\lambda]x$ is equivalent to scale invariant feature transform [14] coefficients. It builds translation invariant representations that are stable to deformations. The translation invariance of output scattering signals $S[p]x$ is due to the averaging of $U[p]x$ by $\varphi_2{}^J$, similar to average pooling in CNNs. The information lost during the averaging operation is then recovered by using wavelet coefficients at the next layer, which explains the importance of a multi-layer network structure. Also, with appropriately chosen wavelets [12], ScatNet can be made to preserve the signal norm.

Hence, we use ScatNet in the context of ear recognition to extract features of the ear image.

In general, various real or complex wavelets ψ can be used to build a ScatNet. In order to capture local orientation information present in ear images effectively, we use an oriented complex wavelet called Morlet wavelet as defined in equation (12.3). For angular sensitivity, the circular envelope of the wavelet is replaced with an elliptical one by introducing a parameter for eccentricity (ε) as shown in equation (12.3).

$$\psi_{Morlet}(x, y) = \frac{\varepsilon}{2\pi\sigma_\psi^2} * \exp\left(\frac{-(x^2 + \varepsilon^2 y^2)}{2\sigma_\psi^2}\right) \times (\exp(i\omega x) - \beta) \tag{12.3}$$

where the constant β is selected so that its mean becomes zero.

The family of oriented multi-scale wavelets is constructed from the above wavelet as shown in equation (12.4).

$$\psi_{\theta,j}(v) = 2^{-2j}\psi(2^{-j}R_\theta v) \tag{12.4}$$

where $v = (x, y)$ and R_θ is the rotation matrix with $\theta = [0, 2\pi)$.

For a Morlet wavelet, the averaging filter φ is chosen to be a Gaussian as defined in equation (12.5).

$$\varphi(x, y) = \frac{1}{2\pi\sigma_\varphi^2} * \exp\left(\frac{-(x^2 + y^2)}{2\sigma_\varphi^2}\right) \tag{12.5}$$

Figure 12.8 shows the family of multi-scale wavelets with number of scales (J) and orientations (L) equal to 3 and 8, respectively. The figure is obtained using the ScatNet MATLAB toolbox (https://www.di.ens.fr/data/software/scatnet/). We have taken help from the same toolbox for our ScatNet experiments in this work. The size of the scattering vector of the pth layer is given by $L^p\left(\frac{J}{p}\right)$. Since all the layers up to layer m are concatenated, the scattering feature vector size becomes $\sum_{p=0}^{m} L^p\left(\frac{J}{p}\right)$. For an image of size $N \times N$, scattering transform yields a total of $N^2 2^{-2J} \sum_{p=0}^{m} L^p\left(\frac{J}{p}\right)$ coefficients and with fast Fourier transform (FFT) implementation, the computational complexity is $O(N \log N)$. The ScatNet based feature extraction technique

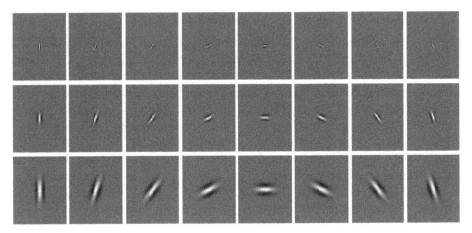

Figure 12.8. Family of multi-scale Morlet wavelets (real part) with $J = 3$ and $L = 8$.

proposed in this chapter for extracting ear features is an extension and modification of our previously published work [13].

The steps for ScatNet feature extraction are as follows:
- The images are first converted to grayscale.
- Since the ScatNet features are not rotation invariant by themselves, we pre-process the images by flipping them to one side and aligning them to a fixed orientation. They are then resized to $2^d \times 2^d$ pixels, where $d = 7$, with bilinear interpolation. This is followed by adaptive histogram equalization for contrast enhancement.
- The preprocessed image is then given as input to a three-layer ScatNet, with Morlet wavelet to extract scattering features. The number of scales of the ScatNet (J) is set to 3 where $2^J = 2^{d-4}$. Scattering coefficients are thus averaged over spatial domains covering 1/16 of the image width which preserves some coarse localization information. The values of σ_φ, σ_ψ and ω are chosen as in [12] for all the ScatNet experiments in this work and the number of orientations (L) is set to 8.
- Then, a logarithm nonlinearity is applied to the scattering feature vector to linearize exponential decay of the scattering coefficients across scales.
- Finally, a supervised features selection is performed using orthogonal least squares regression (OLS) [15], which reduces the dimensionality of the feature vector by selecting K scattering features for each class, which are then linearly transformed into K decorrelated and normalized features. We use the train set of the target dataset for supervised feature selection. For a total of C classes in the dataset, the size of the transformed feature vector becomes $M = KC$, which are basically linear combinations of the original log scattering coefficients. The value of K governs the bias-variance tradeoff and is set to 50 after a few experimentations.
- The reduced feature vector is then used for identification or verification purposes.

12.4.2 Deep learning technique for feature extraction

CNN is a class of neural networks defined using a sequence of convolutional layers consisting of a set of learnable filters (of much smaller size compared to input) which are used to detect the presence of specific patterns in the input image. The earlier convolutional layers typically learn to detect simpler patterns such as lines, curves, etc and deeper layers learn more complex patterns such as objects. Several filters are first convolved with the input image and a set of activation maps is outputted. An activation function which is a non-linear transformation is then applied to every activation map and the transformed output is then sent as input to the next convolutional layer of the CNN and so on. Typically used activation functions are relu, sigmoid and tanh. Pooling layers are typically inserted between convolutional layers to control overfitting by progressively reducing the number of model parameters and also to reduce the number of computations. Average pooling and max pooling are widely used pooling strategies. Finally, a fully connected (fc) layer is then used to learn a non-linear combination of the high-level features as represented by the output of the final convolutional layer which can then be used to classify images.

Various CNN architectures such as LeNet, AlexNet, VGGNet, GoogLeNet and ResNet have been proposed in the literature to perform various computer vision tasks such as object detection, classification, segmentation and so on. They have outperformed previously existing benchmarks by a huge margin.

In the ear recognition literature [7, 8], various CNN architectures have been used and compared. Among various CNN architectures, deep residual networks (ResNet), in particular, ResNet18, have shown to perform better in terms of recognition accuracies [16]. ResNets [17] allow us to build deep networks with increasing accuracy. Also, they have a relatively much smaller number of learnable parameters despite having more convolutional layers. Hence in our analysis, we used ResNet18 as our base model and build upon it.

Data augmentation

Small size of datasets leads to getting overfitting and might lag generalization capability on the testing data. In order to satisfy the requirement of large data size, we perform augmentations [18] of the original dataset with various transformations. We use several image enhancement techniques to transform the pixel values such as histogram equalization, adaptive histogram equalization and the technique proposed by Fu *et al* [21]. We also perform several affine transformations such as scale/zoom, translation, rotation and shear, addition of small Gaussian blur with random sigma between 0 and 0.3, random crops, horizontal flips, addition of Gaussian noise and brightness variations using an open-source image augmentation tool 'Imgaug' [23]. We either apply a single transformation technique or a combination of them to augment each and every image in the dataset.

Domain adaptation

While using deep CNNs for ear recognition, it has been shown [20] that domain adaptation strategy leads to a significant increase in accuracy. Hence, we employ a similar strategy, i.e. adapt the ImageNet pre-trained ResNet18 network using an unconstrained ear dataset to make the network understand the domain of ear images. We use a combination of two unconstrained ear datasets, namely EarVN1.0 and WPUT. EarVN1.0 [9] is a new large-scale ear dataset which is constructed by collecting ear images of 164 Asian people. It consists of a total of 28 412 color images of 98 males and 66 females. The images contain large variations in pose, scale, and illumination. The West Pomeranian University of Technology (WPUT) [10] ear database contains 2071 ear images of 501 individuals (254 women and 247 men) of various ages with at least two images per ear (profile and half-profile) for each person. Various kinds of variations such as hair covering, earrings, glasses, dust, birth-marks, ear-pads, motion blur, etc can be seen in the data. Since the number of images per identity is comparatively less in WPUT as compared to EarVN1.0, we perform data augmentation on the WPUT dataset so as to have a roughly equal number of images for all the 665 (164 + 501) identities. The merged dataset is then split into test and train sets with four images per identity in the test set and the rest in the train set.

The last fc layer of the pretrained ResNet18 network is replaced with a new fc layer (also called softmax layer) with the number of output neurons equal to 665, which is equal to the total number of identities in the above dataset. The parameters of the new fc layer are initialised by Xavier initialisation. We then train the network using stochastic gradient descent with a learning rate of 0.1 and a momentum of 0.8 for a total of 10 epochs. The best rank-1 softmax accuracy obtained on the test set is 96.5%. The training was performed using a desktop machine having Nvidia GeForce GTX 1080 Ti GPU (graphical processing unit) with 12 GB GPU memory and 64 GB RAM. We use the same machine configuration for all the deep learning experiments in this work.

The steps for deep-learning based feature extraction are as follows:
- We use the domain adapted ResNet18 network to perform final finetuning on the target ear datasets.
- The final fc layer of the model is again replaced by a new fc layer with a number of output neurons equal to the number of classes of the target ear dataset. The parameters of the fc layer are initialised by Xavier initialization. The learning rate of the new fc layer and the rest of the network is set to 0.1 and 0.01, respectively.
- We include centre loss [19] supervision along with softmax loss during the final fine-tuning to improve the discriminative power of the deep features. Specifically, a centre having the same dimensions as the features is learned for each class. During training, the distances between the features and their corresponding class centres is minimized and the centres are simultaneously updated. Intuitively, the softmax loss helps to keep the features belonging to different classes staying apart while the centre loss tries to pull the features of the same class to their centres which not only increases the inter-class features separation but also reduces the intra-class features variations.
- The models are thus fine-tuned for a total of 10 epochs using an SGD optimizer with a momentum of 0.9 using the train set of the target dataset.

- Heavy augmentation is applied to the train sets of target datasets to prevent overfitting while fine-tuning the Resnet18 model.
- The learning rates are decayed by 0.1 after 5 epochs.
- We thus obtain trained models for each dataset. In this case, the output of the final convolution layer of the model is used as feature representation of the input ear image, which we shall refer to as the deep features which are then used for identification or verification purposes.

12.4.3 Identification and verification experiments

The following datasets are used for all the identification and verification experiments.

1. AWE

The AWE dataset [3] contains ear images of 100 subjects with each subject having a total of 10 ear images of different quality and size. All the images are collected from the web and are tightly cropped. The average size of the ear images is roughly 83 × 160 pixels. The dataset is packaged with train-test split consisting of six images and four images per person, respectively. The ear images from AWE dataset used in this work have been provided by the University of Ljubljana, Slovenia [3, 25, 26].

2. UERC

The UERC dataset [7, 8] consists of a total of 11 804 ear images of 3706 subjects. The images contain various extents of head rotations, occlusion, gender, ethnicity, and others. The dataset is divided into train and test sets with disjoint identities. The train set contains 2304 images of 166 subjects, whereas the test set contains 9500 images of 3540 subjects. We use only the UERC train set (containing 2304 images of 166 subjects) for closed-set identification experiments. We use 60% images of each of the 166 subjects to train our models and use the remaining 40% to evaluate the models. This scheme gives a total of 1375 train images and 929 test images. The ear images from UERC dataset used in this work have been provided by the University of Ljubljana, Slovenia [3, 7, 8, 25–27].

3. IITB

The IIT Bombay dataset [13] contains ear images of 100 subjects with each subject having five left and five right ear images. All the images are captured using a smartphone with a fixed resolution of 540 × 820 pixels. The images contain varied illumination conditions and poses. We use 60% images of each of the 100 subjects to train our models and use the remaining 40% to evaluate the models.

Identification experiments

We perform identification experiments using AWE, UERC and IITB datasets with the train-test configuration as described above. We first extract features from all the images in the train and test sets of the target dataset using the two feature extraction techniques described in section 12.4.1 and 12.4.2. We then train a support vector machine (SVM) classifier using the feature vectors of the train set images. A trained SVM is then used to classify the features of all the test-set images directly into one of the classes and report the corresponding Rank-1 and Rank-5 accuracy. Rank-n accuracy refers to the fraction of images for which the true class of the image is contained in the top n classes predicted by the classifier. In the case of deep learning-based feature extraction technique, we obtain three CNN and SVM models for each dataset and perform ensembling of the SVM confidence scores to report the rank-1 and rank-5 accuracies. The confidence score for a sample is the signed distance of that sample to the separating hyperplane. Min-max normalization of the confidence scores is performed before ensembling.

Similarly, we extract features using standard texture descriptors such as BSIF, Gabor, HOG, LBP and LPQ and train SVM classifiers using the train sets of the target datasets and obtain the rank-1 and rank-5 accuracies using the respective test sets for comparison. The features for BSIF, Gabor, HOG, LBP and LPQ are obtained using the AWE toolbox [3]. We then use Scikit-Learn [22] machine learning libraries to train the SVMs classifiers. Accuracies obtained using different feature extraction techniques existing in the literature and the two techniques discussed in this work are tabulated in table 12.1. Figure 12.9 shows the corresponding cumulative match characteristics (CMC) curves we obtained by plotting the accuracy at various ranks.

We can observe that the proposed ScatNet and CNN based approaches outperform most of the other techniques by a significant margin. Further, it can be noted that the accuracy of the CNN features is significantly higher as compared to the ScatNet features in the case of AWE and UERC datasets. This can be mainly explained by the capability of the CNN features in efficiently handling various kinds of variabilities and variable image sizes present in these datasets. In the case of the IITB dataset, which contains fixed size good quality images, the performance of ScatNet and CNN features is almost comparable.

Table 12.1. Results of identification experiments on AWE, UERC and IITB datasets.

Methods	AWE		UERC		IITB	
	Rank-1	Rank-5	Rank-1	Rank-5	Rank-1	Rank-5
BSIF	72.25	88.50	64.58	80.95	92.75	96.00
Gabor	69.00	86.75	57.05	76.21	94.75	96.25
HOG	72.25	89.25	66.20	81.38	91.25	94.25
LBP	71.50	88.50	64.48	80.73	92.50	96.00
LPQ	68.00	85.25	63.08	79.12	93.50	96.75
ScatNet (ours)	**77.00**	**89.50**	**64.48**	**82.02**	**94.00**	**96.75**
CNN (ours)	**85.00**	**95.25**	**76.10**	**90.53**	**96.00**	**100.00**

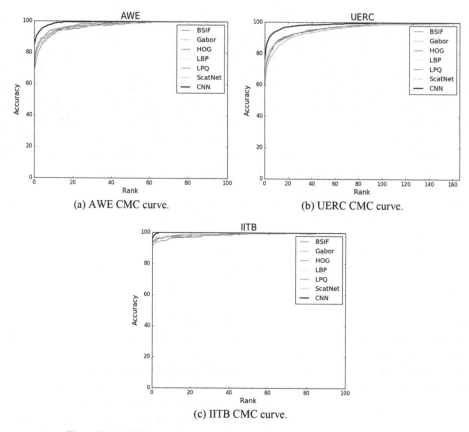

(a) AWE CMC curve.

(b) UERC CMC curve.

(c) IITB CMC curve.

Figure 12.9. CMC curves for the (a) AWE, (b) UERC and (c) IITB datasets.

Verification experiments

We perform verification experiments using the test sets of AWE, UERC and IITB datasets. We generate all possible pairs of genuine and imposter ears from each test set and obtain match scores for each pair using cosine similarity between its features obtained using the proposed feature extraction techniques. The match score is then thresholded to make a genuine/imposter decision. We calculate true positive rates (TPR) and false positive rates (FPR) for various values of the threshold and thus obtain receiver operating characteristics (ROC) curves, equal-error-rate (EER) and area under the curve (AUC) for all the three datasets. We compare the performance of the two feature extraction techniques discussed in this work with the techniques already existing in the literature. Table 12.2 tabulates the EER and AUC values, while figure 12.10 shows the ROC plots which we obtained for all the techniques.

We can observe that our ScatNet and CNN based features perform significantly better as compared to other descriptors. In particular, the CNN features have the lowest EER and highest AUC values. This shows that the CNN features are highly discriminative, which can be mainly accounted for by the inclusion of centre-loss during the training of the CNNs.

Table 12.2. Results of verification experiments on AWE, UERC and IITB datasets.

Method	AWE		UERC		IITB	
	EER	AUC	EER	AUC	EER	AUC
BSIF	0.35	0.70	0.31	0.76	0.11	0.93
Gabor	0.35	0.70	0.34	0.71	0.12	0.93
HOG	0.32	0.73	0.32	0.74	0.15	0.91
LBP	0.36	0.70	0.33	0.74	0.16	0.91
LPQ	0.36	0.68	0.34	0.72	0.13	0.92
ScatNet (ours)	**0.26**	**0.82**	**0.29**	**0.79**	**0.06**	**0.97**
CNN (ours)	**0.09**	**0.97**	**0.08**	**0.97**	**0.01**	**0.99**

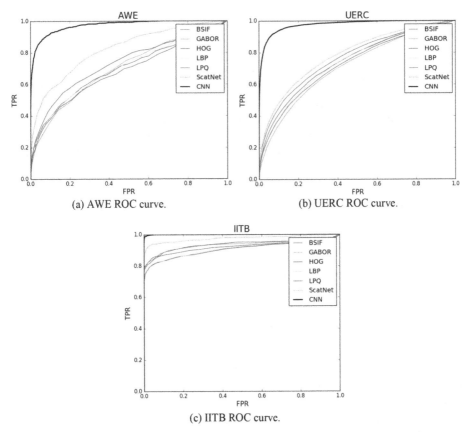

(a) AWE ROC curve.

(b) UERC ROC curve.

(c) IITB ROC curve.

Figure 12.10. ROC curves for the (a) AWE, (b) UERC and (c) IITB datasets.

12.5 Conclusion

In this work, we have developed an end-to-end system for recognizing a person using an image containing the person's ear. The YOLO framework for detection is capable of detecting objects at multiple scales and in real time. The two techniques for feature extraction, namely ScatNet and deep learning based approach have shown remarkable performance on AWE, UERC, and IITB datasets and outperformed several existing texture descriptors such as BSIF, Gabor, HOG, LBP, and LPQ in both identification and verification experiments. In future, ScatNet and CNN features can be fused to use the mutual capabilities and build an even more accurate and robust system. Also, the initial layers of the CNN can be replaced by ScatNet layers while training the CNN which can help in better generalizability and faster training convergence. The ear recognition technology has significant potential in applications such as providing secure access to multimedia by authenticating the ear or in identifying persons from CCTV footage using the person's ear. Also, the ear can be combined with other modalities such as the face or iris to build a multimodal system.

Acknowledgements

We would like to thank National Center of Excellence in Technology for Internal Security (NCETIS, IIT Bombay) for providing all the necessary hardware and software resources which helped us to perform all the experiments efficiently. We would also like to thank the creators of all the publicly available datasets used in this work. We are grateful to all the IIT Bombay people who actively participated in creating the IIT Bombay ear dataset.

References

[1] Anil K J 2011 *Introduction to Biometrics* (Berlin: Springer)

[2] Iannarelli A 1989 *Ear Identification, Forensic Identification Series* (Paramount, CA: Paramount Publishing Company)

[3] Emersic Z, Struc V and Peer P 2017 Ear recognition: more than a survey *Neurocomputing* **255** 26–39

[4] Redmon J, Divvala S, Girshick R and Farhadi A 2016 *You only look once: unified*, real-time object detection *IEEE Conf. on Computer Vision and Pattern Recognition (CVPR) (Las Vegas, NV)* pp 779–88

[5] Redmon J and Farhadi A 2017 YOLO9000: better, faster, stronger *IEEE Conf. on Computer Vision and Pattern Recognition (CVPR) (Honolulu, HI)* pp 6517–25

[6] Redmon J and Farhadi A 2018 YOLOv3: an incremental improvement ArXiv abs/1804 02767

[7] Emersic Z, Stepec D and Struc V *et al* 2017 The unconstrained ear recognition challenge *Int. Joint Conf. on Biometrics (IJCB)* pp 715–24

[8] Emersic Z, Kumar A and Harish B S *et al* 2019 The unconstrained ear recognition challenge 2019 *Proc. of the Int. Conf. on Biometrics, IAPR, 2019 (Crete)*

[9] Hoang V T 2019 EarVN1.0: a new large-scale ear images dataset in the wild *Data in Brief* **27** 104630

[10] Frejlichowski D and Tyszkiewicz N 2010 ICIAR The West Pomeranian University of technology ear database—a tool for testing biometric algorithms *Image Analysis and Recognition Part IILecture Notes in Computer Science* vol 6112 ed A Campilho and M Kamel (Berlin: Springer) pp 227–34

[11] Mallat S 2012 Group invariant scattering *Commun. Pure Appl. Math.* **65** 1331–98

[12] Bruna J and Mallat S 2013 Invariant scattering convolution networks *IEEE Trans. Pattern Anal. Mach. Intell.* **35** 1872–86

[13] Birajadar P, Haria M, Sangodkar S G and Gadre V 2019 Unconstrained ear recognition using deep scattering wavelet network *IEEE Bombay section Signature Conf. (IBSSC) (Mumbai)* pp 1–6

[14] Lowe D G 2004 Distinctive image features from scale-invariant key-points *Int. J. Comput. Vision* **60** 91–110

[15] Oyallon E and Mallat S 2015 Deep roto-translation scattering for object classification *IEEE Conf. on Computer Vision and Pattern Recognition (CVPR) (Boston, MA)* pp 2865–73

[16] Dodge S, Mounsef J and Karam L 2018 Unconstrained ear recognition using deep neural networks *IET Biometrics* **7** 207–14

[17] He K, Zhang X, Ren S and Sun J 2016 Deep residual learning for image recognition *IEEE Conf. on Computer Vision and Pattern Recognition (CVPR) (Las Vegas, NV)* pp 770–8

[18] Emersic Z, Stepec D, Struc V and Peer P 2017 Training convolutional neural networks with limited training data for ear recognition in the wild *12th IEEE Int. Conf. on Automatic Face and Gesture Recognition (FG 2017) (Washington, DC)* pp 987–94

[19] Wen Y, Zhang K, Li Z and Qiao Y 2016 A discriminative feature learning approach for deep face recognition *Computer Vision – ECCV 2016* (Lecture Notes in Computer Science vol 9911) (Cham: Springer) pp 499–515

[20] Eyiokur F I, Yaman D and Ekenel H K 2018 Domain adaptation for ear recognition using deep convolutional neural networks *IET Biometrics* **7** 199–206

[21] Fu X, Zeng D, Huang Y, Liao Y, Ding X and Paisley J 2016 A fusion-based enhancing method for weakly illuminated images *Signal Process.* **129** 82–96

[22] Pedregosa *et al* 2011 Scikit-learn: machine learning in Python *JMLR* **12** 2825–30

[23] Jung A B *et al* 2020 Imgaug https://github.com/aleju/imgaug

[24] Lin T, Dollár P, Girshick R, He K, Hariharan B and Belongie S 2017 Feature pyramid networks for object detection *IEEE Conf. on Computer Vision and Pattern Recognition (CVPR)* 2017 *(Honolulu, HI)* pp 936–44

[25] Emeršič Ž, Gabriel L L, Štruc V and Peer P 2018 Convolutional encoder-decoder networks for pixel-wise ear detection and segmentation *IET Biometrics* **7** 175–84

[26] Emeršič Ž, Meden B, Peer P and Štruc V 2018 Evaluation and analysis of ear recognition models: performance, complexity and resource requirements *Neural Comput. Appl.* **32** 15785–800

[27] Emeršič Ž, Križaj J, Štruc V and Peer P 2019 Deep ear recognition pipeline *Recent Advances in Computer Vision* (Studies in Computational Intelligence vol 804) (Cham: Springer) pp 333–62

Chapter 13

Secure multimedia management: currents trends and future avenues

Vishal Rajput and Sunil Kumar Jauhar

With the passage of every year, more and more people are getting connected to the internet. There is no denying that internet consumption is growing every day. The Covid-19 pandemic has shown us all that we need an even better infrastructure to connect people. Connecting people over the internet also means that we need entertainment to bring new users and keep the existing ones. Entertainment covers a sizable amount of internet traffic. Over-the-top (OTT) media platforms like Amazon Prime, Netflix, and Hulu are the top entertainment providers over the internet. These platforms provide original content to end-users at far cheaper rates than traditional televisions (TVs). A few production houses have even shifted their focus to OTT instead of theatres because of these platforms' lucrative user base. This research will discuss the current trends in the OTT media market and how they manage their content and users. As more platforms rise, managing users becomes a crucial task to keep the entire entertainment industry streamlined. Using bibliometric analysis, we will analyze the trends in different genres of entertainment. Other parameters like rate of content creation, from where it is being produced, in which countries OTT are gaining their customer base, are also included in this research. Furthermore, analysis of other similar articles and journals is also compared to keep track of the progress made in OTT platforms' management.

13.1 Introduction

The internet is considered one of the most important inventions in recent history since its advent and has only seen an increase in user numbers, as shown by Shin *et al* [1]. In June 2020, it had 4833 million users worldwide, which accounts for 62% of the world population. According to the Global Phenomenon report [2], videos account for 60.6% of the web traffic, followed by web, gaming, and social, 13.1%, 8.0%, and 6.1%, respectively. These numbers indicate that majority of the internet's traffic comes from video. Video is also divided into several categories, like entertainment, academic, or infotainment. HTTP media streams amount to 17.3% of traffic, followed by Operator IPTV, Netflix, and YouTube at 15%, 12.87%, and 6.3%, according to Mishra et al [3]. These statistics indicate that entertainment is the most significant part of video traffic. The global OTT market accounted for $110.1 billion in 2018 and is growing at a steady rate of 19.1% to reach $438.5 billion by 2026. Due to the unforeseen pandemic of Covid-19, the entertainment sector has seen a growth of 30% in its user base. Covid-19 has helped the entertainment industry to garner $115.6 billion in recent times, according to the Global Phenomenon report [2]. The OTT global market is expected to grow steadily in the coming years due to more people subscribing to these OTT services, according to Usman et al [4].

Moreover, during this worrisome time, governments are helping several agencies move their work over to cloud-based OTT services, according to Hutchins et al [5]. Fitzgerald [6] and Pandey et al [7] show that in recent times, many digital media and broadcast providers have stepped up their efforts to build new channels for users to access movies, shows, music, etc. The emergency of Covid-19 has positively impacted OTT-business growth worldwide. Furthermore, the lockdown period created a massive demand for OTT-based entertainment, and as a result, these platforms like Hotstar, Amazon Prime Video, and Netflix saw an increase in their viewership, as shown by Ramli et al [8].

13.2 Data collection and screening

Academic interest has grown significantly in the field of OTT forms of entertainment. This study aims to look at the current trends and the future of OTT platforms. The research was carried out using the Web of Science (WOS) database since it holds the most considerable numbers of publications, according to Carvalho and Rabechini [9] and Carvalho et al [10]. For this study, research papers from the year 2006 to 2020 are considered for the analysis. Initially, 293 documents were selected from the WOS database using the two keywords Over-the-top and multimedia management. After manually screening, 252 documents were chosen for further analysis. Out of the 252 selected documents, there were 62 articles, one book chapter, three articles (Proceedings papers), 185 Proceedings papers, and one review. In terms of collaboration, only 11 papers were single-authored, and, on average, there were 2.83 authors per article.

13.3 Results

13.3.1 General performance of selected publications

With the internet reaching every part of the globe, multimedia management is becoming more and more critical. Preliminary information about the data is shown in table 13.1. BiblioShiny software was utilized for bibliometric analysis, which was developed by Aria and Cuccurullo [11]. From one article in the year 2006 to 49 in 2016, articles in multimedia management show how the field has grown over the

Table 13.1. Preliminary information about data.

Description	Results
Main information about data	
Timespan	2006:2020
Sources (journals, books, etc)	198
Documents	252
Average years from publication	3.97
Average citations per documents	3.484
Average citations per year per doc	0.7001
References	4543
Document types	
Article	62
Article; book chapter	1
Article; proceedings paper	3
Proceedings paper	185
Review	1
Document contents	
Keywords plus (ID)	114
Author's keywords (DE)	737
AUTHORS	
Authors	714
Author appearances	930
Authors of single-authored documents	11
Authors of multi-authored documents	703
AUTHORS collaboration	
Single-authored documents	11
Documents per author	0.353
Authors per document	2.83
Co-authors per documents	3.69
Collaboration index	2.92

years. Since 2016 it has seen a little downward trend, but a significant number of articles are still being published to this day. Documents considered in this analysis had an average citation of 3.484. Mean total citations per article also followed an upward trend to 2017 and saw a decline since then. The same is true for the mean total citations per year. The year 2014 had the largest mean total citations per year and mean total citations per article. Figure 13.1 shows the annual scientific production trends from 2006 to 2020; for the year 2020, articles published before July 2020 only are included in this study.

13.3.2 Performance of countries, institutions, and authors

The higher number of publications by a respective author, country, or institute indicates how much research is happening in a field by an individual, country,

Annual Scientific Production

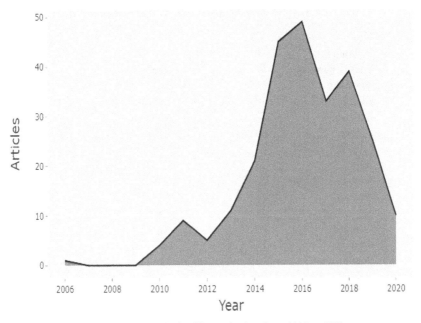

Figure 13.1. Annual scientific production from 2006 to 2020.

or institute, but it does not necessarily mean having more influence in that field. To determine the influence, the *h*-index is reported in this study. It tells about the significance, importance, and broad impact on a researcher's overall field. A large gap between publication and *h*-index for a country/institute/individual shows a high research output but minimal influence.

13.3.2.1 Performance of countries

Scholars from all over the world contributed to the field of multimedia management studies. Table 13.2 shows the top-20 countries with the number of citations and average citation per document. In terms of published articles, China leads the way with 37 publications, followed by the USA and Portugal with 31 and 18 publications, respectively. Although China has an extensive research output, its impact is relatively less, with only 1.892 citations per document. The USA has the maximum number of citations with 179 total citations and with 5.774 average citations per document, followed by Belgium, the United Kingdom, and Germany with 104, 82, and 81 citations, respectively. In terms of quality of research, Belgium leads the way with 13 citations per document. Indonesia scored lowest in both the number of citations and average citation per document in the top-20 countries. Figure 13.2 shows the country-wise contribution to the field of multimedia management and OTT.

Table 13.2. Top-20 countries with the number of citations and average citation per document.

Country	Total citations	Average article citations
USA	179	5.774
Belgium	104	13
United Kingdom	82	6.833
Germany	81	5.4
China	70	1.892
Portugal	61	3.389
France	60	4.286
Canada	43	3.583
Italy	33	3.667
Korea	25	1.786
Austria	21	4.2
Spain	21	3.5
Denmark	20	10
Sweden	13	3.25
Poland	10	2.5
Ireland	9	4.5
Finland	7	7
Japan	7	1.4
Hungary	6	3
Indonesia	5	0.625

13.3.2.2 Performance of institutions

In terms of the most relevant affiliation, University of Aveiro, Portugal tops the list with 28 articles. University of Cagliari, Italy comes at second place with 14 associated articles, followed by Instituto de Telecomunicações, Portugal, with 13 associated articles. Although these universities have produced many articles, this in no way indicates the quality of their work. Table 13.3 gives the list of the top-20 associated affiliations, and figure 13.3 shows institute-wise contribution to the field of multimedia management and OTT.

13.3.2.3 Performance of authors

The most influential author Atzori L tops the list with the h-index of 3 and 32 total citations. Atzori L is associated with the University of Cagliari, Italy, and works in multimedia networking and the Internet of Things (IoT). The second and third in the list are Ahmad A and Leon-Garcia A, both having h-index of 3 and total citations of 29 and 19, respectively. Table 13.4 also indicated other indexes like g-index and m-index and the number of publications (NP). For calculating the g-index, the distribution of citations received by a given researcher's publications is considered to give a set of articles ranked in decreasing order of the number of citations they

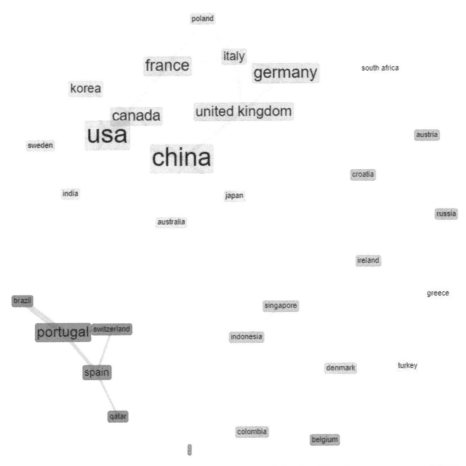

Figure 13.2. Country-wise publications contribution to the field of multimedia management and OTT.

received. The *g*-index is the unique largest number such that the top *g* articles received together at least *g*2 citations. Figure 13.4 also shows the top authors' production over time.

13.3.3 Performance of journals, citations, and keywords

Articles on multimedia management and OTT platforms have been published in a wide variety of journals. This section examines journal titles, citations and keywords to identify key themes, topic areas, and influential articles.

13.3.3.1 Source analysis
Out of all the published articles, *Telecommunications Policy* published the maximum number of articles, followed by *IEEE Access* and *IEEE Transactions on Network and Service Management*, and they published 5, 4, and 4 articles, respectively. Table 13.5 shows the top-20 publishing sources based on their *h*-index and the number of

Table 13.3. Top-20 associated affiliations.

Affiliations	Articles
University of Aveiro	28
University of Cagliari	14
Instituto de Telecomunicações	13
Beijing University of Posts and Telecommunications	12
Technical University of Darmstadt	11
University of Toronto	11
Altice Labs S.A.	9
Orange Labs	9
Columbia University	8
Communications University of China	8
Ghent University, iMinds	8
Nanjing University of Posts and Telecommunications	8
Alcatel Lucent Bell Labs	7
University of Zagreb	7
Bonch Bruevich St Petersburg State University of Telecommunications	6
Hasselt University (tUL)	6
University of Cauca	6
University of Surrey	6
E (Corresponding Author)	5
Kings College London	5

Figure 13.3. Institute-wise publications contribution to the field of multimedia management and OTT.

Table 13.4. Top authors' production over time.

Author	*h*-index	*g*-index	*m*-index	TC	NP	PY_start
Atzori L	3	5	0.6	32	8	2016
Ahmad A	2	5	0.4	29	7	2016
Leon-Garcia A	3	4	0.429	19	7	2014
Li W	3	4	0.5	22	7	2015
Sargento S	2	3	0.4	12	7	2016
Zucherman L	3	4	0.429	19	6	2014
Chignell M	2	3	0.333	12	5	2015
Floris A	2	5	0.4	28	5	2016
Haryadi S	0	0	0	0	5	2014
Hausheer D	3	5	0.5	33	5	2015
Jiang J	2	3	0.333	12	5	2015
Latre S	3	5	0.375	102	5	2013
Nogueira J	3	5	0.6	25	5	2016
Spachos P	2	3	0.333	12	5	2015
Abreu J	2	4	0.333	16	4	2015
Antonopoulos A	3	4	0.75	38	4	2017
Blendin J	3	4	0.5	32	4	2015
De Turck F	3	4	0.429	92	4	2014
Elagin Vs	0	0	0	0	4	2018
Guardalben L	2	3	0.4	11	4	2016

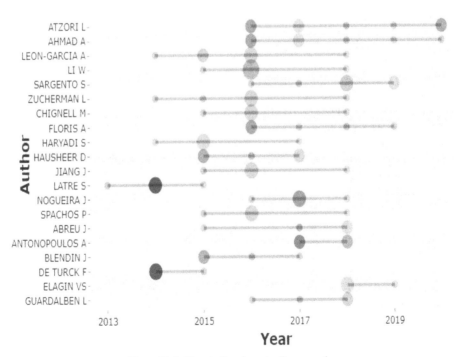

Figure 13.4. Top Authors' production over time.

Table 13.5. Top-20 publishing sources based on their *h*-index and the number of publications.

Source	*h*-index	*g*-index	*m*-index	TC	NP	PY_start
Telecommunications Policy	3	4	0.5	20	6	2015
IEEE Access	1	1	0.5	1	4	2019
IEEE Transactions on Network and Service Management	3	4	0.6	47	4	2016
2015 11th International Conference on Network and Service Management (CNSM)	2	3	0.333 333	14	3	2015
2016 IEEE Global Communications Conference (Globecom)	1	3	0.2	13	3	2016
2018 IEEE Globecom Workshops (GC Wkshps)	1	1	0.333 333	3	3	2018
Journal of Network and Systems Management	2	3	0.25	25	3	2013
Journal of The Institute of Telecommunications Professionals	1	1	0.2	1	3	2016
Multimedia Tools and Applications	1	3	0.2	10	3	2016
Proceeding Of 2015 1st International Conference on Wireless and Telematics (ICWT)	0	0	0	0	3	2015
Proceedings of the 27th Acm International Conference on Multimedia (MM'19)	0	0	0	0	3	2019
2013 IEEE Wireless Communications and Networking Conference (WCNC)	2	2	0.25	9	2	2013
2014 Sixth International Conference on Wireless Communications and Signal Processing (WCSP)	0	0	0	0	2	2014
2015 IEEE 16th International Symposium on A World of Wireless, Mobile and Multimedia Networks (WOWMOM)	1	1	0.166 667	2	2	2015
2015 IEEE International Conference on Communications (ICC)	1	2	0.166 667	7	2	2015
2015 International Conference on Computing, Networking and Communications (ICNC)	1	2	0.166 667	8	2	2015
2016 17th International Telecommunications Network Strategy and Planning Symposium (Networks)	0	0	0	0	2	2016
2016 Asia Pacific Conference on Multimedia and Broadcasting (Apmediacast)	1	2	0.2	26	2	2016
2016 IEEE International Conference on Communications (ICC)	1	2	0.2	4	2	2016
2017 IEEE International Conference on Communications (ICC)	0	0	0	0	2	2017

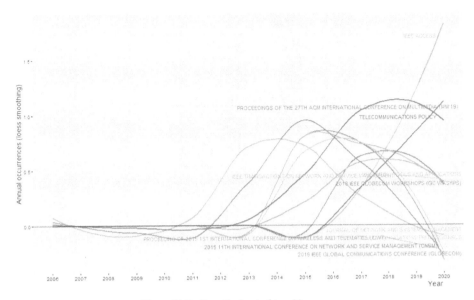

Figure 13.5. Growth chart of top-20 sources.

publications. Figure 13.5 also shows how each source has grown over the years in terms of the number of publications each year.

13.3.3.2 Citation analysis

In terms of the most cited global document, the Claeys *et al* [12] publication in *IEEE Communication* tops the list with 54 citations with total citations per year of 7.71. The Nam *et al* [13] publication in 2014, IEEE Global Communications Conference (Globecom 2014) received the second-highest number of citations, followed by Foukas *et al* [14] publication in 2017, Proceedings Of The 23rd Annual International Conference On Mobile Computing And Networking (Mobicom '17), with 51 and 35 citations, respectively. The total number of references used by all 252 documents is 4543. Mok *et al* [15], IEEE International Symposium on Integrated Network Management (In 2011), P485 became the most referred to document with ten citations.

13.3.3.3 Keywords analysis

Keyword analysis shows that OTT is an essential author keyword with 39 occurrences. QOE (quality of experience) and video streaming follows it with 26 and 12 occurrences, respectively. Table 13.6 gives the list of top-20 keywords used by different authors. Figure 13.6 also shows the growth of different keywords over the years. Figure 13.6 shows how different keywords are related to each other and their overall impact given by the size of each keyword's bubble. Interlink between different keywords is shown in figure 13.7. This gives us an idea about the themes or topics trending overall. Table 13.7 shows the most prominent keywords over the

Table 13.6. Most prominent keywords over the years.

Words	Occurrences	Words	Occurrences
OTT	39	ISP	6
QOE	26	LTE	6
Video streaming	12	Management	6
QOS	11	NFV	6
Quality of experience	9	Quality of experience (QOE)	6
Quality of service	9	OTT applications	5
SDN	9	OTT services	5
5g	7	Over-the-top (OTT)	5
Dash	7	Video	5
IPTV	6	WebRTC	5

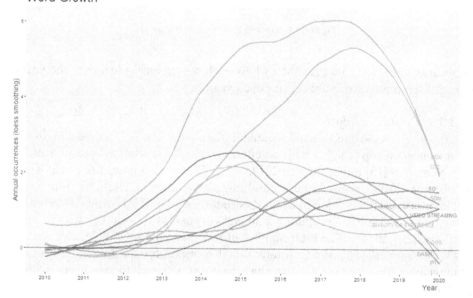

Figure 13.6. Growth of different keywords over the years.

years, and 7 gives us a rough estimation of the thematic evolution of the different subfields in multimedia management.

13.3.4 Factorial analysis

Factorial analysis is a statistics-based method, and it uses unobserved variables called factors to describe the variation among observed, correlated variables. For instance, variations observed in six variables may reflect the variations in two unobserved (underlying) variables. Factor analysis is meant to search for such joint variations in response to unobserved variables. Linear combinations of observed

Figure 13.7. Interlink between different keywords.

variables give the potential factors, plus error terms. Factor analysis aims to find independent latent variables. Table 13.8 gives the result of co-word factorial analysis by the cluster.

13.3.5 Co-citation network

Table 13.9 talks about the 12 major co-citation clusters and which author contributed to which cluster. Cluster 2 is the most significant cluster among the 12 clusters, and in that cluster, Ahmad A contributed the most with four contributions. On the other hand, cluster 12 is the smallest cluster, with Yang J as the only contributor to the cluster.

13.3.6 Collaboration worldwide

This section gives information about which countries are involved with which other countries. Both China and Germany have the maximum number of collaborations with different countries, tallying to 9 each, followed by Italy and Canada with 8 and 5, respectively, whereas France is the one with whom most other countries collaborated. Brazil collaborated five times with Portugal, which is the highest number of collaborations between a set of two countries. Results of all the country-wise collaboration are given in table 13.10.

Table 13.7. Thematic evolution of the different subfields in multimedia management.

From	To	Words	Weighted inclusion index	Inclusion index	Occurrences	Stability index
CDN—2006–2016	QOE—2017–2020	CDN	0.13	0.08	2	0.02
Cellular core networks content delivery—2006–2016	Machine learning—2017–2020	Classification	0.13	0.13	1	0.03
Component—2006–2016	Interoperability—2017–2020	Broadband	0.17	0.17	1	0.06
DVB—2006–2016	Interoperability—2017–2020	DVB	0.13	0.14	2	0.05
IPTV—2006–2016	Interoperability—2017–2020	Broadcast	0.07	0.08	1	0.04
IPTV—2006–2016	OTT—2017–2020	IPTV; HEVC	0.20	0.08	2	0.02
IPTV—2006–2016	QOE—2017–2020	Over-the-top (OTT)	0.13	0.08	2	0.02
IPTV—2006–2016	QOS—2017–2020	H.264	0.07	0.08	1	0.03
OTT—2006–2016	OTT—2017–2020	OTT; telecommunications; over the top; progress	0.34	0.03	21	0.01
OTT—2006–2016	Over-the-top—2017–2020	Television	0.06	0.07	1	0.02
OTT—2006–2016	QOE—2017–2020	QOE; ISP	0.13	0.03	9	0.01
OTT—2006–2016	QOS—2017–2020	QOS; quality of; experience	0.15	0.04	7	0.02
OTT—2006–2016	Quality of service—2017–2020	Quality of service	0.11	0.04	4	0.02
OTT—2006–2016	Security—2017–2020	OTT VOIP	0.13	0.14	1	0.03
OTT—2006–2016	Technological change—2017–2020	Regulation	0.10	0.10	2	0.02
OTT applications—2006–2016	Machine learning—2017–2020	OTT applications	0.33	0.20	2	0.04
OTT applications—2006–2016	Quality of service—2017–2020	Energy efficiency	0.17	0.20	1	0.04
OTT services—2006–2016	IMS—2017–2020	IMS	0.17	0.17	2	0.03
OTT services—2006–2016	Interoperability—2017–2020	MPEG dash	0.07	0.08	1	0.03
OTT services—2006–2016	QOS—2017–2020	MPEG-dash	0.03	0.04	1	0.02
Pricing—2006–2016	Interoperability—2017–2020	Interoperability	0.13	0.08	2	0.04
Pricing—2006–2016	QOS—2017–2020	Web	0.06	0.08	1	0.03

(Continued)

Table 13.7. (*Continued*)

From	To	Words	Weighted inclusion index	Inclusion index	Occurrences	Stability index
Value-chain—2006–2016	QOS—2017–2020	Evaluation	0.17	0.17	1	0.03
Video—2006–2016	Mobility—2017–2020	Virtual network embedding; network virtualization; DMM; network optimization	0.57	0.17	1	0.03
Video—2006–2016	QOE—2017–2020	Video quality; management	0.05	0.03	1	0.02
Video—2006–2016	QOS—2017–2020	Video; wireless; networks	0.10	0.04	3	0.02
Video—2006–2016	Quality of service—2017–2020	Virtualization; LTE-A	0.09	0.04	2	0.02
Video streaming—2006–2016	Machine learning—2017–2020	Applications	0.03	0.04	1	0.02
Video streaming—2006–2016	OTT—2017–2020	Multimedia; systems	0.05	0.03	2	0.01
Video streaming—2006–2016	QOE—2017–2020	Quality of experience; video streaming	0.08	0.03	7	0.01
Video streaming—2006–2016	QOS—2017–2020	HTTP adaptive streaming	0.02	0.04	2	0.02
Video streaming—2006–2016	Quality of service—2017–2020	Network neutrality	0.03	0.04	1	0.02
WebRTC—2006–2016	OTT—2017–2020	CSP	0.03	0.05	2	0.02
WebRTC—2006–2016	Over-the-top—2017–2020	Standards	0.06	0.07	1	0.03
WebRTC—2006–2016	QOE—2017–2020	NFV; SDN	0.18	0.05	3	0.02
WebRTC—2006–2016	QOS—2017–2020	Dash	0.09	0.05	3	0.02

Table 13.8. Co-word factorial analysis by the cluster.

Word	Dim 1	Dim 2	Cluster	Word	Dim 1	Dim 2	Cluster
X5g Mobile Communication	3.53	−0.7	1	H 264	−0.58	0.86	1
Quality Of Service	−0.09	−0.16	1	Http Adaptive Streaming	−0.13	0.75	1
Over The Top	−0.18	−0.05	1	Web	−0.43	3.25	2
Quality Of Experience	1.49	−0.4	1	Security	0.13	−0.03	1
Management	2.68	−0.28	1	Video Quality	−0.39	0.71	1
Monitoring	3.93	−0.35	1	Ott Services	−0.26	0.06	1
X5g	1.29	0.73	1	Mos	0.68	0	1
Quality of Experience Qoe	2.96	−0.23	1	Qos	−0.58	1.03	1
Qoe Management	3.65	−0.63	1	Over The Top Services	0.44	−0.47	1
Video Streaming	1.39	−0.02	1	Catch Up Tv	−0.39	−0.18	1
Over The Top Ott	2.84	−0.28	1	Iptv	−0.33	−0.15	1
Classification	−0.53	0.03	1	Multimedia	−0.11	0.14	1
Qoe	0.14	0.22	1	Interoperability	−0.08	−0.02	1
Ott	−0.48	−0.48	1	Video	−0.51	3.18	2
Isp	0.19	−0.85	1	Dash	−0.39	1.1	1
Sdn	−0.68	−1.62	1	Wireless	−0.31	4.11	2
Nfv	−1.03	−1.98	1	Networks	−0.36	5	2
Network Slicing	−0.11	−1.45	1	Crowdsourcing	−0.09	−0.03	1
Resource Management	0.77	−0.44	1	Lte	−0.05	0.36	1
Regulation	−0.45	−0.32	1	Telecommunications	−1.04	−1.03	1
Http Streaming	0.07	0.57	1	Csp	−1.94	−2.55	1
Mpeg Dash	−0.33	0.83	1	Over The Top 1	−1.61	−0.54	1
Machine Learning	−0.51	0.06	1	Quality Of	−1.41	−0.1	1
Dataset	−0.57	−0.16	1	Ims	−0.02	−0.2	1
Ott Applications	0.04	−0.12	1	H 264	−0.58	0.86	1
Cdn	−0.17	−0.15	1	Http Adaptive Streaming	−0.13	0.75	1

Table 13.9. 12 Major co-citation clusters and which author contributed to which cluster.

Node	Cluster	Betweenness	Closeness	PageRank
Bampis C G 2017—2	1	0	0.000 497 265	0.025 254 384
Barman N 2018—2	1	0	0.000 497 265	0.025 254 384
Mittal A 2013	1	0	0.000 497 265	0.025 254 384
Mittal A 2012	1	0	0.000 497 265	0.025 254 384
Moorthy A K 2010	1	0	0.000 497 265	0.025 254 384
Reith B 2018	1	0	0.000 497 265	0.025 254 384

(*Continued*)

Table 13.9. (*Continued*)

Node	Cluster	Betweenness	Closeness	PageRank
Soundararajan R 2013	1	0	0.000 497 265	0.025 254 384
Wang Z 2004—1	1	15	0.000 497 76	0.036 524 543
Apple 2017 2017—1	1	0	0.000 495 786	0.006 854 761
Bouten N 2012—1	1	0	0.000 495 786	0.006 854 761
Afolabi I 2018	2	0	0.001 005 025	0.024 913 353
Ahmad Arslan 2017	2	4.746 5192	0.001 007 049	0.028 189 418
Ahmad A 2018—1	2	0	0.001 005 025	0.024 913 353
Ahmad A 2017	2	0	0.001 005 025	0.024 913 353
Ahmad A 2018—2	2	4.746 5192	0.001 007 049	0.028 189 418
Ahmadi A 2019	2	0	0.001 005 025	0.024 913 353
Barakovic S 2013	2	17.945 542	0.001 008 065	0.029 228 796
Bentaleb A 2017	2	4.861 426	0.001 007 049	0.028 781 066
Cofano G 2017	2	0	0.001 005 025	0.024 913 353
Ge C 2016	2	0	0.001 005 025	0.024 913 353
Gramaglia M 2016	2	0	0.001 005 025	0.024 913 353
Hossfeld T 2017	2	18.342 855	0.001 009 082	0.030 955 721
Liotou E 2018	2	0	0.001 005 025	0.025 500 639
Rodriguez DZ 2014	2	0	0.001 005 025	0.024 913 353
Seufert M 2015	2	21.263 734	0.001 009 082	0.033 476 947
Skorin-Kapov L 2018	2	0	0.001 005 025	0.024 913 353
Wang Y 2017	2	0	0.001 005 025	0.024 913 353
Li Y 2015–1	3	0	0.000 408 163	0.003 405 221
Abdelwahab S 2016	4	0	0.000 408 163	0.003 405 221
Fischer A 2013	5	0	0.000 408 163	0.003 405 221
Agyapong PK 2014	6	161	0.001 012 146	0.038 745 527
Akyildiz I F 2015	6	56	0.000 991 08	0.025 435 704
Feng Z Y 2015	6	0	0.000 989 12	0.016 174 985
Foukas X 2017–1	6	0	0.000 964 32	0.011 293 639
Gudipati A 2013–1	6	0	0.000 989 12	0.016 174 985
Joseph V 2014	6	0	0.000 964 32	0.011 293 639
Trakas P 2017	6	0	0.000 989 12	0.016 174 985
Nguyen V G 2017	6	0	0.000 989 12	0.016 174 985
Varela M 1741	7	34.387 055	0.001 010 101	0.034 453 115
Awobuluyi O 1658	7	0	0.000 984 252	0.007 463 501
Hossfeld T 2015—1	7	17.768 869	0.000 990 099	0.019 524 626
Liotou E 2015	7	13.937 48	0.000 989 12	0.019 131 053
Passarella A 2012	7	0	0.000 986 193	0.010 141 955
Wamser F 2015	7	0	0.000 965 251	0.008 107 512
Nygren E 2010—1	8	0	0.000 408 163	0.003 405 221
Pinson M H 2004	9	0	0.000 408 163	0.003 405 221
Palomar D P 2006	10	0	0.000 416 493	0.022 701 476
Rainer B 2016	10	0	0.000 416 493	0.022 701 476
Sullivan G J 2012	11	0	0.000 408 163	0.003 405 221
Yang J 2015—1	12	0	0.000 408 163	0.003 405 221

Table 13.10. Country-wise collaboration.

From	To	Frequency	From	To	Frequency
Austria	Norway	1	Germany	Spain	1
Brazil	France	1	Germany	Switzerland	1
Brazil	Portugal	5	India	USA	2
Brazil	USA	1	Indonesia	Singapore	2
Canada	Denmark	1	Iraq	Malaysia	1
Canada	Japan	1	Ireland	South Africa	1
Canada	South Africa	1	Italy	Belgium	1
Canada	Sweden	1	Italy	France	2
Canada	USA	2	Italy	Germany	2
China	Australia	2	Italy	Korea	1
China	Austria	1	Italy	Poland	2
China	Canada	2	Italy	United Kingdom	3
China	Greece	1	Italy	USA	1
China	Italy	1	Japan	Greece	1
China	Japan	3	Korea	Canada	2
China	Pakistan	1	Korea	USA	3
China	United Kingdom	3	Lebanon	Switzerland	1
China	USA	3	Poland	Brazil	1
Germany	Belgium	1	Poland	France	3
Germany	Croatia	1	Poland	USA	1
Germany	France	1	Portugal	France	1
Germany	Greece	1	Portugal	Spain	3
Germany	India	1	Portugal	Switzerland	2
Germany	Poland	1	Spain	Ecuador	1

13.4 Conclusion

In this study, a comprehensive review of the scientific literature has been performed on multimedia management and OTT platforms. In our approach, we combined complex network analysis along with bibliometric analysis. Research articles from 2006 to 2020 were analyzed using citations, affiliations, h-index, and many more. Country/institute/author-wise assessment showed how much literature is being produced in this field by each country/institute and author. Further analysis was done on the keywords. It gives us the idea of how this field is evolving with time and current trends. Journal analysis tells us which research articles contributed most to the field of multimedia management. This study was done to organize the ever-growing field of multimedia management. It provided us with details about the critical sub-topics, authors, country, and institutes in multimedia management.

References

[1] Shin J, Park Y and Lee D 2016 Strategic management of over-the-top services: focusing on Korean consumer adoption behavior *Technol. Forecast. Soc. Change* **112** 329–37
[2] Global Phenomenon Report 2019 https://sandvine.com/phenomena

[3] Mishra, Mishra D, Vijayakumar P, Sureshkumar V, Amin R, Islam S H and Gope P 2018 Efficient authentication protocol for secure multimedia communications in IoT-enabled wireless sensor networks *Multimedia Tools Appl.* **77** 18295–325

[4] Usman M, Jan M A, He X and Nanda P 2016 Data sharing in secure multimedia wireless sensor networks *2016 IEEE Trustcom/BigDataSE/ISPA* (Piscataway, NJ: IEEE) pp 590–7

[5] Hutchins B, Li B and Rowe D 2019 Over-the-top sport: live streaming services, changing coverage rights markets and the growth of media sport portals *Media, Cult. Soc.* **41** 975–94

[6] Fitzgerald S 2019 Over-the-top video services in India: media imperialism after globalization *Media Ind. J.* **6** 206

[7] Pandey S, Choi M J and Park S 2019 The evolution of Over the Top (OTT): standardization, key players and challenges. *Majlesi J. Electr. Eng.* **13** 81–7

[8] Ramli T S, Ramli A M, Adolf H, Damian E and Palar M R A 2020 Over-the-top media in digital economy and society 5.0 *J. Telecommun. Digital Econ.* **8** 60

[9] Carvalho M M D and Rabechini Junior R 2015 Impact of risk management on project performance: the importance of soft skills *Int. J. Prod. Res.* **53** 321–40

[10] Carvalho M M, Fleury A and Lopes A P 2013 An overview of the literature on technology roadmapping (TRM): contributions and trends *Technol. Forecast. Soc. Change* **80** 1418–37

[11] Aria M and Cuccurullo C 2017 Bibliometrix: an R-tool for comprehensive science mapping analysis *J. Informetr.* **11** 959–75

[12] Claeys M, Latre S, Famaey J and De Turck F 2014 Design and evaluation of a self-learning HTTP adaptive video streaming client *IEEE Commun. Lett.* **18** 716–9

[13] Nam H, Kim K H, Kim J Y and Schulzrinne H 2014 Towards QoE-aware video streaming using SDN *2014 IEEE Global Communications Conference* (Piscataway, NJ: IEEE) pp 1317–22

[14] Foukas X, Marina M K and Kontovasilis K 2017 Orion: RAN slicing for a flexible and cost-effective multi-service mobile network architecture *Proc. of the 23rd Annual In. Conf. on Mobile Computing and Networking* pp 127–40

[15] Mok R K, Chan E W and Chang R K 2011 Measuring the quality of experience of HTTP video streaming *12th IFIP/IEEE International Symposium on Integrated Network Management (IM 2011) and Workshops* (Piscataway, NJ: IEEE) pp 485–92

CPSIA information can be obtained
at www.ICGtesting.com
Printed in the USA
BVHW092205211121
622067BV00003B/67